Not the Seasons I Expected

Blant Hurt

All the best,

Blant Hurt

Fairbourne Publishing
1223 W. Matthews Avenue
Jonesboro, Arkansas 72401

Cover by Rodrigo Corral Design
Text design by Asya Blue

Not the Seasons I Expected is a work of nonfiction. The events and places in this memoir have been recreated from the author's recollections. The conversations are not written to represent word-for-word transcripts, though in all instances the essence of the dialogue is accurate. Some names and identifying details of people described in this book have been altered to protect their privacy.

Printed in the United States of America

Print ISBN: 978-0-9973256-4-5
Digital Edition ISBN: 978-0-9973256-5-2

www.blanthurt.com

For my mother, and for my father.

A special thanks to Jim Morgan for his
editorial guidance and expertise.

Also by Blant Hurt

HEALER'S TWILIGHT
THE AWKWARD OZARKER

Contents

Prologue

On the occasion of my 59th birthday, which fell in the middle of the college football season, my mother gave me a plaque that read, "Thankful, Blessed, & Football-Obsessed." At first, I didn't think much about her little gift. This plaque, the size of a thigh pad, was like those throwaway wall hangers that say, "What Happens at the Cabin Stays at the Cabin." Yet the words in bold type stuck with me and I wondered how it had come to pass that my mother—at this advanced stage of my life, much less hers—viewed one of her son's defining qualities as being "Football-Obsessed." Wasn't such a take on me rather narrow? After all, like all of us I considered myself a man of varied talents and interests. Even so, I couldn't deny that the words on this plaque, which bore a $4.00 price tag from TJ Maxx, my mother's favorite store, were indeed accurate.

Since I was 9 years old, I have been thrilled, tantalized, and tormented by my favorite college football team, the Arkansas Razorbacks. What an exhausting half-century it has been. My fandom—you could even call it a fanaticism—took root in my youth with one game that captured my imagination, in no small part because my father was a fan too and, given his example, my passion was as inevitable as the removal of the training wheels from my bicycle.

The idea of writing this book came to me in the wake of the 2016 Belk Bowl, which, like so many football games and practically any football season, and even with life itself, had not gone as I had expected. The Arkansas Razorbacks blew a 24-0 halftime lead against Virginia Tech. This collapse, which I likened to a 100-Year Flood even though it came just one game after a similar second-half collapse, left an ugly watermark on my psyche. But it also agitated my curiosity: Why did the outcome affect me so much? Why, as a man well into my 50s, couldn't I just shrug off this loss? Why did it color my entire holiday season?

In the spirit of self-discovery, I made a few notes. At first, the act of writing about the tenacious grip that Arkansas football has had on me for nearly half a century seemed wasteful. Didn't Razorback football already occupy enough space in my head? Only months before this Belk Bowl meltdown, I'd penned a column for the local newspaper in which I had half-jokingly suggested that during football season my IQ drops at least 20 points.

On the other hand, what else had ever affected me so viscerally? What, save the very thump-thump of my heart itself, was such an integral part of my past, present, and future? The more I thought about it, the more I came to see that my fandom was a unifying theme of my life, if not *the* unifying theme. It has colored and infused my entire being, and it's never been something I could compartmentalize. There's always been an interplay between it and every epoch of my life, and it has affected every significant relationship I've had, including those with my father and mother, my sister, my grandparents, my uncles, my childhood friends, my frat brothers near and far, my current wife and stepchildren, my ex-wives, my business colleagues, my beloved teachers. No one I've ever been close to has escaped the turbulence of my fandom.

So I pressed on. And as I wrote I sensed that my story, while rooted in specifics unique to me and my state and my times, also touched on aspects of the universal. It's never been lost on me that if I'd been born 70 miles to the east, just across the Mississippi River, I would surely have lived my life as a Tennessee Volunteer fan. Ditto if I had grown up in Youngstown, Ohio, and was nutty about the Ohio State Buckeyes. So I invite all who are similarly afflicted to read on—like it or not, I suspect you'll find a bit of yourself in my story.

1

The Big Shootout

I was born on October 19, 1960 or, as it was known in our household, three days before the Arkansas-Ole Miss football game. My father, a 21-year-old die-hard Razorback fan, faced a dilemma: Would he tend to his wife and newborn son in Jonesboro, or abandon us for the game down in Little Rock, some 120 miles south? When he wasn't harvesting cotton with his new one-row John Deere cotton picker, my dad served as an aide-de-camp to a gubernatorial candidate who lived down the street. Dad's side job was to drive this candidate wherever he desired to go, and on this particular Saturday both of them desired to be at Little Rock's War Memorial Stadium.

I've never had a problem with Dad's choice, especially considering that Ole Miss was ranked number two in the nation, while Arkansas, under head coach Frank Broyles, was ranked 14th and had just beaten Texas 24-23. It was indeed a pivotal matchup. Besides, if Dad had stayed home, what exactly could he have contributed to my care? All I was doing was eating and sleeping, peeing and pooping. My mother, stricken with postpartum depression and coming from a family of non-football fans, didn't see it that way. She was further put out that Dad had changed my name on my birth certificate to his name, his father's name, his grandfather's name: I, therefore, became William Blant Hurt, IV, cementing my line going back to a 20-year-old man from Bristol, England, who'd boarded a ship to Virginia in 1701.

In hindsight, I have to believe that both my dad and the erstwhile gubernatorial candidate, who eventually decided not to challenge Orval Faubus in the Democratic primary of 1962, were on to a good thing. Little Rock had suffered through the desegregation crisis in 1957, and the national perception of Arkansas was quite unfavorable. In 1958, Frank Broyles was hired and lost his first six games. But in 1959, the Hogs had gone 9-2, their most wins ever in a season.

Though the Razorbacks lost this first-of-my-life matchup against Ole Miss on a controversial call (my father, to this day, swears the game-winning field goal was wide), the Hogs went 8-3 in the year of my birth; then 8-3 in 1961; 9-2 in 1962; 5-5 in 1963; 11-0 in 1964, including the national championship; and 10-1 in 1965. The cover of the November 8, 1965, *Sports Illustrated* carried the headline "Arkansas—The New Dynasty."

My life throughout the 1960s was almost idyllic. I went to a good public school where all the boys played Red Rover on the black-topped playground. My mother made sure my sister and I were regularly attendees of the First Methodist Church. My enterprising father found lucrative outlets for his prodigious energies and imagination. Our new one-level brick house was surrounded by open fields, where the kids in our neighborhood came together to play sandlot baseball. When it rained, we frolicked in the ditch banks and spent days at our hideaway in the nearby woods that we called Rattlesnake Camp. Our idea of being mischievous was to throw crab apples at one another. As the fireflies and mosquitos came out in the evenings, my mom and dad watched Walter Cronkite on *CBS News*. My paternal grandparents lived just up the hill, and my maternal grandparents lived only two miles away, out near the gladiola farm. I knew it was my bedtime when I heard Johnny Carson's opening monologue on *The Tonight Show*.

I really latched on to Razorback football only near the end of the 1969 season, after the Hogs had echoed the dynastic years of 1964 and 1965 by reeling off nine in a row. It's odd, but before the 10th game of that season I have few memories of Razorback football. A kid learns when he's ready to learn. From this game on, I can remember more than I sometimes wish to.

The date was December 6, 1969, a Saturday. I was rapt as the announcer on television gravely delivered the lead-in: *"Razorback Stadium, Fayetteville, Arkansas, where the unbeaten and top-ranked Longhorns of Texas, with the nation's most awesome rushing attack, meet the unbeaten and second-ranked Razorbacks of Arkansas, led by quarterback Bill Montgomery, in a game that should decide the national championship."*

With my mom and dad at a game-watching party, I was at my grandmother's house, which smelled of roast sirloin, her specialty. I darted in from her living room to nab a thick-cut end piece full of peppery flavor, then hustled back to one of the throne-like easy chairs. This living room of my grandmother's was a citadel of comfort with her state-of-the-art Zenith TV (complete with a remote control, rare in those days), huge ottomans for the feet, plastic drinking glasses that didn't sweat when filled with ice water, table-top buttons to turn the lamps on and off with minimal strain and, within arms' reach, her mail-order catalogs, including *Hammacher Schlemmer* and *Horchow*, dozens of magazines like *Sports Illustrated* and *National Geographic* and *Southern Living*, and stacks of the *National Enquirer* and *The Star*, which she referred to as her Funny Papers.

Dark-haired and hazel-eyed, my grandmother was dressed

in a drapey, red-tinged muumuu and black slippers adorned with red rhinestones. Yet despite all of her creature comforts, she was hardly a softy. Years before, my grandfather had taken her to a gathering of John Deere dealers, where she'd refused to shake the hand of one of the executives in the receiving line because he wore an "I Like Ike" button. On this particular game-day Saturday, I'm confident she hated the Texas Longhorns at least as much as she did any random button-wearing Republican.

The images flicked by on my grandmother's television. There was the pregame prayer by the Reverend Billy Graham, the panning shots of the Razorback cheerleaders, the overflow crowd set against the leaden December sky. In a quaint humanizing touch, 11 players from each team were introduced, one by one, in front of the camera, each posing without his helmet when his name was called. A helicopter landed near Razorback Stadium and soon images of President Nixon appeared. *My gosh,* I thought, *if the Arkansas Razorbacks are important enough for the President of the United States to helicopter into the Ozark Mountains to watch them play, then aren't I justified in giving my heart and soul to this team?* Before the 1969 season, the legendary Roone Arledge of ABC Sports had made a bet that Arkansas and Texas would be the two best teams in college football, so he had asked them to move their game, typically played in mid-October, to the end of the season. Both Arkansas and Texas had won their first nine, setting up what was billed nationally as The Big Shootout.

The Big Shootout. Boy, did this speak to me. It was two heavily armed gunslingers at the OK Corral, good guys versus bad guys, light against dark. The quarters clicked by: At the end of the first, it was 7-0 Arkansas. At halftime, it was still 7-0. By the end of the third, the Hogs led 14-0. As all this unfolded, my grandmother's living room was filled with her shouts, cheers, her oohs and aahs. Her favorite expletive was a rapier-sharp "dammit," and beside her, at the ready, were the white dinner gloves she sometimes donned to keep from biting her fingernails.

Then came the final score: 15-14 Texas.

Looking back, many of the finer points and mind-bending absurdities of this so-called Game of the Century were lost on me. How did my team lose a game in which the other team turns the ball over six times? Why, with 10:34 left in the fourth quarter, did Coach Broyles decide to throw a pass, subsequently intercepted, when Arkansas had the ball inside the Texas 10 yard line? Why didn't he just play it safe and kick what would've been the game-clinching field goal? How did James Street, facing a fourth-and-three with 4:47 left and his team down 14-8, fit that pass over two cozy defenders and into the outstretched arms of tight end Randy Peschel?

I had no idea where my 5-year-old sister was. I was just glad she wasn't in the living room to annoy me by standing in front of the television, as she sometimes did when I watched *Little Rascals* at our house after school. She was probably taking a long nap, as was my grandfather. Nothing got between him and his afternoon nap. Regardless, from my vantage point, truly bad forces had been loosed upon the world—namely, that tawny-haired clarinetist in the Texas Band. As the dramatic fourth quarter unfolded, a close-up of her face kept appearing on the TV screen as she cried and cheered and ultimately flashed the Hook 'Em Horns sign in victory. It was as if this tearfully jubilant gal was shooting me the middle finger even before I understood what it meant.

I teared up when President Nixon, brandishing a wooden plaque of some sort, went to the Texas locker room to declare the Longhorns national champions. "For a team to be down fourteen to nothing and not to lose its cool," he said, "proves that you're number one, and that's what you are." At that moment, I can't say that I actually disliked Nixon, but years later it hardly surprised me to learn that he was sometimes called Tricky Dick. All I knew was that my team had lost The Big Game, and the purported Leader of the Free World was in the wrong locker room.

My grandmother fixed me a roast beef sandwich and, with her red rhinestone slippers in hand, retired to her bedroom. I poured myself a glass of milk, alone with nothing on the TV except *The Lawrence Welk Show* and *Hee Haw.* I picked up a copy of *National Geographic,* which I typically found boring, and I even read the garish headlines in the *National Enquirer.* Anything to divert me. Such torment, the gloom after losing a momentous game, the haunting what-ifs, the realization that the outcome can never ever be changed and there will be no second chance. I missed my mom and dad.

The following Tuesday, after school, I went back to my grandmother's house to see the latest *Sports Illustrated.* There, atop the knee-high pile of magazines on the floor beside her easy chair, was the new issue featuring a cover photo of quarterback James Street on his pivotal 42-yard touchdown run early in the fourth quarter. My eyes went to the headline: "Texas Gambles Its Way Past Arkansas." Back then, any story on the cover of *Sports Illustrated* was a big deal. I picked up the magazine but couldn't bear to open it, so I just placed it back on top of the pile. For good measure, I covered the *SI* with one of my grandmother's *National Enquirers.*

Even in my crushing disappointment, I had been captivated by the high-stakes drama of The Big Shootout, the frenzied spirit of the home-state crowd, the full-throated build of the Woo Pig Sooie call, the cheerleaders in crimson sweaters, the players in their red helmets bearing the logo of the charging Razorback. I relished the sense that my team was at the center of what I took to be the entire universe, and I was somewhat justified in this: The Big Shootout was viewed by one in four Americans, and drew a Nielsen rating of 52.1, swamping *Rowan & Martin's Laugh-In,* the era's highest rated TV show at 31.8.

And so, with this game, the 1960s came to an end. Over the decade, even with this stinging loss, Arkansas had won more games than any college football team except Alabama. No wonder my father was so into it. As a kid, I just assumed the Razorbacks' reign near the top of college football would go on forever and prove as immutable as my parents' love. But what the hell does a third-grader know?

2

Looking Long
for Jimbo

Inspired by The Big Shootout, in the fourth grade I played peewee league football. The Whirlwinds of South School wore white jerseys with red numerals, which somewhat resembled the Hogs' away uniforms. The coach put me at quarterback, chiefly because I could remember the plays and help the other boys get lined up in the right spots. The only downer was that I never actually threw the football, which, at regulation size, was too big for my hands. Whenever our coach called a pass-play, I took the snap from center and lateraled to the halfback, our best runner and passer. My role thusly circumscribed, you could say I was little more than a game manager.

At my insistence, I wore number 10, same as Bill Montgomery, the Hogs' dapper quarterback. On television, I had noted everything about him: the shape of the white facemask on his red helmet, the white sweat bands up his forearms, the slash of eye black on each cheek, the hand towel that hung out of the front of his white pants. Bill Montgomery was who I wanted to be. One day I, too, would quarterback the Hogs, a dream as vivid to me as was the Ponderosa Ranch on the *Bonanza* TV show: *Facing a crucial third down, I signal timeout to the referee and trot to the sideline to confer with Coach Broyles. I wipe my face with a towel, then put my helmet back on and, with my chinstrap dangling, trot back to the huddle where I take one knee and look up into the expectant eyes of my Razorback teammates and bark out the play call.*

My goodness, how fantastic was that going to be!

Actually, the odds of any such future for me were quite long. My father was five feet eight, and my mother stood at five feet—both of them the smallest of their several siblings. When my mother was pregnant with me, she and my father had fretted over whether they'd have a boy or a girl, a concern my plainspoken grandfather had considered misplaced. "You two had just better worry about not having a damned midget," he declaimed.

Like The Big Shootout the previous December, the opener in 1970 against Stanford was also broadcast on national television, thus perpetuating my belief that Razorback football was a matter of world-shaping influence. Led by Jim Plunkett, Stanford jumped out to a 27-0 lead. Then in the second quarter, with the score 27-7, a black Razorback player named Jon Richardson caught a 37-yard touchdown pass from Bill Montgomery to cut the lead to 27-14. Until that day, it had never occurred to me that a black guy would play for the Razorbacks—or for any opposing team, for that matter. All players on both sides in The Big Shootout were white, and rest assured when the Hogs had played Ole Miss in the Sugar Bowl the previous January, all the Mississippi players had been white as well.

Did I realize that Jon Richardson's appearance in this game represented something momentous? No, I did not. Jonesboro was still mostly segregated, with a so-called "colored" neighborhood just east of downtown. Sure, there were two black girls in my fourth-grade homeroom class, but I didn't think of them as symbolic in any way. They liked me and thought I was cute, and I liked them and thought they were cute, too. There were no black boys on my peewee league football team, and the only black man I knew did odd jobs for my grandfather. Nevertheless, sports can open minds: If a black player wore a Razorback jersey and lined up at running back behind Bill Montgomery, that was fine by me.

Late in the fourth quarter, the Hogs cut the lead to 34-28, but Bill Montgomery came up inches short on fourth-and-two inside the five-yard line. While this took some of the shine off of my number 10 peewee-league jersey, I still then dreamed of quarterbacking the Razorbacks one day. But that lingering ambition was soon to suffer a mortal blow.

One Saturday morning, the South School Whirlwinds, in our white helmets, were pitted against a crosstown rival, the black-helmeted East School. The dew-soaked grass was tracked with footsteps, and as the sun rose higher my team faced a crucial fourth and one. We all huddled with our coach, a gaunt man with what I took to be the world's largest Adam's apple. He called a quarterback sneak. This was to be my moment to shine. All 11 of us fourth-graders broke the huddle with an almost synchronous clap.

I lined up under the center, but across the line of scrimmage, staring at me with his pit bull eyes, was a thick-necked linebacker named Scott Reed, a savvy player whose father was the football coach at Jonesboro High. Certainly, Scott Reed knew I was about to attempt a quarterback sneak. In an effort to confuse me, he darted around behind his nose guard, crouching off his left rump, then his right rump, then back and forth like a madman. I glanced at our coach, who, in a show of confidence, declined to call a timeout. My eyes went back to Scott Reed in his dastardly black helmet, and I knew that one of two things was going to happen when the ball was snapped: I would either go left of the center and Scott Reed would go right and I'd easily pick up the first down. Or I would go left and he would go left, too, and it would get ugly. Obviously, if I went right of the center, the same calculus of limited possibility applied. Only when the ball was snapped did I decide which way I would go.

Woozy and likely concussed, I walked slowly to the sideline. After I gathered my wits, I examined my heretofore scuff-free white helmet and was impressed by the long black scar near the crown; there was even a rough-grained chip in the white of my helmet. Meanwhile, the game went on and whenever one of my teammates came to the sideline, I showed off my scarred helmet as if to justify why I hadn't picked up the crucial first down. But our peewee league coach didn't call any more quarterback sneaks, and my duties as the team's signal caller were even further narrowed. I became a caricature of the quarterback as game manager.

During fourth grade, I also encountered challenges away from the peewee-league football field. Mrs. Elkins, my homeroom teacher, decided she'd seen enough of my oddball handwriting. I was a left-handed hooker, meaning I slanted my paper backwards, contorted my arm into a half circle, and wrote with my thumb and forefinger pointed back at my chest instead of away from my body like every other kid.

Mrs. Elkins, prim and gray-haired, was correct: The way I wrote was overly labored, even goofy. She likely wasn't thrilled that I was writing left-handed in the first place. This was before America had a string of presidents who wrote left-handed, including Gerald Ford, George H.W. Bush, Bill Clinton and Barak Obama. Not all left-handers are hookers. Only Ford and Obama hooked, which can be cured—people can learn to write normally as left-handers, and Mrs. Elkins, bless her heart, was determined to make sure that if I wrote with the wrong hand, then at least I would use proper form.

To assist her, she positioned Jimbo Osment, one of my best friends, at the desk next to mine with instructions to raise his hand if he caught me hooking. The first time I broke ranks, he punched me in the arm. One of the biggest bruisers in peewee football, Jimbo wore number 44 because he idolized Donnie Anderson, the lumbering running back and punter for the Green Bay Packers. Nevertheless, Jimbo wasn't the kind to abuse his power over me, nor did he have to. His mere presence at my side was enough to reform my penmanship.

Near me and my guard dog Jimbo sat Bob Childress, small and bespectacled, and Neal Harrington, black-haired and waif-thin. If I could assign friends grades of permanence, Jimbo, Bob, and Neal would score most highly—and, critically, each of them totally got Razorback football. The bond between the four of us was such that we'd formed the HOCH Club, an acronym comprising the first initials of each of our last names. Our Club included a membership card as well as a little ditty of a song, coined by Jimbo, that's too embarrassing to recount here. But, most of all, our Club was our way to declare that we were above the other boys at South School Elementary.

Yet we HOCH Clubbers had no reason to be uppity. Like all of our classmates, we were the products of our decidedly modest environment. Set along a ridge amid a featureless agricultural landscape, our hometown of just over 27,000 seemed to have no reason to exist, except to fill a hole in the map in the imaginary triangle between Little Rock, Memphis, and St. Louis. There was no river, no nearby lake of any size, not even one of the new interstate highways of the era. So it had to be the people, right? The sturdy, the hardworking, the enterprising, the dutiful, the devout, descendants of those in work boots and chore coats and soiled shirts who'd cleared the vast surrounding land of hardwood trees, rebuilt the modest downtown after a devastating fire in 1889, tended mercantile stores, and generally brought civilization west with a theater, a newspaper, a hospital, and, eventually, a land-grant university. Like the rest of America, Jonesboro had emerged from a post-War War II slumber. Anyone who drove through town couldn't help but notice the preponderance of banks and churches, the physical manifestation of the dogged pursuit of commerce and faith—which, as it happened, turned out to be my parents' abiding passions.

As the lunch bell rang, all 30 of us fourth-graders surged towards the lunchroom, where the girls sat apart from the boys at long eight-seater tables. Here too, Jimbo sat beside me because he knew I never ate everything on my plate. He waited patiently, and then just before I returned my lunch tray, gobbled up my untouched applesauce and the last soggy French fries.

Out on the playground, several lithesome girls climbed on the monkey bars, while we HOCH Clubbers went down the hill past the playground to either the baseball diamond or the makeshift football fields, depending upon the season. We played games of some sort all the time—in spring and summer it was Little League baseball and backyard whiffle ball; fall brought peewee league and sandlot football, and winter was Y-league basketball and after-school pick-up games. There was no expectation that we specialize in one sport, or quit another if we weren't any good—we played for the pure fun of it. It didn't matter that Bob was ungainly, or that Neal had bum knees, or that I was perennially undersized, or that Jimbo, while gifted, was slow of foot.

Schoolyard touch football games were my realm, my domain. I played all-time quarterback, and while my 10-year-old hands couldn't properly grip a real football, I could really sling around a toy football. I could perfectly time a down-and-out, gun a pass on a crossing route, or take something off a short throw and hit my intended receiver in a spot where he could easily catch it. I loved to dial up my favorite play, on which Jimbo went long down the sideline and I threw the toy football into the sky as far as I could. Though lacking in foot speed, Jimbo had a knack for getting behind defenders Neal and Bob, plus his hands were as sticky as Fred Biletnikoff's. Jimbo and I had a telepathic connection, not unlike that between Bill Montgomery and his favorite target, Chuck Dicus.

Then the bell rang at the schoolhouse up the hill. Lunch break was over, time for just one more play: I dropped back again and looked long for Jimbo.

3

Dad & Mom & Me

My father had a talent for spotting opportunity. Years ago, while working at my grandfather's John Deere dealership in Jonesboro, he'd noticed that the coffin-sized tool boxes of the kind mounted behind the cab of a pickup truck were hot sellers. So Dad ordered a few from the manufacturer, loaded up my mother's wood-paneled Ford Country Squire Station Wagon with them (two in the back and two on the roof), and drove around Craighead County selling them to farmers. Emboldened by his initial success, he took a gamble and ordered 100 more tool boxes. When they arrived, my grandfather, who'd fronted most of the money, said, "Okay, you little shit, you wanted 'em, now you'd better sell 'em." So my father traveled all over the Mid-South hawking these tool boxes. After this scrappy beginning, he launched a company called Stor-All Tool Box.

Dad was a busy man with the patience of an entrepreneur, which is to say he didn't have it in abundance. To him, time was precious and it was a challenge to hold his attention. But during football season, when he got home from work in the evenings, he and I played a pitch-and-catch game we called Hut-Two. Out in our front yard, I assumed the three-point stance of a flanker, and when Dad called, "Hut-Two!" I raced ahead as he lofted the football, putting plenty of air under it while I strained to reel it in. Then I jogged back, tossed the ball back to Dad, returned to the imaginary line of scrimmage, and waited for him to say, "Hut-Two" again. When I tired of running deep routes, I executed down-and-outs along the sideline, using the street for a boundary as I tried to snag the football while dragging one foot to stay in bounds. We played Hut-Two until daylight faded, or until Mother called us inside for supper. But even after we finished eating, I pestered my father to toss me the football while he sat under the lamplight reading his trade journals.

It was September of 1971, a dark time in this country—in the world, for that matter. On some Sundays, I played sandlot football in my grandparents' front yard with several of my uncle's friends. One of them, in recognition of my pass-catching skills (or at least my enthusiasm for endlessly playing pass-and-catch), called me "Bambi," the nickname of Lance Alworth, the All-American wide receiver for the Razorbacks in the late 1950s. I liked being called Bambi, and I envied my uncle and his friends because they were older. Yet only two years before—the week before The Big Shootout, in fact—President Nixon had instituted the first draft lottery since World War II. So I had no reason to envy these older young men. To avoid being sent to Vietnam, my uncle was serving as a cook in the Army Reserve, and I had heard him say he could cook a meal for two hundred soldiers, yet couldn't prepare one for a family of four. It was the year of the May Day protests in Washington and the publication of the Pentagon Papers. But none of this marked my world. Arkansas football was at the outer limits of my understanding, and even this was proving dark enough for my young mind. And though I couldn't know it, I was only days away from one of the biggest disappointments of my youth.

Kids are often derided for developing a personal fable in which the child is said to feel as if he's the only one who has ever experienced what he's going through. The child thinks he's invincible and that nothing bad will happen to him. This notion of a personal fable is intended to denote the child's narcissistic immaturity. But isn't this the ideal mental state for every sports fan? Doesn't the fanatic want to live in a world in which his team is truly special, even historic in some sense—a world in which bad things happen only to *other* teams and their less-deserving fans?

Of course, we do.

Over the previous two years, Arkansas had lost only to Texas (twice), to Archie Manning's Ole Miss Rebels in the Sugar Bowl, and to Heisman Winner Jim Plunkett's Stanford team, which went on to beat Ohio State in the Rose Bowl. None of these losses wrecked my so-called personal fable.

But when the Hogs lost their 1971 home opener to Tulsa, any sense I had of being bulletproof was demolished. I had been so confident of a victory that I hadn't even bothered to listen to the game on the radio. My father announced the final score as I fetched an errant Hut-Two pass from my mother's shrub garden. I was stunned that Arkansas had fallen to such a decidedly lesser team. It was late afternoon on a Saturday and I had hours to stew on this loss, to turn it over in my mind as I lay in bed that night. It was the first thing I thought of when I awoke the next morning, and I lugged it to school on Monday: Tulsa 21, Arkansas 20. Had I jinxed my team by not listening to the game? At some point, every fan must reckon with superstition. But even at age 11, my gut told me that wins and losses were not decided by whether or not I had on my lucky red T-shirt, or if I ate the same Swanson TV dinner of turkey, green peas, and whipped potatoes on the night before each game (Mother typically cooked these dinners on Friday evening when she and Dad went out). Such nonsense was for weaker souls. Still, I had the same feeling I get every time the Hogs lose to any lesser opponent, which is that the world can be a dark place indeed.

On the weekend of my 11th birthday, my father and I headed to Little Rock to attend my first Razorback game. Even better, it was against the Texas Longhorns. Under a heavy sky, Dad sped southward on the two-lane road in his Cadillac; all around us, the endless fields of rice and soybeans and cotton had mostly been harvested. On the side of the road was a John Deere tractor, its huge black tires throwing off mud, and, near it, another tall green contraption full of fluffy cotton. "That's a two-row cotton picker," Dad said.

"Really," I said, not as interested as I should've been, considering how much I'd benefited from my father's knowledge of farm equipment.

When I was three, before Dad had started Stor-All Tool Box, he and my grandfather had made a killing with a savvy bit of harvest-related arbitrage. One day a young man had pulled into my grandfather's John Deere dealership with a two-row cotton picker in the back of his bob truck. Obviously, a two-row cotton picker was a step up from a one-row cotton picker, but my grandfather further learned from the young man that, owing to the introduction of a new style of cotton picker called a stripper, there was a surplus of two-row cotton pickers in west Texas, where the young man was from. So my grandfather and my dad flew out to west Texas and bought 100 of these two-row cotton pickers from various farmers for $6,000 each. Then, while my grandfather went back home to get the money to cover all of the checks they'd just written, Dad loaded these two-row cotton pickers on a train and shipped them back to northeast Arkansas, where he and my grandfather sold all 100 of them in just a few weeks for $9,500 each. That was big money back then.

This father-son trip to Little Rock was my dad's way of sharing his past with me. He had first been to War Memorial Stadium

back in 1954, when he and his teammates from his junior high football team had sat in the north end zone where the Hogs' Preston
Carpenter, wearing no facemask, ran right towards them to score
the winning touchdown against Ole Miss. This thrilling ending
was said to be the moment the Razorbacks became a statewide
obsession.

When Dad and I got to War Memorial Stadium, we passed
through the turnstile and entered a subterranean expanse of
concession stands, bathrooms, and various ramps that led to the
stands. The air smelled of popcorn, hotdogs, imminent rain. We
found our ramp, and I followed as we fell in line with the throng
of fans shuffling ahead. I inched closer to the daylight, and then
boom! Down on the perfect-green AstroTurf, the red-shirted Razorback players warmed up on one side of the 50-yard line, and the
white-shirted Longhorns scurried around on the other. The passes
of the quarterbacks zipped through the air, the receivers ran their
crisp routes, the running backs practiced their sharp cuts. *Was
I really here?* I could scarcely believe how close I was to these
players. As my father and I climbed the stairs to our seats, I stole
backward glances and tried to recognize familiar jersey numbers
from past games I'd watched on TV. Jim Bertelsen, number 35
for Texas, was one of the players introduced on camera before the
kickoff of The Big Shootout (he'd also scored the winning touchdown). Bill McClard, the Hogs' All-American field goal kicker, stood
at the 40-yard line. Wasn't number 26 Mike Reppond, the wide
receiver who was quoted in *Dave Campbell's Arkansas Football* as
saying the first time he'd tried to catch a pass from the rifle-armed
Joe Ferguson, the ball went through his hands and shattered his
shoulder pad?

From the onset, I loved the coziness of War Memorial Stadium. It was perfectly bowl-shaped, with risers of the same height
all the way around. After the players headed towards the locker
room, the Razorback Marching Band formed into a giant Arkan-

sas "A" that stretched across half the field. The Band played the national anthem, and then marched up and down the field as they blared the stirring cadence of the Arkansas Swing March. Kickoff drew closer and my adrenaline surged higher when I spotted the jumpy Razorback players gathered in a knot in the tunnel. Framing the tunnel, red-clad fans banged the railing like maniacs. With a surge, the knot of players broke and charged through the "A" as they took the field to the sound of Arkansas Fight, and all 56,000 fans in the stadium stood for the opening kickoff and Called the Hogs (Woo Pig Sooie!) with a swelling intensity so loud the roar vibrated in my chest.

Then it began to sprinkle. I slumped when Texas returned a punt inside the 10-yard line and went up 7-0. Oh my gosh, was this going to be a repeat of the previous season when the Longhorns beat the Hogs 42-7, a mere continuation of the last seven quarters going back to the fourth quarter of The Big Shootout, as Texas had outscored the Razorbacks 64-7? My dad bolted from his seat to go get a box of popcorn and two Cokes.

Then the rain came down harder. But as the red of the Razorbacks' water-logged jerseys turned several hues darker than the red of their shiny helmets, Joe Ferguson got busy. At halftime, the Hogs led 21-7. Late in the third quarter, the sky fell in a torrent, and with each tackle along the sidelines the players skidded great distances in sprays of water. It reminded me of whiffle ball games in Jimbo's backyard after we had soaked the base paths for hours with a garden hose, just to enjoy the sloppiness.

After spotting Texas a touchdown, the Hogs reeled off 31 straight points, a stunning reversal. Throughout the game, I slipped my dad nuggets of Razorback trivia: Hog quarterback Joe Ferguson was only a sophomore; Mike Saint, the Hogs' bruising fullback, was a converted tight end (I'd read that in the *Arkansas Gazette*); and then, in a what-if zinger, I reminded him of how much sweeter this victory would be if only the Hogs hadn't lost three weeks before to Tulsa.

We left War Memorial Stadium early, understandable given the rain. I was disappointed, but Dad, for all his long history with Arkansas football, wasn't as emotionally attached to the Razorbacks as I was. He didn't pore over the sports pages of the *Arkansas Gazette* or religiously watch *The Frank Broyles Show* on Sunday afternoons. He hadn't committed the entire Razorback roster—every player's name, number, height, weight, hometown—to memory. In such matters, I was the teacher, he, the pupil. Always, I took Things Razorback a quantum level further. It was a world I could master and lord over the less knowledgeable, including my dad.

We returned to Jonesboro happy, which pleased Mother because she knew life at our house would be calmer. She had prepared a late dinner of cold chicken and mashed potatoes—Mother took great joy in doing for others, and one of the chief goals of her life was to get a good meal down the throats of my sister and me. As we enjoyed our meal together, I spotted the chocolate-covered angel food cake my mother had made for my birthday. I hugged her and squeezed her playfully. "Did you watch on TV?" I said. In some ways, I wished I could've seen the game as it came across on national television, to have heard the commentary of Chris Schenkel and Bud Wilkinson, to have basked in the nationwide acclaim that had surely been heaped on the Hogs that afternoon.

"It was just great," Mother said, even though she didn't offer any game-related specifics, except that it had rained, which was when I knew she still had no idea who Joe Ferguson was.

Certainly, my mania for Razorback football put my mother in a tough spot. In high school, she had lived in Louisville, Kentucky, where her father worked as an engraver for the *Louisville-Courier Journal*. There, she'd been named Basketball Queen, a high honor, she noted, because basketball was a bigger deal in Kentucky than football. But, sports-wise in the state of Arkansas, all there was of any consequence was Razorback football, and in the wake of the victory over Texas, my joy was deep, almost rapturous. To have sat in War Memorial Stadium and watched the Hogs beat Texas was like I'd drunk from a magic potion. The images coursed through my mind and if I thought about it very long I got goosebumps over how the Razorbacks had finally vanquished their hated rival.

Yet my mother could only look on as if I'd fallen into a world she didn't understand and would never be able to identify with, no matter how much she loved me, which was a lot. She had attended a few Razorback games, and while she enjoyed all the socializing, she had no interest in the game, or the team, itself. Her experience of Razorback football was almost entirely second-hand, and to the extent that she paid attention to it at all, she did so only because my dad and I were in its thrall. Nevertheless, she was wise to the world and wise to people, and I suspect she knew that with her son, she had a budding head case on her hands. Yet she never undercut or belittled me, or implied that my passion was misplaced. She just accepted my love for the Hogs as an unalterable expression of my personhood, like the fact that I punted with my left foot.

Just before Thanksgiving that season, the made-for-TV movie *Brian's Song* came out. Our family gathered in our living room to watch it, the lights dim, our feet in the pale-green shag carpet of the era, with Blossom, our beloved golden lab, on the lush sofa between me and my mother. My father, in his usual chair, peered up only occasionally from his trade journals, while my 7-year-old sister, barely interested in the movie, was wrapped up like a mummy in what she still called her "cubby," a worn-to-tatters dingy-white polyester blanket she literally could not live without.

Brian's Song is the story of Brian Piccolo, a running back for the Chicago Bears who'd played alongside Gayle Sayers, and his brave fight with cancer. The final scene, during which Piccolo's wife sobs at his deathbed, just tore my guts out. I sniffled uncontrollably and turned my face to try to hide my tears. But it was hopeless, my awkwardness amplified because I was the only one in our living room engrossed in *Brian's Song*. Mother slipped me a Kleenex, while my sister, her eyes wide with disbelief, regarded me as if I, her elder brother, was the biggest whiny baby she'd ever seen. I mumbled about how my hay fever was bothering me, my mouth such a quivering mess of emotion that when I tried to get the words out I blew a spit bubble. What I really wanted to do was curl up in the fetal position, with dear Blossom at my side, and bawl like an infant.

4

DNA of a Fanatic

Despite the win over Texas, the 1971 Razorbacks were relegated to the lesser Liberty Bowl in Memphis, which presented another opportunity for my father and me to take a road trip.

I had been to Memphis many times, but usually with my mother and sister. Those visits, more like scavenger hunts, were for the purpose of buying things that were unavailable in a small town like Jonesboro. How well I remember those trips, piled into my mother's wood-paneled station wagon with Mother smoking a cigarette (a habit she later quit), my sister and I roaming freely throughout the car because no one wore seatbelts in those days. We crossed the flat Arkansas delta and then, suddenly, the ragged skyline of the River City came into sight. Crossing the long bridge, the water below coursing in great swirls of brown wash, was like being transported into another world.

Our usual first stop, at my urging, was James Davis, a well-known haberdashery, where the neatly folded boys' shirts were stacked in a wall of wooden cubbyholes. Locating the one marked with my size, I pulled out every shirt and chose my favorites, which I then presented to Mother. She would tell me I could only have three shirts and even that was pushing it, but she was ultimately fighting a losing battle: My father was well dressed, and my grandfather was a veritable clotheshorse.

After lunch at Britling's Cafeteria on Poplar Avenue, we would resume our shopping at department stores like Goldsmith's and Julius Lewis. Later, we would hit Seessell's Supermarket for date bread, French horns, and chocolate éclairs, and then we would double back for a stop at Mednikow's Jewelers. By this time it would be getting dark and my sister and I would be getting cranky, so to placate us Mother would take us to TGI Friday's in Overton Square for fried shrimp dipped in cherry sauce. On the drive back to Jonesboro, Mallory would fall asleep under the glow of the car's dashboard and I would tell Mom that I was never going back to Memphis with her ever again. But inevitably, as Christmas drew closer, I would rethink that position.

This December trip to Memphis with my father, however, was no mere pre-Christmas shopping excursion. He and I were headed to a Razorback post-season bowl game against Tennessee. It would be a game my dad would never forget—the game in which his son's once-private fanaticism first showed its rabid face in public.

The night was cold and misty, and the brooding atmosphere in Liberty Bowl Stadium evoked what I imagined to be the feeling of war. My pulse quickened when the Razorback players charged the field like a white-clad army. I've always easily surrendered to the grandeur, pageantry, and formality of college football. No other sport offers quite the same sense of scale and drama and clash, and at any game involving the Arkansas Razorbacks, I've also always—since this Liberty Bowl game against the Tennessee Volunteers—had a problem with self-control.

It happened late in the fourth quarter, when, with the Hogs up 13-7, Arkansas running back Jon Richardson fumbled. The fumble happened on the far sideline, but I swear I saw a Razorback player (specifically, number 74) rise from the pile with the football cradled to his chest. He handed the ball over to the referee, who promptly awarded possession to Tennessee.

At which point I snapped like The Incredible Hulk.

I stood on my seat and booed and stomped. My squeaky 11-year-old voice carried to all those around us as I, incredulous, implored my father to make sense of what had just happened. "They can't give the ball to Tennessee! Can they? Huh? Huh? How can the referee do that? This isn't right! *Can't somebody do something?*"

I brayed and brayed. I would not let it go. (I have never let it go.)

By this point, my father was less interested in what had happened on the field than in what was happening right beside him. Even he was taken aback by my sustained outrage. Yet he did nothing to deter me—didn't even offer a calming pat on the back. He just let my berserker fit play out, regarding my tantrum with eyebrows raised and perhaps—as I've gathered during his many retellings of this story through the years—some kind of twisted pride.

As fans, it's interesting to ponder just what influences our behavior. How much of what we do owes to nature? How much is due to nurture? My dad has always been a moderate man. He drinks a bit, but never overdrinks. He likes good food, but seldom overeats. He rarely ever uses a bad word. Yet, like his mostly-Irish mother and two younger brothers, he can get hot when his temper is stirred. Growing up, I remember Dad's ongoing war on mosquitos. Each summer, as these pests swept in from the flooded rice fields that encircled Jonesboro, Dad would say, "So many mosquitos, they fly in formation!" Inevitably, over the course of any summer, my sister or I would carelessly leave the screen door ajar, and each time the house became infested with mosquitos my dad would come unhinged. Tormented by the thought of even one mosquito in his bedroom, he would stalk it like a demon and smack it against the white ceiling with my mother's flyswatter. Yet throughout this blatant rip-off at the Liberty Bowl, my father, the crazed mosquito hunter, kept his cool. My outrage was enough for both of us, apparently. And my anger burned even hotter when, after being gifted this fumble, the Vols scored to win the game.

Dad and I walked silently to the outer parking lot. It was late, and with the gloomy weather and the winter solstice, I felt as though it had been dark all day. The fact was, my sense of right and wrong had been deeply offended, and any lingering joy I felt in being with my father was buried beneath my disappointment over how the Hogs had been jobbed. As we crossed over the Mississippi River, the lights of Memphis receded and the sprawling cotton fields of eastern Arkansas were as black as my mood.

When I walked into our house, my mom said, "I'm so sorry, hon," as if I'd been mugged in Memphis. Her hair was matted on one side—she had fallen asleep while waiting up for Dad and me—and the TV was still on. I doubted that she had watched the game; she'd probably heard the result on WMC's 10 o'clock sports report with that loudmouth Jack Eaton.

"Are you hungry, hon?"

"No," I replied, even though I was indeed hungry. But I was in no mood to be agreeable. I plopped down in front of the TV. Who cared what was on? It was only five days before Christmas, always an exciting time because school was out. The previous Christmas, my mother, ever the Good Samaritan, had spiced things up by arranging for us to be joined by Darryl Hamilton, a rough-edged 15-year-old from juvenile detention down at Cummins Prison. I hadn't asked Darryl any questions about his checkered past, though it didn't take me long to discern that he wasn't a Razorback fan. Despite our lack of common interests, over the course of his two-week stay I realized that the only true difference between Darryl Hamilton and me was that I had been born to a good family and he had not.

Through the doorway to the kitchen, I saw my mother and father huddled in conversation. On the wall near the refrigerator hung her flyswatter, the same one that Dad used to stalk mosquitos and Mother sometimes used to rap my sister's bare legs. I turned down the TV and overheard Dad telling Mother about my brattish behavior during the game—how I'd stood up on my seat, my yelling, my sustained upset. He seemed more pleased than when I'd brought home top marks on my mid-year fifth-grade report card. But as he spoke, I saw a look of consternation spread across my mother's face, and I knew she wished she'd been sitting beside me earlier that night at the Liberty Bowl with her flyswatter in her hand.

"I'm going to bed, y'all," I called from the living room. I offered this in a conciliatory tone as I'd decided it was best to end my pout. "Night all. Nite-nite."

In the following summer of 1972, my mother and I went to Keller's Sporting Goods to buy me a new football helmet for the upcoming peewee league season. This store had a big sign that fronted Jonesboro's Main Street, a gumball machine inside its doublewide front door, and unvarnished hardwood floors throughout. For a young sports junkie like me, it was as treasure-laden as the vault at Fort Knox. I was entering sixth grade and was determined to make my mark on the gridiron, notwithstanding my demotion to second-string halfback during fifth grade. Plainly, I needed some sort of a leg-up.

I first tried on a helmet that was too much like the rinky-dink helmets I'd worn in past seasons. It was solid white, like an egg, with thin padding inside and an uncool plastic facemask that resembled no facemask I'd ever seen on any Razorback player. As I wandered the store, hoping to come upon a better option, I spotted a genuine Chicago Bears helmet high on a shelf. I had no idea why Keller's Sporting Goods had such a helmet, but this shiny black beauty looked exactly like the helmet Brian Piccolo (played by James Caan) wore in *Brian's Song*. It was a shocking sight, for sure.

"Can I try on that one, please?" I said to the clerk.

I waited while he fetched a ladder, which took seemingly forever. Meanwhile, my mind raced. More than anything, I wanted a helmet like those I'd seen on television. I craved authenticity, and this time I was not going to be denied. When I was seven, I had asked Santa Claus (who by then I had long known was my parents) for a Batman costume. It was to be an *exact* replica, in miniature, of the get-up Bruce Wayne wore on the *Batman* TV show—pointy-eared mask, sleek knee-high boots, tight leggings, flowing cape, wide gold belt. But the Batman costume I found under the Christmas tree was more like a cartoonish pair of loose-fitting pajamas. In an especially underhanded trick of design, the pants were black from the knees down, as if this dark-colored cloth was supposed to pass for Batman's knee-high boots.

The clerk finally descended the ladder with the prized helmet in hand.

"It doesn't have a facemask," he said. Certainly, I knew this. The fact that it was the only one in the store that lacked a face-mask only made it more desirable. This bona fide Chicago Bears helmet, emblazoned on both sides with the trademark Bears "C," was as heavy as a bowling ball. When I put it on, the weight of it caused my head to titter from side to side as if I were a bobble head.

I glanced at Mother, who was nibbling at her lower lip to keep from laughing. I had a pretty good idea of how dorky I looked: The previous autumn, Razorback quarterback Joe Ferguson had appeared on the cover of *Street & Smith's Official 1971 College Football Yearbook* in a red Hog helmet with no facemask. Ferguson lacked the movie-star good looks of his predecessor, Bill Montgomery, and in that tight-fitting red helmet with no facemask, he'd looked like an old Russian woman with her head wrapped in a babushka.

"I'll be really safe in this helmet," I said to my mother, even as I imagined the ferocious blows I would deliver to thick-necked boys like Scott Reed. The helmet still felt heavy on my head, but I figured I'd get used to its heft, which I took to be further proof of its invincible quality.

"I'm not sure that's the helmet for you, hon."

I sighed at my mother's killjoy reluctance. It was probably about the money, since this helmet cost about four times as much as one that was age-appropriate. In our family, my mother was the penny pincher; my father, confident of his money-making abilities, spent more freely.

"But I really want *this* helmet," I said, convinced fate was with me on this. After all, what were the odds of my finding a helmet like this in Jonesboro, Arkansas? "Just look at this thing," I went on as I rapped my fists several times above each earhole, like I was christening the hull of some unsinkable ship.

When the clerk again noted that the helmet lacked a face-mask, I glared at him, frustrated by his lack of imagination. I had the perfect one in mind: gunmetal gray and shaped like the one worn by Gayle Sayers (as played by Billy Dee Williams) in *Brian's Song.*

"I just don't know about this helmet," Mother said more firmly.

"But Mom."

Eventually, my mother's wiser head prevailed, and later, though not immediately, I was thankful. Most boys want to fit in, and the cinematic wonders of *Brian's Song* notwithstanding, I'd have looked silly showing up for my first sixth-grade practice wearing a helmet that looked as if it had been lifted from the locker of an NFL player.

In the fall of my sixth-grade year, I was beside myself with excitement about Razorback football. My fervor had been stoked by the summer issue of *Dave Campbell's Arkansas Football*, with this banner on the cover: "1972: Blockbuster Year for Joe Ferguson and the Razorbacks." Inside was an article entitled, "A Dream Team Takes Shape at Arkansas," and, on page 13, a prediction that this Razorback team would go on to be crowned national champions.

Certainly, that prophecy suffered a serious setback when the fourth-ranked Hogs lost their season-opener to the USC Trojans. But over the next month, the Porkers reeled off four in a row, and it was during this stretch that my enthusiasm, and to a lesser degree that of my football-savvy HOCH Club friends, spilled over onto the playground at South School Elementary. These were the halcyon days of Dickey Morton, who, at five feet ten and 160 pounds, was the leading rusher in the Southwest Conference. On his Sunday television show, Frank Broyles sometimes mentioned the "Inside Belly Series," a package of running plays that were propelling an itty-bitty white guy to a place as one of the greatest running backs in Hog history. Thus inspired, the full HOCH Club membership imitated the Razorbacks' offensive attack as best as we could.

During both the morning and afternoon recess, Jimbo, Bob, Neal, and I lined up in the wishbone formation (invented at Texas in 1967 and, trust me, quite popular back in the early 1970s) and ran various phantom plays of our own devising: some runs, some passes, some run-pass options. We used unsuspecting classmates as defensive obstacles, darting and weaving among them on the blacktopped playground. I took the phantom snap and ran at half-speed down the imaginary line of scrimmage, then I inevitably encountered (or sought out) a classmate on the crowded blacktop and, at this "decision point," I either cut up field or pitched the football to the trailing halfback. In another go-to play, I faked the fullback handoff to Jimbo, dropped back seven steps, and fired a long pass as he lumbered down the blacktop.

As my friends and I executed our skeleton offense—as quarterback, it all revolved around me—it's hard to imagine what our elementary-school teachers thought of us. Mr. Dobbs, impossibly large at six foot six, stood on the fringe of the playground in arms-folded silence, smothering a smile. He was a with-it dude—in that era of Bobby Fischer and Boris Spassky, he let us to play chess in his homeroom class, and we also got to shoot BB guns in a school-sanctioned program (we actually fired at targets in our classroom!). Nevertheless, even for the with-it Mr. Dobbs, our phantom wishbone attack was probably a little surreal.

5

Football Factions

Friendships can be strained by football loyalties, and I can see now that the riving of us HOCH Clubbers into football factions was as inevitable as the splintering of a major religion into various offshoots.

It was October, the Saturday of the Arkansas-Texas game, and the eyes of my buddies lit up when they spotted my mother's bounty of fried chicken drumsticks, potato salad, coleslaw, and a chocolate-covered angel food cake topped with 12 red candles. Ostensibly, we were all gathered for my birthday, but even I will concede that they likely considered my mother's cooking to be among the most consequential benefits of our friendship.

We sat around the dining table and waited for the feast. Though all four of us HOCH Clubbers played peewee league football, only Jimbo had achieved any sort of glory. Yet even his peewee league career had recently been pockmarked by a notable moment of humiliation. "Did you hear what ole Perry Jones did to Jimbo?" Bob said, referring to the only boy in the league who was a bigger bruiser than Jimbo; Perry Jones was a hulking figure, like that Lennie character in Steinbeck's *Of Mice and Men*.

"Not *that* story again," groaned Jimbo.

Bob gave a guttural laugh, then launched: "I'll never forget this play as long as I live. Jimbo broke through the line on a fullback dive and was running ahead, when from behind ole Perry Jones jumped on his back and drove him to the ground."

"Yes! Yes!" Neal said, red-faced with laughter. "Oh, Jimbo, who could forget! We all saw you crying after Perry Jones piled on top of you."

I hadn't borne witness to this now legendary play because I wasn't on Jimbo's peewee league team. Yet for Bob, an undersized cornerback, and for Neal, a gangly offensive tackle with bad knees, this fullback dive and its brutal aftermath represented a remarkable show of vulnerability from a boy we all considered indestructible. Jimbo not only ruled the football fields at South School, he was also a dominant pitcher in Little League baseball—to the point that Bob often said that the proudest moment thus far in his Little League career was to have connected on a late-swing, line-drive foul off one of Jimbo's fastball pitches.

"I wasn't crying, guys," Jimbo protested.

I loved all this—it was rare that we ever got to Jimbo. Typically, he dished it out rather than took it.

"You *were* crying," Bob and Neal said in mock disgust. "We saw tears. Boo-hoo-hoo!"

"I'd just had the breath knocked out of me," Jimbo said. "My eyes were just watering, that's all. Come on, guys."

I laughed like a hyena too, even as I smothered any mention of how the week before, in my role as a backup running back, I'd scored my only touchdown in three years of peewee league football when I overpowered a boy named Barry Cato. On his knees when we'd met at the goal line, Barry had wrapped his scarecrow arms around my short, churning legs, but because I was running at full speed I fell over him into the end zone—a feat which, had I revealed it, would have been met with guffaws about what a lousy football player Barry Cato was.

In time my mother brought in her food, prompting the clank of plates and the ting of silverware to blend with the ongoing chatter of rough teasing and derisive laughter. Jim, Bob, and Neal went hard after the potato salad, made from my grandmother's recipe. Yet with the approach of the opening kickoff, my gut was jittery with anticipation, and my appetite for my mother's cooking—which, of course, I took for granted—was hardly up to that of my friends.

Eventually, we all gathered in the living room to watch the game. I turned up the TV to hear the voices of Chris Schenkel and Bud Wilkinson, who were, to me, the epitome of college football. Whenever they were on, I knew it was a big-time game. But after I had turned up the volume, my friends only talked louder.

"Quiet, guys," I said. "Hush! Hush!"

But such seriousness—*my* seriousness—could not be tolerated.

"Gonna beat *Tejas* today?" Jimbo said, pronouncing it Spanish style. He knew that despite last year's cathartic 31-7 win in Little Rock, the Longhorns were still my bête noire.

"Yes, Jimbo," I said in a lame attempt to shut him up, "*Tejas* is going down."

Then Bob and Neal chanted, "Beat *Tejas!* Beat *Tejas!* Beat *Tejas!*"

"All right, all right," I said, scooting my chair closer to the TV, which for some reason offended Jimbo.

"Is Steve Wooster still playing for *Tejas?*" he said, deadpan.

"You know good and well that he graduated."

"Woo Woo Wooster on a Rampage."

This was Jimbo's sly reference to the subtitle on the cover of *Sports Illustrated* the week after the Horns had stomped the Hogs 42-7, the same cover with the headline "Texas Slaughters Arkansas." "Woo woo," he repeated, imitating the horn of a freight train. "Woo woo woo."

I cut my eyes at him. "We're going for two in row over Texas,

Jimbo. Domination."

"That's right," Bob chimed in, taking up for the Razorbacks.

During a TV timeout, I turned to Jimbo and, still stung, began to chant, "Perry Jones! Perry Jones! Perry Jones!" as Bob and Neal joined in.

At halftime, my mother swept into the living room with my birthday cake and vanilla ice cream and Coca-Cola. Unfortunately, the game down in Austin was not looking good. Though the Horns and Hogs were evenly ranked (15th and 17th, respectively), the Hogs appeared overmatched.

When the second half began, Jimbo, fearing that he'd acted like an ungrateful guest, feigned sincere interest in the game. "So, Joe Ferguson can really sling it, can't he?" Then, after watching several plays, he punched Bob in the arm and said, "So, who are the Oakland Raiders playing tomorrow?"

"Who cares about the Oakland Raiders?" I said.

"*I* care about the Raiders," Bob said, with mock anger. "I care a *lot* about the Raiders."

"I care about Alabama," Neal said. "Roll... Roll," he went on, not even bothering to say Roll Tide. The previous New Year's Eve, all of us HOCH Clubbers had stayed at Neal's house on the night that Bear Bryant's undefeated Crimson Tide was matched up against undefeated Nebraska in the Orange Bowl. As we'd sat around the Harringtons' fire-lit living room, I, just to be contrary, openly rooted for the Cornhuskers. I resented Alabama's success all the more after the Razorback loss in the lesser Liberty Bowl, but it was a wonder that Neal's father, a native of Talladega who'd met Neal's mother in History class at the University of Alabama, didn't grab me by my shirt collar and toss me out into the cold—especially considering that his alma mater lost to Nebraska 38-6.

Texas was up 28-8 by the end of the third quarter—so much for celebrating my 12th birthday with a victory over the hated Longhorns. This just wasn't fair. I had *so* looked forward to this season, and now the Porkers were headed for their second loss. The only drama remaining in this game was how much longer my friends and I would continue to sit, increasingly silent, in front of the TV.

As if our stomachs were bottomless pits, Mother brought in a plate of her warm chocolate chip cookies. They were soft, with the chips still gooey on the inside, just the way I liked them. But after they scarfed down the cookies, my friends totally lost interest in the game. Jimbo and Neal got up and went outside, but I stayed glued to the chair—as with any Razorback game, I wanted to watch every last minute, down to the coaches meeting at midfield after the final whistle. Bob, bless his heart, was the last to abandon me, and as the game clock ticked down I heard my mother's voice from the kitchen: "Honey, shouldn't you join your friends out in the front yard?"

"Coming, mother," I said with an edge. As I passed through the kitchen, she said, "Sorry, hon," and while I appreciated her concern, she didn't understand the pain of losing to Texas. She couldn't. She never would.

6

Roots of Inferiority

D aybreak brought odd sights across Jonesboro: a canoe protruding from the second floor of a house; strands of straw blown with such a fury that they were embedded in brick walls; boys on rooftops who'd been instructed by their otherwise-sane fathers to shoot any looters who wandered into their yard.

As the tornado of May 1973 tore through town, I was safe in my basement bedroom at our new house. My mother had let me sleep. Yet I'd been awakened by the sobs of a woman, a dark-haired chain smoker and friend of our family—her house was gone and she still wasn't sure where her husband was.

Over the long summer, the town healed. While my house was unscathed, the storm had torn the roof off Bob Childress's house, skipped over Neal Harrington's only because it was down in a swale, then hugged the upslope and demolished the high school on the hill. The tornado's selective ruin set up a trying seventh grade year. Because I lived in a different school district in the southwest part of town, I didn't attend the same junior high that my three HOCH Club buddies went to. Yet the school I was supposed to go to was also damaged. So all the kids in town were forced to go to the only other junior high school in Jonesboro, though in different shifts; my school went from 7 a.m. to noon, while my HOCH Club buddies went to school in the same building from 12:30 p.m. to 5:30. We were like factory workers, passing one another during the noon-hour shift change.

Above all, 13-year-old boys need to stay busy, and I'm sure my mother worried about what she would do with me through the long afternoons. Mother and I were not on good terms at the moment, having butted heads over my growing collection of Alice Cooper records, which she eventually confiscated. She was pushed over the edge by songs like *Raped and Freezin'* and *Dead Babies*, not to mention that devil-red cover on the *Killer* album, with its close-up of a snake's head with forked tongue.

Fortunately for both of us, over the previous summer I had become acquainted with a simulated board game called Strat-O-Matic Baseball. I'd played this game at Jimbo's house and was intrigued by the stat-driven numbers on the batter and pitcher cards, the roll of the three dice, the thrill of competition against an opponent. But I didn't have a Strat-O-Matic Baseball board game, and I had no idea where I could get one. So I created my own version, using index cards to make batter and pitcher cards for my own All-Star roster, including Lou Brock, Willie Mays, Hank Aaron, Ron Santo, Bob Gibson, Juan Marichal, and Steve Carlton. For competition, I enlisted a bright-eyed boy from down the street whom everyone called Skipper. I set up my homegrown board game in a cramped closet just outside my bedroom, where Skipper and I spent endless hours absorbed in Strat-O-Matic baseball.

At my new junior high, I made other new friends, among them a blond-headed boy with the improbable last name of Gschwend, first name Chuck. We both played golf at the Jonesboro Country Club in the summer (my mother would drop me off in the morning and I'd play until my hands were blistered), we both were short in stature, and we both, owing to unrelated bicycle wrecks, had one crowned front tooth that was ringed with silver. Chuck, whose father was an Arkansas State fan, had never been to a Razorback game, but I would eventually remedy that—in our eighth-grade year, he came with me to Little Rock for the 1974 season opener against Southern Cal.

In my mind's eye, I can see Chuck and me, along with my grandmother, in a crowded bus on our way to War Memorial Stadium. I'm no longer exactly sure why we were riding this bus, but it was probably because we were staying at the Coachman's Inn in downtown Little Rock where my grandmother, our chaperone, had attended a pregame party of some sort.

In any case, our bus, full of hearty Razorback fans, rolled along—but then, as we neared the stadium, traffic slowed, and slowed, until we were hardly moving. Meanwhile, my grandmother, who had no doubt knocked back several shots of Canadian Club whiskey at the Coachman's Inn, had a mighty urge to pee, and her polite yet increasingly urgent requests to be let off the bus fell on deaf ears. Plainly, this bus driver was determined to deliver us all to the stadium without opening any doors on the way. Meanwhile, my grandmother sat in her seat and stewed, her ire rising. When she could take her discomfort no more, she stood up, grabbed the leather strap above her head, drew a labored breath, and yelled, "Let me off this damn bus!" A pause followed. Then louder, *"Let me off this damn bus!"*

All eyes turned to my grandmother, as if she were protesting some sort of civil rights injustice. Chuck had moved to a seat across the aisle to gain distance, and underneath his bang of blond hair he was wide-eyed. When our glances met, I silently, needlessly, mouthed the words, "She really has to go to the bathroom," and shrugged.

Again, "Let me off this damn bus!" Another pause. Then, with exquisite enunciation: "Let. Me. Off. This. Damn. Bus!"

Finally, the driver opened the doors and she got off.

I gazed out through the tinted windows as my grandmother, dressed in a blowsy Razorback-red outfit, trundled up the sidewalk to a stranger's house. There was a brief conversation punctuated by her emphatic hand gestures, then the stranger opened the front door and she disappeared inside. As our bus pulled away, I slunk down into my seat and tried to vanish.

From the opening kickoff, this game against USC was sheer magic. Coached by John McKay, the Trojans were led by such stars as Pat Haden, Anthony Davis, and Lynn Swann. They arrived ranked fifth in the nation, yet departed on the short end of a 22-7 outcome.

As Chuck and I left the bright lights of War Memorial Stadium that night, the magic trailed us. It was mid-September and the air was warm and humid, like every night of the long Indian summer. But this wasn't just any other night. Something momentous had happened, and even outside the stadium the atmosphere was buzzy and jubilant, with spontaneous Hog Calls breaking out here and there. I don't remember how Chuck and I got back to our hotel in downtown Little Rock—we rode a magic carpet, I guess. As for my grandmother, she was waiting for us when we got there.

The next morning, I went to the lobby of the Coachman's Inn to pick up a copy of the *Arkansas Gazette*. But because the game had ended late in the evening, the coverage in that morning's newspaper was thin, with only a front-page headline and a brief summary and no in-depth stories in the sports pages. But on Monday morning, back home in Jonesboro, I eagerly fetched the *Arkansas Gazette* from our driveway, stuffed it in my backpack, and then headed to school. Later, in math class, I pulled out my newspaper, tossed away each section but the sports pages, then pored over every game-related article in sight, all the while hoping the math teacher didn't notice what I was up to.

I especially relished the column written by Orville Henry, who had a unique relationship with Frank Broyles, essentially serving as Boswell to his Dr. Johnson. On Sundays during the football season, Broyles flew down to Little Rock to film his coach's show, and while he was in town he spent several hours with Henry, explaining the hows and whys of the previous day's game. Thus armed, Henry's write-ups in Monday's *Arkansas Gazette* were like tutorials in the ins-and-outs of a college football game. Broyles was cleverly using Henry to educate football fans across the state, and I was among the most attentive of their pupils.

Other tidbits in that day's newspaper: The Hogs had moved up 10 spots in the Associated Press poll, and linebacker Dennis Winston, with his 22 tackles, had won National Defensive Player of the Week. I read and re-read the excerpts from other newspapers around the country, the more glowing and one-sided the better. Something like this from *The Los Angeles Times*: "On a brilliant night in Little Rock, the mighty Trojans were exposed by a gutty group of Razorbacks, who announced themselves on the national stage." Or a similarly fawning snippet from the *St. Louis Post-Dispatch*: "Once again, the Arkansas Razorbacks proved they are the cream of college football."

Today, I'm aware that some of my yearning for recognition from outsiders owed to my sense of my home state's fraught place in the world. Thanks to my father's entrepreneurial successes, my family had travelled a bit: When I was seven, we drove to California in my mom's wood-paneled station wagon. We made a stopover in Las Vegas, where Mother's purse was stolen from our hotel room while we were at the swimming pool, and finally reached southern California and its many famous attractions, such as Knott's Berry Farm and Disneyland. This trip opened my eyes to the vastness of America and Arkansas' comparatively inconsequential place in it. But not *just* inconsequential: backward, to boot—typified by a shorter excursion our family had made to the Ozarks theme park

DogPatch USA, based on Al Capps' Li'l Abner comic strip. Some Arkansans found that hillbilly shtick funny, but it made me wince.

Not surprisingly, then, this fabulous victory over the big-city USC Trojans only amplified my love for the Arkansas Razorbacks. Granted, this love of mine was narrow and tribal—an abiding affection for a region, a land, a team, a mascot. Nevertheless, I knew it was as deep and as important to me as is the love a proud Frenchman feels for his country.

A week after the USC win, however, the Razorbacks lost 26-7 to Oklahoma State, on their way to a 6-4-1 finish. Meanwhile, USC went on to win 11 in a row and finish Number 1 in the final UPI Poll. This is just another example of why my fan's journey has felt like a never-ending trip down Irony Lane.

7

Eyes on Fayetteville

In ninth grade, I sat in class and daydreamed of my first trip to fabled Fayetteville, home of the Razorbacks, where the Hogs were to play Texas on the day before my 15th birthday. Why, I wondered, had it taken so long for me to go worship at the Source?

For one thing, Fayetteville was not an easy place to reach from Jonesboro. Two hours west of our house, less than the halfway point in the trip, the highway ended at Lake Norfork, a place I knew well from summer days of boating and swimming, with fears of long-whiskered catfish nibbling my toes. But now our car had to be transported across the lake by ferry, carrying us over what had been the North Fork River, where my grandfather had fished for small-mouth bass, before the dam was built and the water had risen like a veil over the hollers.

Deposited back on dry land, we drove another three hours across the interior of the Ozarks, through the remote towns of Mountain Home, Harrison, and Alpena. The hillsides were time-worn and unblemished, the trees ablaze in autumn flames of red, orange, and yellow. Along the two-lane road, we passed chicken farmers in pickup trucks and little old ladies in Chevrolets, not to mention an impressive variety of road kill.

When we finally arrived in Fayetteville, I was, to my great shock, decidedly underwhelmed. There wasn't much to the campus: a somewhat imposing student union, a nondescript library, a smattering of other buildings that didn't hold together architecturally. The white-columned Greek amphitheater looked interesting, if for no other reason than I'd heard this was where Friday night pep rallies were held. Maple Street, aptly named, was somewhat impressive in a sylvan sense. The much-ballyhooed Dickson Street was steep on both ends, with a pool hall, a used bookstore, a liquor store, a few restaurants, and, at the easternmost top, a pharmacy and the church that had famously displayed a sign during the lead-up to The Big Shootout: "Football is a game. God is eternal. Nevertheless, Beat Texas." But, really, Fayetteville struck me as achingly modest, not very unlike the backwoods I'd travelled through to get there. My disappointment echoed the feeling I'd had upon receiving that third-rate Batman costume for Christmas when I was seven.

But the excitement of a football game can work wonders on my psyche. When I finally took my seat inside Razorback Stadium, the weather was football-crisp and the crowd was stirred to a Hog-calling frenzy. The players ran through the Arkansas "A" and then spilled out onto the near sideline. Frisky with energy, they jumped around like what I imagined to be a sounder of wild hogs. Then all the Razorback players gathered into a giant red-helmeted knot and any latecomers ran at them and launched themselves on top of the others. I felt connected to each player because, of course, I knew their names, numbers, heights and weights, their hometowns, and whether or not they were sophomores, or juniors, or seniors. I also knew that every Razorback player in that mighty knot wanted to win this game as badly as I did. They were all in just like I was, and football is nothing if not an all-in game.

Looking across the gridiron to the Longhorn sideline, I noticed how beefy the linemen were and how much taller and thicker in general the Texas players were than my Arkansas team. The Razorbacks had a reputation for being feisty and slightly undersized, with the implication that the former made up for the latter. Maybe it did in the 1960s, when Arkansas somehow beat Texas four times even though no defensive lineman weighed much more than 200 pounds. But thus far in the 1970s, whenever the Hogs played the Horns I sensed that the Razorbacks were undernourished, which discouraged me. Was it because Texas is some five times larger than Arkansas? Was it because we're a poor state? Heck, given the arduous trip I'd endured to get to Fayetteville, it even occurred to me that the Hogs might be undersized simply because it was hard to transport adequate supplies of food up here.

My sense of lack was furthered by the modesty of Razorback Stadium, which held only 43,000, had steep metal risers on each side, was mostly open on one end, and had no lights whatsoever. Was this really the hallowed place where just six years earlier President Nixon had watched The Big Shootout alongside Arkansas Governor Win Paul Rockefeller, Senators J. William Fulbright and John McClellan, and George H. W. Bush, then a Congressman from Texas?

The lack of lights totally blew my mind. Was electricity scarce here in the Ozarks? Was somebody trying to keep the light bill as low as possible, not unlike my father, who fussed at my sister and me when we forgot to turn off the lights at home? Regardless, now I understood why, owing to the threat of darkness, every game at Razorback Stadium started at 1 p.m. sharp.

I was seated on the home side (thus launching a lifelong tradition) and beside me were two old salts, dry-witted country lawyers from Pine Bluff or some such place. Early in the fourth quarter, the Longhorns were up 24-3 and by that point the most impressive sight I'd encountered in Fayetteville was Texas running back Earl Campbell, still two years away from winning the Heisman Trophy. Meanwhile, a silver flask passed frequently between the old salts, and as the sour odor of bourbon rose into the fall air, their boozy commentary grew more bitter with every Texas score. With only minutes left, one of them said, "Well, Frank, you've done it again. The next time you play golf with your ole buddy Darrell Royal, ask him just how in the hell he does it."

I was taken aback by such cynicism. Despite serial losses to Texas, plus a run of three mediocre seasons, I still idolized Frank Broyles—and now these drunk old complainers were dressing him down? When the clock expired, I rose from my seat and gave them the stink eye.

8

Teen Transitions

When I was growing up, the Cotton Bowl was the Razor-back fan's Super Bowl. For the big game against Georgia on New Year's Day 1976, my entire family, plus my junior high buddy Chuck Gschwend, stayed at the swanky Fairmont Hotel in downtown Dallas, yet another marker of my father's rising fortunes with Stor-All Tool Box.

Like all families, my family had a complicated relationship with money. My mother, my sister, and I liked money and enjoyed what it brought to our lives, but we didn't always appreciate what my father had to do to earn it.

His entrepreneurial talents—being alert to a certain kind opportunity, imagining possibilities consumers would welcome, launching a business and building it through years of focused toil—are not the kinds of skills that kids, or even a wife, readily appreciate. My immature mindset about this was predictable. Also foretold was that it would take working in his manufacturing plant to give me a better appreciation for the source of all my creature comforts.

That reckoning was more than a year in my future, however; at the moment, we were in glittering Dallas, on New Year's Eve, and my pal Chuck and I weren't allowed to go anywhere without my parents. Mother was especially watchful. Stuck at the Fairmont in an era of no video games, no in-room movies, and no cable television, Chuck and I entertained ourselves by sliding down the long banister of the hotel's grand escalator as if it were the newest ride at Disneyland.

On game day, which had the feel of a momentous party, Chuck and I did not sit with my parents; for some reason, we had separate tickets on the top row beneath the press box. Cotton Bowl Stadium had until recent years been home to the Dallas Cowboys, so the view from there was familiar to me from Sunday afternoon games on TV. At 77,500, the size of the crowd was equal to the population of my hometown times three. I couldn't be more thrilled to be there.

I opened the game program and was soon absorbed in a counting exercise based upon a line of thought I'd picked up from the sports pages of the *Arkansas Gazette*. Under "The Theory of Many Seniors," teams laden with seniors had winning seasons and teams that lacked seniors didn't. This Razorback team was loaded with 21 seniors, which explained why they were co-champions of the Southwest Conference. But that was this season's team, and this season would end after this game. What about next year's team? Well, by my count, the Hogs' roster presently had only 14 juniors.

"Could be a long year ahead," I muttered to Chuck, whose attention was on the man in the aisle peddling confections of pink cotton candy.

"Huh?"

"Nothing," I said, my head still buried in the game program. "Never mind."

The Razorback players took the field and Chuck's pride, as well as mine, swelled when Scott Bull, number 19, a six-foot-five senior from Jonesboro, Arkansas, lined up as quarterback. This was our guy. *Scott Bull*—such a killer name for a football player, a nifty juxtaposition of the civilized and the menacing, like Buck

Buchanan, that lineman for the Kansas City Chiefs.

One's character as a football fan is formed early, and it was not lost on me that Chuck, as a newbie Hog supporter, was rather more excited about the fact that Scott Bull hailed from our hometown. As for me, when it came to the Razorbacks, I always looked at the larger picture: I'd have been just as happy if Mike Kirkland was at quarterback; after all, Kirkland had been featured on the cover of *Dave Campbell's Arkansas Football* the previous summer. Besides, deep down I knew Scott Bull wasn't as talented as Bill Montgomery, much less Joe Ferguson, now playing on Sundays for the Buffalo Bills.

On the first play of the second quarter, the Pride of Jonesboro fumbled. On the previous possession, his wounded-duck pass had bounced off the shoulder pad of a Georgia cornerback. The Bulldogs led 10-0 at the half. Then, after a failed trick play by Georgia, Arkansas scored 10 points in 37 seconds. In the fourth quarter, the Hogs added three more touchdowns. Scott Bull, with BULL in hand-sized letters on the back of his jersey, ran for one touchdown and passed for another. The Hogs won 31-10 in Dallas, a perfect start to my New Year.

By now, I had long moved on from playing organized football. I was into Pete Maravich, the basketball phenomenon from LSU. A fascinating guy, he was, from his shaggy hair down to his trademark floppy socks, a wizard who could spin a basketball on his forefinger until it bled. He was my basketball version of Bill Montgomery.

Spurred by my love for the round ball, my father installed a basketball goal in our driveway. Late into the evenings, I shot basket after basket under the floodlights, and, like Pistol Pete, tried to dribble two basketballs at the same time. Though I was undersized, basketball, with its lack of menacing physicality, suited me better than tackle football. No thick-necked Scott Reeds could crumple me without incurring a foul.

I played point guard on my junior high team, exploiting a brief window of time during which I could beat out a few other boys who, due to late birthdays, were six to 10 months behind me in maturity. But in both eighth and ninth grade, I was surrounded by bigger and better teammates, including several black players.

Basketball was hardly all that was on my teenage brain, however. Thanks to a unique English teacher, Mrs. Hayes, my interests broadened as she dazzled the class—or at least me—with her generous readings of classic books. Over numerous hour-long sessions, she read Charles Dickens' *Great Expectations* aloud to our entire class. I was enchanted. Oh, the childlike joy of having a story read to me, the wonder of Dickens' words in the air. I hadn't expected to be beguiled by Mrs. Hayes. Yet she did it, my mind transported back to Georgian England and overtaken by the picaresque tale of orphan Pip.

What Mrs. Hayes had offered me was a catalyst: At this formative age I could've turned more of my attention to literature and imaginative storytelling, or at least to the diligent reading of good books. Yet the spell she'd cast soon waned, and I got over *Great Expectations*. As the springtime weeks passed, with the Hogs coming off a 9-2 season capped by the thrilling win in the Cotton Bowl, I buried my head even further in the sports pages of the *Arkansas Gazette*. There was little place in my head or heart for much else.

As the new football season unfolded, the 1976 Razorbacks—the team with only 14 seniors—went 5-5-1, and in December the headline in the *Arkansas Gazette* announced that Frank Broyles was retiring. In his melodious Georgia drawl, Broyles often said, "They remembah Novembah," a trope that he had first invoked in 1958, when, after losing his first six games as head coach, the Hogs rattled off four straight. It was his way of encouraging fans, as well as his new boss, Athletic Director John Barnhill, to forget about his initial two months. But over the course of the 1976 season, Broyles had been stalked by his own meme. After the Hogs won five of their first six, they had their most forgettable November during Broyles' 18-year tenure: a tie with Baylor; a loss to Texas A&M; a loss to SMU; a loss to Texas Tech. *They remembah Novembah.*

At some point during this undressing, capped by an early December loss to Texas, Broyles, who for the previous two years had also served as Arkansas' Athletic Director, decided that, as head football coach, he had to go. From here, I literally had no idea where Razorback football was headed. But I trusted that Frank Broyles had a plan.

The following summer, that of 1977, I worked in a factory. Granted, it was my father's new factory with its sheet-metal punch presses, the welders in their hoods, the chemical smell from the paint line and heat radiating out from the massive drying oven. A Stor-All Tool Box was purchased to go on the open back cab of a pick-up truck, so Dad's business was basically a bet on the proliferation of these pick-up trucks: a solid wager. His new factory was so large that the foreman rode around on a golf cart to spare his aging legs. It was a marvel how these tool boxes, still hot to the touch from the drying oven, were boxed up in cardboard and then loaded onto 18-wheeler trucks for transport to all parts of America.

My job was to put a layer of cushioning tape on the underside of the metal lids of the six-foot-long metal tool boxes to prevent the lids from clanging when they were shut. I was helpmate to a snaggle-toothed man named Toe Smith. Toe wasn't his real name, but that's what all the other workers called him. I was mindful not to seek favorable treatment at the factory, lest I not fit in with the blue-collar men. But my father *owned* the factory, a fact made remarkable to me with each day I worked there. I had come to appreciate that he actually *made something*.

My job, however, was a hot, tedious task that paid the minimum wage at just over two dollars per hour, dispensed at quitting time on Friday afternoons. After my previous summer serving as a Congressional page in Washington, DC—a position my father had arranged for me—this factory work was a comedown. The only time I complained, Dad said, "You want to have a car, don't you?"

"Yes, sir." The dove-gray Cougar my dad had bought for me was absolutely essential to my newfound freedom.

"You want to be treated like an adult, don't you?"

"Yes, sir."

End of conversation.

As the long summer days passed, I realized how important it was to do well in school. Unless I wanted to work at a job like this for the rest of my life (or even again the next summer), I needed to do something to improve my prospects, and obsessing over Razorback football wasn't exactly the road to self-betterment. Nevertheless, I grew excited about the upcoming season, the Razorbacks' first under new head coach Lou Holtz, formerly of the New York Jets, who turned out to be Frank Broyles' plan. On some hot afternoons, just knowing that the season opener was drawing closer kept me going. *Only three weeks until the first game!*

It has always been thus: Over the course of my life, there's no telling how many gut-checks of various sorts I've been able to endure because I knew Razorback football was just beyond the horizon. So while sometimes I believe that my love of the Razorbacks hasn't helped me achieve anything worthwhile—that it's only served as a distraction, and even a hindrance—I can just easily convince myself that my fandom has helped me keep my psychological balance.

9

Life Lessons

Owing to my father's ongoing entrepreneurial success—
the vanity plate on his new Cadillac El Dorado read, "2L
Box"—my family had moved into one of the nicest houses in
Jonesboro, with Spanish tile floors, vaulted ceilings, a swimming
pool, and even a pool house. Our new house was across the street
from our old house, which we'd only lived in for five years. But my
father had long coveted this new home of ours.

In addition, Lou Holtz's first year had gone remarkably well,
with only one loss amid 10 wins. A post-season appearance at
the Orange Bowl loomed and, not surprisingly, given my dad's
history with Razorback football, my parents travelled to Miami
for the big game against the Oklahoma Sooners, leaving me and
my 13-year-old sister at home. No big deal. Mallory and I were
generally well behaved. Yet my parents made the uncharacteristic
mistake of hiring a pliable young couple, friends of our family, as
overnight house sitters.

Word soon got out about the vulnerable situation at my new
house, and soon I was host to the most legendary party of my high
school years. Everyone who was anyone in my orbit showed up,
and the spree gathered momentum at roughly the same pace with

which the Hogs overwhelmed the Sooners—which is to say things got deliriously out of hand early.

The events of that night remain a bit hazy. I vaguely recall our house sitters churning out dozens of grilled cheese sandwiches as if they were short-order cooks. Meanwhile, my father's liquor cabinet was invaded with the precision of a military maneuver. I looked out the windows of the pool house and saw Jimbo circling the winterized swimming pool with a Budweiser in hand, remarkable given the fear of alcohol impressed upon him by painful dealings with his alcoholic father.

Weeks before this Orange Bowl matchup, Lou Holtz, invoking his "Do Right Rule," had suspended three players who'd accounted for 78 percent of his team's points; reportedly, the police had found a partially clothed woman in the players' dorm room. Accordingly, the Razorbacks entered the Orange Bowl as 24-point underdogs. Top-ranked Texas had lost in the Cotton Bowl earlier that day, so to win the national championship, all second-ranked Oklahoma had to do was to beat an outclassed, depleted Arkansas team. But the Sooners didn't allow for an aroused opponent, featuring a show-stealing performance by Roland Sales, an unknown backup who rushed for 236 yards, an Orange Bowl record. At halftime, the Hogs were up 24-0. *Somebody give me another Bud!*

When my parents returned from Miami the next day, they were transfixed by the deck furniture submerged in the brackish water of our swimming pool. I have no idea why I, or our house sitters, didn't bother to fish the furniture out of the pool before my folks got back. We were like burglars who neglected to wipe off our fingerprints.

I tried to avoid Mother, whose jaw was set. Yet in my father's gentle brown eyes I detected a twinge of understanding. He, like me, was in an upbeat mood after the monumental Hog victory. I could tell he was impressed that my sister and I had pulled off such a happening party. Gone were several fifths of his bourbon and scotch, plenty of Mateus wine in those retrograde green flagons, and numerous bottles of a then-trendy sparkling red wine called Cold Duck. But all this swill was replaceable with a trip to the middling package store down at the county line.

"Everybody still got their fingers and toes?" my dad said, his cryptic way of asking if any of my friends had been injured, ticketed for drunk driving, or even tossed in jail. My mother, however, was solidly in the camp of Lou Holtz and his Do-Right Rule. Three years before, as part of my mom's spiritual awakening, she had heard from God to stop even her modest drinking. To disguise this in front of their friends, my father would pour her a 7-Up, drop a maraschino cherry in her glass, and garnish it with a tiny umbrella.

"How many people came to your party?" Mother said.

"Everybody," I replied, seeking safety in numbers, even though my friends and I, especially my HOCH Club buddies, were hardly hell-raisers. Jimbo and I, along with several other party attendees, had even recently witnessed for the Fellowship of Christian Athletes to a crowd in the main sanctuary of the First Baptist Church. I had felt the Holy Spirit move me, or so I'd thought. Jimbo later viewed his participation in this New Year's bacchanal as a low point of his youth.

Still, my mother's green eyes bore down on me. She was concerned about the impact of such a boisterous party on my impressionable 13-year-old sister, who, it must be said, was smack dab in the middle of it all. (More and more, Mallory reminded me of my grandmother, with her high cheekbones and fierce loyalty towards the Hogs.) There were threats to ground me, and even my not-so-innocent sister, for weeks on end.

In so many areas of life, bright lines can be hard to draw, and those who do so are considered harsh and judgmental. (My sister and I sometimes called my mother a fuddy-duddy.) Not surprisingly, many us lead muddled lives full of gray areas. We tolerate—and are told we *must tolerate*—moral ambiguity, lapses of discipline and loss of focus, underperformance, and general sloppiness. In many realms of life, there's no scorecard, per se. No winning or losing.

Yet one of the satisfactions of being a football fan is that we don't have to put up with such ambiguity. We enter an alternate universe with a tight coupling of cause and effect, with clear-cut winners and unmistakable losers. *Football is not necessarily nice, and it's not supposed to be.*

There was wisdom in Lou Holtz's suspension of three key players for the Orange Bowl, just as there was wisdom in my mother's hard line. Coach Holtz had made a tough decision and, with this unlikely victory, was rewarded for it. Even though I ultimately got off the hook for hosting this rousing party without my parents' permission, the example he set was not lost on me.

After this Orange Bowl triumph, Lou Holtz became somewhat of a national celebrity. On one school night, I stayed up past my bedtime to watch the entire telecast of *The Tonight Show*, where Holtz, as the final guest of the evening, trotted out his skills as an amateur magician. I was as proud as if he were a close member of my family. When asked by host Johnny Carson to describe Fayetteville, Holtz said, "Well, it's not the end of the earth, but you can see it from there," which riled his boss, Athletic Director Frank Broyles, who thought this was a dumb thing to say when a big part of Holtz's job was to lure young men to northwest Arkansas to play football. And, like my discipline-minded mother, Broyles had a point.

Nevertheless, I adored Holtz, with his endearing lisp, his innovative offense, and his rapier wit. (When he'd been asked by a reporter about fans throwing oranges on the field after the Texas

A&M game to celebrate the pending invitation to the Orange Bowl, he quipped, "I'm just glad we weren't invited to the Gator Bowl.")

Most of all, I was pumped that Lou Holtz had won 11 games. The Hogs finished ranked third behind Alabama and national champion Notre Dame. The only loss was to Texas, 13-9 at home and four days before my 17th birthday. If the Hogs had won this one, they probably would've been voted national champions. In any case, this unlikely win in the Orange Bowl only turbocharged my passion. Razorback football was once again ascendant, as further confirmed by the cover of *Sports Illustrated* the following September, their *College Football 1978* edition, which read, "No. 1 Arkansas" and featured a picture of Lou Holtz, Ron Calcagni, and Ben Cowins, one of the three players suspended for the Orange Bowl. But the *Sports Illustrated* cover story jinxed the Hogs, who sustained back-to-back losses in mid-October and a disappointing season overall, given the preseason hype.

The following May, of 1979, I graduated from high school, seemingly destined to matriculate to the University of Arkansas. Everything pointed in that direction. After all, it was, in a sense, my birthright.

10

Unmoored

When it came to choosing a college, my father once said that I could go anywhere my brains and his money could take me. No doubt, he hadn't thought through where his offhanded comment might lead.

In recent years, our family, along with that of my pal Chuck Gschwend, had gone on ski trips to Aspen together. I fell for the pristine majesty of the mountains and long days of skiing on the velvety snow, followed by dinners at The Shaft served on tin plates like the old silver miners had used. My reward to my parents for all their largesse was to pick a university a thousand miles away from home.

My four-man dorm suite in Boulder was on the 10th floor of a tower on the edge of the University of Colorado. From the narrow window near my bed, I saw the Flatirons, the upward-thrusting rock formation at the foothills of the Rocky Mountains that seemed both touchable and unreal at the same time. From the common room nearby, I heard the music of Alan Parson's Project. My roommates, three upperclassmen from southern Colorado, were obsessed with this rock band, much the way I'd been fixated on David Bowie after I'd seen him in concert at the Mid-South

Coliseum when I was 15.

I reached under my bed to retrieve the cardboard box. This box, which looked like it had once held a dress, bore a mailing label in my mother's handwriting. Inside the box were about two dozen chocolate chip cookies packed in unsalted popcorn, with the dark of the cookies sticking up through the popcorn like the Rockies protruding through low clouds.

I resisted eating another of these cookies, which were an irregular handmade size with just the right mix of pecans and chocolate chips, and were soft throughout because my mother knew I liked them that way. I had eaten three cookies the day before. I had to stop. So I nibbled at the popcorn, curiously sweet with its dusting of cookie crumbs, and I wondered who else but my mom had ever thought to pack chocolate chip cookies in unsalted popcorn, as if cushioning tiny plates of china with Styrofoam.

When this box had arrived two days before, I'd carried it to my room and closed the door because I didn't want any of my other three suitemates, especially Peter, with whom I shared a bedroom, to see me teary-eyed over a box of chocolate chip cookies. It made me think of my HOCH Club friends back home—Mother always cooked a fresh batch of cookies whenever they came over to our house—and for some reason I recalled a sandlot football game we'd played in Jimbo's backyard, when one of the chubby kids we'd cruelly nicknamed Dougus Tubbus got cut up pretty bad when a meaner boy had, in a late hit along the sideline, knocked him into a thatch of thorn bushes. But what had made me tear up until my vision blurred was the thought of how much love and care my mother had put into this box of full of chocolate chip cookies, and how she'd driven to the post office in downtown Jonesboro and mailed it to me out here in Boulder.

Finally, I gave in and ate a cookie. Then I hid the box under my bed and thought that if my roommate Peter found this box and ate even one of my mother's cookies, I would have to confront him.

The only person in Colorado I wanted to share these cookies with—the only person besides me who would truly appreciate them—was a friend from high school, Scott Willhite, who was enrolled at a preparatory school for the Air Force Academy in nearby Colorado Springs. Occasionally, he and I hooked up on weekends. Blond-haired, tall, and strong-armed, Scott had seen his promise as a high school quarterback sabotaged by injury, and he was beaten out by the same boy who'd relegated me to the bench as a back-up point guard on the Jonesboro High basketball team. Out here on the front range of Colorado, Scott and I were both unmoored: he, because he had heeded his fathers' wishes that he join the Academy, and I, because I had rebelled against paternal expectations.

But in two weeks, on my birthday, I was headed home to go to the Texas game in Little Rock, and the thought of this caused me to wonder if the Razorbacks would win this weekend against Texas Tech. But wait, didn't Arkansas typically play Texas Tech the last game of every season? Was my memory of this season's schedule for the Hogs even correct? Perhaps, in my excitement to come to school out West, I had underestimated the impact of my voluntary exile. In this pre-digital era, I couldn't get a copy of the *Arkansas Gazette*, much less listen to Razorback games on the radio, or watch on television. My only sniff of Razorback football so far this season had been when the *Rocky Mountain News* had devoted a half-page to Colorado State's game against the Porkers back in mid-September.

That night, on the tiny black-and-white TV in my dorm room, I watched the *ABC News Special Report*. In the wake of the Iranian Revolution, there were ongoing stories about gas rationing. This was disturbingly familiar. Back during the summer, President Jimmy Carter, donning a humble cardigan, had addressed the nation about our malaise during an era of inflation, unemployment, and the energy crisis. All this introduced a world of limits that was in stark contrast to my upbringing, with my father's mentality of abundance, optimism, and plentiful opportunity.

The following morning, I rode the bus to the center of the University of Colorado campus. I looked out at the Flatirons, their angularity all the more striking under the direct sunlight, and just above, high on the blue horizon, I saw the white plume of a jet tracing across the Colorado sky. Hundreds of such planes traversed the sky every day, and I wondered if, oil crisis aside, I was really going to be able to fly back to Arkansas to attend the Texas game.

Across the aisle from me sat Amy Redford, who also lived in my dormitory. Her father, Robert Redford, had long ago been a baseball player at Colorado. I was quite taken with Robert Redford—when I was 13, I had gone to see *The Sting* four times at the Malco theater back home—and each time I saw Amy Redford on this bus, I furtively stared at her, trying to see her father in her, or see her in him. Dare I take the seat beside her and try to make conversation? Nah. I couldn't imagine her calling her father, a symbol of the American West, to tell him she'd taken up with a boy from eastern Arkansas. He would flare his jaws and narrow his famous blue eyes.

When our bus arrived at the center of the campus, I got off and walked past a row of buildings with sandstone walls trimmed in limestone. The air smelled of fir trees and pines and it seemed everyone wore a backpack, even the gray-haired man in a suit and tie. On the great lawn in front of Norlin Library, a group of kids played hacky sack, and when a Frisbee darted into my line of vision, I flinched as if it were an incoming missile.

Economics 101 met at Lecture Hall 140, just off the University Memorial Center. This was my favorite class, thanks to Reuben Zubrow, a legendary teacher straight out of Central Casting, with his tousled gray hair and eyebrows like unruly broom bristles.

Even with an audience of over 150 students, he connected. I had arrived early to get a closer seat, so I could better hear Professor Zubrow's low reedy voice. He taught from the classic textbook written by Paul Samuelson with its emphasis on the Phillips Curve, which stipulated that there was a trade-off between inflation and unemployment: When one rose, the other fell. Paradoxically, President Jimmy Carter, along with Democrats in Congress and Fed Chairman Arthur Burns, were at this moment enacting policies that caused both to rise in unison. Unemployment was soon to hit 7.1 percent and inflation ran at 11.3 percent annually. I should've stood up in Reuben Zubrow's class and said, "But professor, what about...?" But I yet lacked the intellectual discipline to pose such questions. (Though, in my defense, most economists and more than a few chairpersons of the Federal Reserve have never come to grips with the contradictions of the Phillips Curve.)

When I emerged from Lecture Hall 140, I heard the sound of chants, so I watched the spectacle as 30 or so students marched in a tight circle and shouted, "*Deport the Shaw, Deport the Shaw, Deport the Shaw.*" These protesters carried placards bearing a grainy photograph of an old gray-bearded man, vaguely literary—a reference not to the Shah of Iran, recently deported to the United States amid much controversy, but rather to George Bernard Shaw, the long-deceased British playwright. In Boulder, as in many college towns, the ironic view of life prevailed. No surprise. Ever since the Stanford band had worn snorkel gear during their halftime performance at War Memorial Stadium when I was 10 years old, I had intuited that the smarter a university is, the more ironic are its students.

Finally, I made my way to the nearest bus stop, which faced Folsom Field, home of the Colorado Buffaloes. The Saturday before, I had sat in the stands as the home team lost 9-7 to Drake University; the Buffaloes were now 0-3. Until then, I'd been confident that I was in capable hands: Chuck Fairbanks, former head coach at

Oklahoma, and most recently the New England Patriots, was the new Colorado football coach. At Oklahoma, Fairbanks had won 10 or more games in three of his six seasons. But with the loss to lowly Drake, I realized that Colorado football didn't matter to me. After all, it wasn't as if my father had left my mother only three days after my birth to attend a Colorado Buffaloes game. Did he, now?

From high in War Memorial Stadium, I spotted the yellow ABC Sports sign in the south end zone. ABC Sports was the only network that broadcast college football games, so this meant I was at the heart of that Saturday's football action and only further justified my long trip from Boulder.

Beside me was Bob Childress, my pal since grade school. Blessed with a late-teens growth spurt, Bob almost kneed the back of the man seated on the row in front of us. I, of course, had ample legroom, yet one of my shoulders touched that of the chunky fellow beside me and my other shoulder touched Bob's, all of us packed in so tight we had to stand up in order to raise our arms when we Called the Hogs. Bob was attending hometown Arkansas State University, as were our fellow HOCH Clubbers, Jimbo Osment and Neal Harrington. While Jimbo and Neal were unreliable Hog fans, Bob had always loved the Razorbacks, though for reasons I've never entirely understood, he also had a thing for the Oakland Raiders. The walls of his bedroom back in Jonesboro were decorated with black-and-silver pennants.

I examined the game program, noting the heights and weights of the Texas linemen. Ugh. Then I scanned the Razorbacks' roster. I knew uncomfortably little about these players and their storylines. I couldn't name a single offensive lineman, much less who played nose guard. Yet I had enough residual knowledge of these Hogs to be optimistic. Kevin Scanlon was an all-Southwest

Conference quarterback, and running back Gary Anderson could deliver. Plus, Lou Holtz was a proven big-game coach.

Down on the field, the Razorback Band marched and Arkansas Fight blared. I fixed my eyes on the mouth of the north end zone tunnel where the peppy Razorback players were ready to burst forth through the Arkansas "A." Finally, the kickoff of the Texas game was here, and I felt the adrenaline surge down to my toes.

Since matriculating to Boulder, I'd become even more aware of what outsiders thought of Arkansas, and the second-class status accorded my home state wasn't helped by the fact that Texas had won the last seven in a row against the Hogs. Never mind the fact that nobody out West cared much about the fate of my team. This was the era of *Mork and Mindy*, the television sitcom set in Boulder, and just as the otherworldly Mork took little on Earth seriously, few folks at the University of Colorado took football seriously either. Regardless, I was certain that somehow my home state would be a better place if the Razorbacks could somehow beat the Longhorns.

Texas went up 7-0 in the first quarter. But the Razorbacks tied it up when Gary Anderson scored on a 28-yard scamper. At halftime, I fought the crowd to buy a Coke and a box of popcorn, and when I returned to my seat I nervously tore all four flaps off the top of the box of popcorn while I mentally prepared for the second-half in which Texas would wear down the Hogs. I glanced up at Bob, whose face seemed sunburnt even with the cloudy weather, and he blew out his cheeks as if he, too, sensed what was coming.

Despite our expectation of the worst, the Razorbacks scored twice in the second half to go up 17-7 with only eight minutes left and held on to win 17-14, when the Longhorns' barefooted kicker missed a game-tying field goal in the last minute. In unison, all of us delirious Hog fans counted down the final seconds: "Five! Four! Three! Two! One!"

The energy of the crowd carried over outside the stadium, with a great swell of people walking in one direction and another great swell walking in the other. Bob and I passed by the gate outside the Razorbacks' locker room, where the fumes from the nearby charter buses made me think of how much fun the players would have on their ride back to Fayetteville. "Hurry, hurry," I said to Bob, over my shoulder. "We gotta get a move on!"

My urgent mission was to get to his car in a faraway parking lot, so I could hear the postgame show on the radio. If I missed the opening segment when the announcers went over the stats, then I wouldn't be able to get any stats until the Sunday edition of the *Arkansas Gazette* came out the next morning, and there was no possible way I could wait that long.

We got to his car just in time and the stats confirmed what I suspected: Texas had dominated the game in every way possible except the final score. They had more total yards (312 to 189), more first downs (19 to 14) and had punted only five times, while the Razorback had punted 10 times. But somehow, for once, the Hogs had won the game.

Bob and I inched along in traffic, which gave me plenty of time to listen to Lou Holtz's post-game comments. But Coach Holtz was so amped up and talked so fast—and in that Yankee accent of his, to boot—that I was only able to catch about half of what he said. Then after the announcers gave the scores from other college football games played that day, including the Colorado Buffaloes' home loss to Missouri, Bob and I pulled into the parking lot of The Buffalo Grill. Speaking of irony.

The Buffalo Grill was—is—a broken-in restaurant with red-and-white checked tablecloths and the odor of grilled hamburgers. Bob studied the menu through his horn-rimmed eyeglasses, no doubt honing in on the prices—he had an aptitude for numbers, and had already declared a major in accounting.

"Good win," he said, as he looked up with a smile.

"Yes, well worth my trip back. I'm just glad their field goal kicker is foolish enough to try to kick barefooted. I tried that once in Jimbo's backyard and almost broke my foot."

"Great to finally beat *Tejas*," he said, invoking the Spanish pronunciation so favored by Jimbo.

I raised my glass in a toast of iced tea, since neither of us was old enough to order liquor and we didn't have fake IDs, either. "Beat *Tejas* forever."

As momentous as this game had been for Bob and me—for all our love of the Razorbacks—we didn't further rehash it. I knew what I felt, which was a fleeting euphoria, and I knew he felt the same thing, and to go on about the particulars of the game would only diminish the highly-desirous emotional effect. Besides, deep down both of us had come to understand that there were more consequential things in life than Razorback football, especially Bob. His mother had died of breast cancer and his father of a heart attack, but he wasn't letting himself be defined by it. He and his older sisters had just bravely gone on, basically raising themselves in the same house damaged by the 1973 tornado.

The waitress brought our cheeseburgers, and, while we were eating, a family walked in and the youngest boy was wearing one of those red plastic hats shaped like a charging Razorback with its sharp snout and tiny curlicue tail. Bravo! I loved the in-your-face spirit of these Hog hats; occasionally I wore one of them myself. This boy was about the same age I'd been when my dad and I had come to Little Rock for the Texas game eight years earlier, and this made me want to call Dad and gloat over the Hogs' win. But the Buffalo Grill didn't have a pay phone, or not one that I saw, anyway.

Late that night, Bob and I drove back to Jonesboro, and the next

day I caught a plane in Memphis to return to Boulder, the inter-
mountain capital of lousy college football. Though only two months
into my freshman year at Colorado, I knew I was going to transfer
to the University of Arkansas. But that would come later. For better or worse, I took pride in not being a quitter. I hadn't quit high
school basketball, even though I was undersized and spent most
of my senior year on the bench. I was going to finish my freshman
year at the University of Colorado, even if my time there had an
expeditionary feel to it, like when I'd gone away to a two-week
summer camp when I was 12.

Soon after I returned to Boulder, the Iranian hostage crisis
hit the news, and the scarcity mentality and professed pessimism
of President Carter again overtook me. I worried mightily that all
of the fun at the University of Arkansas would somehow end before
I could even get there. The life of a college student as I imagined
it in Fayetteville would never be the same as it was back when
gasoline was cheap and plentiful. I even wondered if, in such an
energy-starved world, frivolous activities like football games would
continue to be played.

Despite my homesickness, it was only late October. I had
almost a whole school year left in Boulder. Resolved to make the
best of it, I immersed myself in my classes, studied hard, and
drew deep the Colorado experience, all the while drifting further
from my roots. One night, over the pay phone in my dormitory,
my father, in exasperation, said, "Do you want me to tell you what
kind of car you drive?" This was his response to my insistence that
the man on the other end of the phone line did not sound like my
father.

"Is that really you, Dad? I'm sorry. We must have a bad
connection."

I could tell I'd hurt his feelings, but apparently I had wandered so far from my raisin' that I didn't even recognize my own
father's voice. Out in Boulder I'd become immersed in the dialect

and speech patterns of Other America, and the man I was talking to sounded too Southern, as if he were from *Arkansaw.*

—————— 11 ——————
Ground Zero

Finally I was at a university that took football seriously. So, did I wind up at the University of Arkansas based upon my lifelong allegiance to Razorback football? The inescapable conclusion is that, yes, I most certainly did. I wanted to get in on all of the football-related fun: the Friday night pep rallies at the Greek Theater, the buzzy atmosphere of home-game Saturdays, the feeling that I was finally at the center of it all, or at least as near to the heartbeat of Hog football as I could get. I belonged here, where my father had always wanted me to go to college. (With higher matters in mind, my mother had always urged me in the direction of Oral Roberts University.)

But soon into my first season in Fayetteville unforeseen challenges arose.

At any Football School, having a date for the upcoming game was a major deal. Though I had only been on campus for a month, I had no intention of once again joining the small but all-too-visible group of losers at the Sigma Chi house, my new fraternity, who were dateless. For the first home game against Tulsa, I'd given myself a pass. No need to rush such things. But into the first week of October, the leaves on the majestic maple tree on the front lawn of the Sigma Chi house had begun to yield their green. I had to get with it.

For upcoming game against TCU, sympathetic friends set me up with a sorority girl named Darla, Lacey, who hailed from central Arkansas. She was blond and cute and had a good reputation. That's about all I knew, but I figured I'd learn more about her when we sat together at the Razorback game, not to mention the parties at the Sigma Chi house on Friday and Saturday night.

All week, I made plans for our date: I had gotten seats next to the couple who'd set us up, so at least she would have somebody to talk to during lulls in the game, or when the conversation between us dragged. I was mindful that during the game I wasn't going to evince so much insider knowledge of Razorback football that I came across as a stunted young man with limited career prospects. I wouldn't gush about how that stud Billy Ray Smith, Jr., whose daddy had also played for the Hogs, was on his way to becoming one of the greatest defensive players in the history of college football. I would keep to myself the backstory on Razorback cornerback Kim Dameron, number 44, who'd played quarterback on the Rogers team that Jonesboro destroyed two years before in the state high school playoffs, and how Dameron had been hit so hard during that game by a friend of mine that this single hit had earned my friend a football scholarship to Arkansas State University—even though he, like every other kid in Arkansas, had wanted to play for the Hogs. But most of all, I was going to control myself when something aggravating inevitably happened down on the football field and I got the irresistible urge to yell my head off about it.

On Friday night, before the party cranked up at the fraternity house, I purchased from a friend a six-pack of Budweiser, just to make sure I had my bases covered, assuming my date was a beer drinker. But I wasn't going to be drinking any beer. The mere thought of it gave me cold sweats, because the night before, I, along with a gaggle of mostly-underage fraternity brothers, had played nickel beer—that's right, free-flowing beer for mere nickels—at a bar off the Square. I was a lightweight drinker and, generally speaking, I knew my limits. But this Dionysian frenzy went on into the wee hours. I hadn't risen from bed that day until well after lunch.

By 11 o'clock that night, the party was in full roar. Any parents who had hung around after the early spaghetti dinner were long gone, and there was no one down any of the crowded hallways over the age of about 23. I walked past a room with music blaring so loudly—*Celebration* by Kool & the Gang, over and over—that it seemed the walls might crumble. Finally, I reached my two-man room, which overlooked the interior courtyard, where a band played.

My relationship with my two-man room at the Sigma Chi house was unique. Technically, I lived here, but in reality I only slept here occasionally, treating it like a hotel room. I could do this because I had been taken under the wing of a tall, sallow frat brother affectionately known as Bone Man. (Whenever he entered a crowded room, always wearing his black penny loafers, all the frat guys would chant, "Bone, Bone, Bone…"). He lived next door in a yellow Victorian, and I had lapsed into the habit of sneaking over to his air-conditioned house to sleep, a godsend, particularly since the Sigma Chi house was both noisy and lacked air conditioning.

My putative roommate came into our room and informed me that he'd seen Darla Lacey down on the dance floor, so I went to the window and peered down into the courtyard but couldn't make her out among the throng of coeds. My putative roommate grabbed two beers from his cooler and left, and I turned off the light and lay down on the lower bunk bed. I was still sick to my stomach; all I'd eaten that day were a few saltine crackers and a bite of a Snickers bar. I shut my eyes, and through the Babel-like cacophony of noises coming from all directions, I overheard several upperclassmen laughing in the hallway right outside the closed door. All I could do was hope they didn't come into my room and find me lying on the bunk as sober as a preacher.

I never saw Darla Lacey that night, and I had zero contact with her on the day of the game—because she didn't show. So instead of a cute coed sitting at my side at Razorback Stadium, there was nobody to serve as a proxy for my mother, who, in the past, had a way of tempering my in-game outbursts whether she knew it or not. Just the thought of her perched in miniature on my shoulder, glaring at me, was sometimes enough to make me pull back. Other times, even that imagery wasn't enough.

Early in the first half, I bolted up and yowled at the Hogs' quarterback, Tom Jones. "My gosh, Derek Holloway was wide-ass open! Come on! Let's go!"

When I finally sat back down, I felt the stern gaze of the young lady who'd set me up with Darla Lacey in the first place, and that's when I wondered if rumors of my antic passion for the Hogs had scared off my date. Then, I thought, nah. There were thousands of students in Fayetteville just as nutso about Razorback football as I was. Well, dozens anyway. More likely it was Darla's dread of breaking the ice, her preference for the company of her sorority sisters, her desire to claim she had a date to the game and just leave it at that.

The Hogs had not lost to TCU since two years before my birth, an astonishing run of dominance. The game was a blowout, so, lacking female attention, I sat in the stands and watched the Razorback pompom girls with their short red skirts that flared when they made their high kicks. By my lights, several of these girls had great legs, so when there was a break in the football action, my eyes drifted in their direction.

Heretofore, my romantic life had been characterized by youthful crushes and near misses. In grade school, I had made goo-goo eyes across the classroom at a blond cutie, and I'd always had a soft spot for the eldest of the Pryor girls who lived down the street. In ninth grade, my role as a starter on the basketball team led to a romance with a vivacious cheerleader, which lasted until an athletic 11th-grader set his sights on her. In high school, though popular, I inevitably was interested in some older, untouchable girl, or, alternatively, was pursued by girls I wasn't crazy about. At the University of Colorado, the young women were a worldlier breed, and I hadn't connected. Besides, I wasn't going to stay in Boulder, anyway. In Fayetteville, though, I had counted on upping my game. But siting alone in the stands at Razorback Stadium and gawking at pompom girls down on the sideline was hardly the way to go about it.

All through my freshman-year sojourn in Boulder I had never tried drugs, not even marijuana. But during my junior year in Fayetteville, a once-in-a-generation calamity prompted a breakdown.

Counting the previous season's 44-7 thumping of TCU—the game during which I'd had the non-date blind date with Darla Lacey—the Razorbacks had beaten the Horned Frogs 22 straight times, and I had no reason to think that this year would be different; after all, the Hogs were rolling along at 3-0. But down in Fort Worth, the lowly Horned Frogs had other ideas.

I listened to this night game on the radio in the parking lot behind the yellow Victorian where Bone Man lived. He and I had spent the better part of the afternoon arguing about President Ronald Reagan. "So, you're a Carter fan?" Bone Man had said, twisting a cigarette in his pale, thin fingers. *"Jimmy Carter?"*

Midway through the fourth quarter, the Hogs led TCU 21-13 and, in my mind, this game was basically over. Certainly it was with TCU down 24-13 with 5:20 left and the ball on TCU's five-yard line. Then came a quick TCU score, an ensuing fumble by

Hog running back Jessie Clark, and then another touchdown pass by TCU. Done deal.

This was an out-and-out travesty. Here I had transferred to the University of Razorback Football and now the Hogs had lost to TCU for the first time since before I was born. *How could this possibly happen?* I was despondent and searching for some way to cope.

Deep in my postgame funk, I sat out in the parking lot in a stationary Oldsmobile Cutlass with two frat brothers (not Bone Man, who was too square to smoke pot) who had launched into a pot-induced laugh attack. They passed a blunt back and forth and giggled like tipsy sorority girls. Certainly, I was in no mood to participate in their stoner silliness, yet I was intrigued by the way they had so blithely blown off this hard-to-take defeat. So, with no beer readily at hand....

So why was this the only time I've ever smoked pot? Well, dear reader, it seems I was just not very good at inhaling. Heredity factors in. My father claims he can't inhale either, which accounts for one of his sayings: "If cigarette smoking isn't the dumbest thing ever invented, it's the second dumbest thing ever invented." As usual, he has a point.

This silly loss to TCU notwithstanding, I was enjoying my student days at the University of Arkansas. Any experience of college is largely attitudinal. It is what you make of it. I had an active social life and was doing well academically. I'd even figured out how to circumvent the math requirement for a Bachelor's Degree by taking a course in Logic. Due in part to the inspiration of Mrs. Hayes, my junior high teacher and devoted reader-out-loud of Charles Dickens' *Great Expectations*, I had declared a major in English. The English Department at the University of Arkansas was well regarded nationally, with distinguished teachers like Ben Kimpel, poets such as Miller Williams and James Whitehead, novelist and screenwriter William Harrison, and Beat Generation writer John Clellon Holmes. It was a fairly heady milieu for a young man who was drawn to books and fashioned himself to be a decent writer. Moreover, the contrarian in me liked that I was the only member of my fraternity, save one other upperclassman, who'd dared major in a subject as impractical as English.

12

Peak Razorback

espite the shock of the TCU loss, my junior year of college was the best. I knew the ropes in Fayetteville, yet I was still a year away from serious worry about getting a job. But during this stretch, one weekend in particular stood out and, not surprisingly, it centered on a football game against the Texas Longhorns.

I had no date for this game. I didn't want to fool with it because my dad, mom, and 17-year-old sister were in Fayetteville for the weekend, arriving on Friday night in time for the spaghetti dinner at the Sigma Chi house. Texas Week brought a buzz to campus, and even to the entire state of Arkansas. Everyone was caught up in it, with the possible exception of my mother who was more concerned with how many square meals I was eating (numerous at the D-Lux on Dickson Street, thanks to extra spending money from my father), and where and how often I was getting my laundry done (eek!), and if I was attending Sunday morning services at the local Methodist church (no).

After dinner, Mom, Dad, and Mallory came by my new apartment, which was conveniently located near the frat house, and there they met my roommate, Rick Angel, a fraternity brother with whom I'd developed a strong bond—in part because we were both Type A strivers and in part because he was among the most knowledgeable and rabid Razorback fans I had ever encountered. Among our Sigma Chi brethren, Rick and I were considered studious, steady, mature young men. Yet when it came to Razorback football, we could really gin each other up.

Our apartment was cramped, with grungy carpet and a shared bathroom. While Mother was in the tiny kitchen looking through the largely-empty drawers and cabinets, I pulled my father aside. "Um," I said, tentatively, "I'm planning to sit with Rick at the game tomorrow, okay?"

"Sure," he said. "I'd do the same thing."

"Thanks," I said, relieved. "We've got good seats, right behind the Texas bench."

"Fine, fine."

Game day was balmy and overcast with a warning of tornadoes, which was unusual for mid-October. One way or another, it felt like something surreal was about to go down at Razorback Stadium, and I just hoped it wasn't another loss to top-ranked Texas, winners of eight of the last nine in this series.

With their first possession of the game, Longhorn quarterback Rick McIvor fumbled. When he came to the sideline, my roommate and I, from only a few rows behind the Texas bench, razzed him. This was the only game I've ever talked trash to opposing players, though not because I'm philosophically or morally above it; I just never had sat this close to the bench of any opponent. And now it was as if I were possessed by that demon from *The Exorcist*. I was thankful none of the Longhorns could climb into the stands and get their hands on me, and if there had been even a remote possibility of that, I'd have kept my mouth shut.

Hey, McIvor, you suck!

On the Longhorns' second possession, the football was snapped over the punter's head for a safety. Just like that, they were down

8-0. On the Longhorns' third possession, they fumbled inside their 10-yard line. By halftime, the Hogs led 25-3, and into the fourth quarter it was 42-3. I was witnessing the football equivalent of a Biblical miracle. Coming only two weeks after the Hogs' first loss to TCU since 1958, this supernatural occurrence confirmed the wisdom of my decision to transfer to Arkansas.

This was sweet revenge for The Big Shootout, played on the same field 12 years earlier. Almost every Razorback fan sensed this, and more than a few of the Longhorn players no doubt realized it too. All these players were roughly my age and, like me and practically everyone else in America, they'd watched the so-called Game of the Century on television. Certainly, Texas head coach Fred Akers grasped the karma involved, since he hailed from Blytheville, Arkansas, and had played halfback for Frank Broyles' first teams of the late 1950s. My mind flashed back to that young lady in the Texas Band—the one the ABC cameraman had been obsessed with and who had repeatedly flashed the Hook 'em Horns sign on the TV in my grandmother's living room back in 1969. I'd been wanting to give it back to this gal in the white cowboy hat ever since. So where was she now?

Yet this game was decidedly not The Big Shootout. Granted, Texas had come in as the nation's top-ranked team, but Arkansas wasn't even in the top 20. Whereas The Big Shootout had been a slugfest between two heavyweights, this game was a fired-up David smiting a mistake-prone Goliath. Nevertheless, it was a delight to sit behind the Texas bench and watch the Longhorns suffer. Revenge is a complex emotion that reflects poorly on those who revel in it. For Arkansas fans, this rout created the rare challenge of how to act when bringing mighty Texas low. Behaving like a graceful winner was apparently too much to expect.

Go home, McIvor! You loser!

With two minutes left on the game clock, a gaggle of Hog fans started to tear down one of the goal posts. Coach Lou Holtz fussily ran onto the field and tried to stop the mob, but as the final seconds ticked down, the bile of the crowd only rose. The Hogs had ruined the Longhorns' season—this was their only loss all year, and, really, it was like two losses rolled into one. We were determined to rub their bovine noses in it.

When the scoreboard flashed 0:00, I watched from behind the Texas bench as the mob headed towards the goalpost at the other end of the field. At first, these fans were content to sit on the horizontal beam, but then like unruly zoo animals they climbed each upright. This goalpost came down too. A fistfight broke out amid the Texas Band, a carryover from the previous day when they had brazenly marched into Brough Commons and mocked the Hogs by chanting, "TCU!...TCU!" The Band had to be escorted out of Razorback Stadium under the protection of the Arkansas State Police.

Eventually, the mob down on the field carried one of the fallen goalposts all the way to Dickson Street, a hilly mile or so away, where they had the presence of mind, not to mention a movie director's sense of atmospherics, to lean it upright against a tall-enough building. Throughout the night, bonfires clogged Dickson Street, which was covered with broken glass, and 70 people were arrested.

Never one for mayhem, I participated in none of this. I had played my part in this catharsis by taunting Texas players all afternoon, and to prove it my voice now sounded like Froggy's from the *Our Gang* TV show. My idea of a proper celebration was to have a nice dinner with my mom, dad, and sister at Herman's Ribhouse, my usual Saturday-night spot, where the tall, stern Herman Tuck manned the grill with a white rag hanging from his back pocket as he churned out hamburger steaks, hash-browned potatoes, and salad for five dollars and seventy-five cents. The dark dining room, full of giddy fans, was dramatically lit by giant fish tanks filled with orange and white koi. With my father along to pick up the tab, I ordered a plate of ribs and a glass of ice water, mindful that the next time I came to Herman's I could legally buy a cold Budweiser, and there was nothing my mother could do to stop me.

My dad sipped a Dewar's-and-water as he and I and Mallory, a University-of-Arkansas-student-in-waiting, talked on about what had happened that day. Already, in our little world, this game had taken on a history-making hue, much as when Neil Armstrong walked on the moon. There was practically no end to the joy the three of us got from this unexpected win, which is always the best kind. For me, there was also the deep joy of experiencing all this with my family. The day before, when they had arrived in Fayetteville, I'd worried about keeping them entertained for two days. Whatever would we do on Saturday night when all of us were disappointed over another loss to Texas? The whole weekend had been an experience that I would never have had if I'd chosen to stay at the University of Colorado.

The following Monday was my 21st birthday, and I would like to report that this milestone prompted me to reflect and take stock of my life. But with the game still topmost in my mind, how was that even possible? One of joys of any great victory is to hold on to it for as long as possible. I couldn't quit thinking about the win over Texas, nor did I want to.

There can come a point at which deep fandom results in the relinquishing of one's life to the team, and on my 21st birthday I came as close to handing over the keys of my life to the Arkansas Razorbacks as I have ever come. If a map of my psyche were drawn, almost every jot of land would've been claimed by Arkansas football, a stake more intensely held because I knew several of these Razorback players: Wide receiver Derek Holloway was in my chemistry class; backup safety Cliff Henry was a fraternity brother; the thick-necked Scott Reed, who'd stuffed me on a quarterback sneak back in peewee league football, was the Hogs' third-team quarterback. These dudes were my peers, and they had pulled off a feat that had eluded Razorback players across my entire teen years, excepting the win over the Texas Longhorns two years ago in Little Rock. And what had I done so far in college? Take a course in Shakespeare? Ace Western Civilization? Learn about specious macroeconomic concepts like the Phillips Curve? Get initiated into Sigma Chi?

By the next week, my Hog mania had calmed considerably as the Porkers lost to the Houston Cougars for the third straight year. Soon, I was engrossed in a book by Robert Pirsig titled *Zen and the Art of Motorcycle Maintenance*. Though all writers and all books are flawed, it was my habit to seize on a book and fall under its sway. When in Boulder, I had drunk down *The Greening of America* by Charles Reich and *The New Industrial State* by John Kenneth Galbraith, both left-leaning tomes. I'd also digested *Catcher in the Rye*, a book that until then had escaped my attention, probably because it had been banned from the public schools back in Jonesboro. Regardless, I considered my book habit to be good for me. After all, there was more to life than football, wasn't there?

After the season finale, a home loss to SMU, I drove back to Jonesboro for Thanksgiving. By tradition, Thanksgiving lunch was at my grandparents' house. For the occasion, I was well dressed in gray wool slacks, polished black loafers, and a navy cashmere sweater. I didn't want to disappoint my clotheshorse grandfather, who commanded the bar in his tan Oxford pants, open-collared dress shirt with cuff links, and two-tone brogues as he poured Bloody Marys and gin and orange juice concoctions he called Little Darlins'. The living room was crowded with my sister and mom and dad and aunts and uncles and cousins, and on the TV was the

Cowboys-Bears game. My grandmother, clad in one of her many blowsy muumuus, entered from the kitchen, headed for her stool at the bar. On cue, my grandfather poured two shots of whiskey, Old Charter for himself and Canadian Club for her. With a backward flick of her head, my grandmother downed the whiskey, then slammed the little glass onto the bar and said, "Damn!" as if she'd just had a belt of a foul-tasting cough syrup. Then, cat quick, she gulped Coca-Cola from one of those little eight-ounce bottles she always kept in her refrigerator because each of her five grandkids, myself included, thought Coca-Cola somehow tasted better when we drank it from one of those little bottles.

In the dozen years since I'd watched The Big Shootout with my grandmother in this very living room, the way she processed Razorback football had changed. She loved the Hogs with more parochial fervor than ever, but these days she couldn't bear to watch any Razorback games on television at all—her nerves could no longer stand the strain. She'd reached the limit of what she could give, and even the slightest brush with Razorback football in real time caused her to hold her clenched fists near her heart and nervously shake them like a child spooked by a ghost.

Soon, the buffet was covered with heaping plates of roast turkey, mashed potatoes, green beans, sweet corn, sweet potatoes, and cornbread dressing both with and without sage, since one of my uncles claimed to be allergic to it. But the highlight was a dish my mother made (from a recipe she'd seen in *Southern Living)* called Epicurean Peas, which were English peas smothered in mushroom gravy, bacon, and onions. No holiday meal was complete without this dish, and my uncle, the one allergic to sage, affectionately called them Goobered-Up Peas.

But amid this vast cornucopia, somehow the smell of turnips overwhelmed everything. Boiled to an off-white softness and served in a small tureen, these turnips emitted an almost-rank smell that lingered with a pungency like that of battery acid. No one in our extended family ever ate any of these turnips, and I'm not sure my grandmother even ate them. It seemed her chief purpose in cooking them, aside from perhaps upholding a Thanksgiving tradition from her youth in south Arkansas, was to torment her three sons.

Near the buffet, all of us gathered in a big circle, joined hands and bowed our heads. My grandfather started strong with his prayer, but when he got to the part when he thanked to God for the many blessings bestowed upon our family, his voice broke, as always. His eyes were watery and he took out his handkerchief and blew his nose, this pause only heightening the awkwardness. Then in a hoarse whisper he said Amen, and that was the end of his Thanksgiving prayer.

We all started down the buffet, working both sides in silence, as if the sheer volume of the food had mesmerized us. Then, as was tradition, my dad said, "Oh, hello, rah-de-do-dah, I can't wait to have some of these turnips."

"Me too," grumbled one of my uncles.

With my heaping plate of food, I headed for the breakfast room with its white Formica table. All the other grandkids, including my sister, sat at this table. I'd hoped this Thanksgiving to have graduated to the formal dining room and sat at the long oak table and talked with the adults about whatever it was they talked about. Maybe next year.

When we all finished our big meal, the menfolk gathered in the living room to watch the second half of the Cowboys-Bears game. I felt drugged with sleep from all the rich food, but just after I nodded off, I was jolted by my grandfather's sharp voice: "Goshdammit!"

His face was red with anger as he thrust his hands down into the side cushions of his easy chair. He finally found the remote control, aimed it like a pistol at the TV, and hit the mute button. Then, with what seemed to be a great sense of relief, he sank back into his easy chair.

I went to the kitchen to get a bowl of ambrosia, another dish my grandmother made only for Thanksgiving and Christmas. Near the cake stand, I spotted my father, who with the stealth of a ring-eyed raccoon was eating the top layer off the pecan pie my mother had made, leaving only the gooey filling underneath. Every Thanksgiving several of these top-eaten pecan pies could be seen strewn about the kitchen at our house down the street.

"What was that all about?" I asked my father, referring to the mini-tantrum my grandfather had thrown.

"He can't stand John Madden," Dad said. "The sound of his voice drives your grandfather crazy, so he mutes the volume and just watches the game."

I returned to the living room, now so silent that it seemed one of us among my uncles and male cousins should have told a joke. Soon, my grandfather retired to his bedroom for his nap and I slipped into his easy chair and turned up the volume on the TV just loud enough to hear the voices of John Madden and his play-by-play sidekick Pat Summerall, whom I'd always liked because he'd played for the Razorbacks back in the early 1950s.

That night, at my parents' house, I watched yet another football game on TV. Then, on Friday and Saturday, I watched yet more college football games, gorging on them like all those helpings of Goobered-Up Peas I'd eaten.

On Sunday, after church, my dad, mom, sister, and I sat down for a family lunch, a goodbye lunch for me. Mother had washed all my clothes, and my car was packed with Thanksgiving leftovers and various foodstuffs she insisted I take back to Fayetteville. A pro football game flickered on the TV in the den, but my dad, faced with the prospect of another afternoon spent watching games, looked at me across the table and said, "I'm footballed out." I knew exactly what he meant.

But before I left for Fayetteville, he and I addressed the classic division between the practical-minded father and the impractical, somewhat literary-minded son.

He was reading the Sunday edition of the *Arkansas Gazette* and, of course, despite his earlier assertion that he was footballed out, a pro football game was on the TV.

"You know, I'm majoring in English," I said, purposely not tacking on the word Literature because saying "English Literature" made my choice of study sound even more frivolous.

My dad lowered his newspaper and drew a bead on me. "That sounds about as useful as underwater basket weaving."

I'd heard him use this expression many times when referring to something he considered foolish to even attempt. I sat there in silence, hoping he'd follow this up with one of his cryptic cut-to-the-chase qualifiers like, "Well, that two and two makes four," or even say, "Just because I say so, doesn't make it right," as he sometimes did when walking back something he'd said.

"Well, don't worry," I finally said. "A lot of college students who major in English go on to law school," and when these words came out of my mouth I actually believed this just might happen.

13

Chasing the Dynasty Year

I was stoked about my senior year of college. The 1982 edition of *Dave Campbell's Arkansas Football* projected the Razorbacks to be the best team in the Southwest Conference, and the Hogs were slated to play Texas in the final game. The prospect of two top-ranked teams facing off in December in a reprise of The Big Shootout was so tantalizing that during the season I actually rooted for the Longhorns. In October, though, they lost back-to-back games to Oklahoma and SMU.

Meanwhile, the Hogs gallantly rolled along. On a Tuesday morning in early November, I opened the *Arkansas Gazette* to learn that the Razorbacks had climbed to number five in the Associated Press poll. The Porkers hadn't started a season at 7-0 since 1969, and on campus in Fayetteville the air was more electric and the Friday Night pep rallies at the Greek Theater more intense—even the autumnal colors of the tall maple in front of the Sigma Chi house seemed more vibrant. Everyone was in a better mood; at least I was. All of this winning felt more personal and intimate. More than ever, this was my team and I took ownership as the victories piled up: Tulsa, Navy, Ole Miss, TCU, Texas Tech, Houston, Rice. Yessiree, my college-age dreams of Razorback football glory were coming to pass. The long-sought Dynasty Year was actually unfolding.

For reasons having to do with chasing after a young woman whom I'll call my Treasured Girlfriend, I spent the Saturday of the eighth game of the season (the Hogs were playing Baylor in Waco) in Texarkana, Texas. On this particular Saturday afternoon, my Treasured Girlfriend, whom I'd met in Fayetteville over a year ago, had to work at Dillard's Department Store, where she was training to be a corporate buyer. Alone in her apartment, I opened the front door, wearing only gym shorts, and was taken aback by how high the sun was. I had only risen from bed an hour before, and I was pretty much spent.

I believe it was actor Lawrence Olivier who said, "Inside, we're all seventeen, with red lips." Well, I had just turned 22 and was hot-to-trot, as was my Treasured Girlfriend. All to say, my principal focus on this first weekend of November was not on Razorback football. In fact, I'd just had the greatest morning of my life, my Treasured Girlfriend and I having had sex no fewer than three times.

Regardless, the mid-afternoon kickoff of the Arkansas-Baylor game was imminent. My Treasured Girlfriend had a clock radio that she typically kept on her bedside table, and which I had moved to the kitchen counter. I worked the tuning knob to ease the orange needle across the FM dial, listening with the intensity of a safe cracker. Finally, I heard the familiar voice of Paul Eels, the color man for Razorback football. *Thank God!* But when I turned up the volume, the connection weakened. The only sound coming from the clock radio was pulsating static, fading in and out like waves from the outer reaches of the galaxy.

I had already missed half of the first quarter of this game, but I wasn't overly worried: Baylor was 1-5-1, and my Hogs had beaten the Bears 10 of the last 13 times they'd met. I switched to the AM dial and again worked the tuning knob. Once more I thought I heard Paul Eels, but it turned out to be the voice of the color man for the North Texas Mean Green, which on that day were matched up against New Mexico State.

My Lord, I thought, *why isn't the Hogs' game against Baylor televised?* But that was a silly question: I couldn't remember ABC Sports ever televising an Arkansas-Baylor game, because typically the Bears weren't good enough to have one of their games televised nationally, or even to have it broadcast regionally, like ABC Sports sometimes did for games involving lesser teams.

I returned to the clock radio, and on another of my delicate calibrations of the tuning knob, I heard Paul Eels' voice. *Hallelujah!* But then came a swell of static, then his voice, then static—back and forth with the maddening regularity of a metronome. But what choice did I have, even if listening to this game was like trying to assemble a puzzle with half the pieces missing.

Going into the final quarter, the Hogs were ahead 14-7. It was closer than I expected, yet I had confidence in the Hogs' defense, which led the nation in scoring defense, yielding a paltry 10.5 points per game; they hadn't given up a single touchdown in the last four conference games. But so much for statistics: Down the stretch, the Bears scored 17 points and my dreams of a Dynasty Year had gone kablooey.

When my Treasured Girlfriend returned to her apartment after her long day at Dillard's, she was surprised to find me in a foul mood. "We lost to friggin' Baylor," I said grumpily from the couch. "Ruined the whole season."

She frowned. *Wait a minute, buddy, shouldn't you be in the best mood ever?* Really though, she couldn't be expected to understand my plight: Her only connection to the Razorbacks was that she had a Bachelor's degree in Marketing from the University of Arkansas. Her father and older brother were more into car racing. In her defense, however, she wasn't one of those types who was allergic to anything sports-related. The previous spring, during her final semester in Fayetteville, she'd accompanied me to a driving range, where she'd sat in a metal lawn chair with a beer in hand and provided a running commentary on every golf shot I hit: "Whoops, you snatched that one to the left!" "Yuckie, Bub, you took too much dirt on that swing!"

My eyes followed her lithesome figure as she disappeared into her bedroom, the scene of our luscious morning feast. On the TV in the living room was the 6 o'clock news and, like a sadist, I watched the sports report, which showed on the screen: "Baylor 24, (5) Arkansas 17." It was the sight of that little number (5), which denoted the Razorbacks' national ranking before they'd lost that afternoon that made my heart sink even lower.

I closed my eyes, still trying to process the enormity of this defeat. I wasn't superstitious and I'd never believed my actions had anything to do with the Hogs' winning or losing. Nevertheless, I darn sure believed that my mental state could mirror that of the Razorbacks. If I was excited about a game against a particular opponent, then surely the team was stoked as well. Yet, if I was just not into a game because I sensed the opponent wouldn't put up much of a fight, then I feared the team was on the same wavelength. Ergo, if due to my extracurricular morning activities I didn't have enough in my tank for a tight four-quarter game down in Waco, then there you go.

My Treasured Girlfriend came out of her bedroom. "Are you going to put that clock radio back where you got it?" I mumbled about how the reception on her clock-radio was crummy.

"What was that?" When she closed the refrigerator door, her hard gaze returned to me, and I started to explain that when and where Arkansas football was involved, my timbre could quickly and permanently change. But I didn't.

"Let's go out for dinner," I said. I needed a change of scenery. I'd scarcely left her apartment all day.

"I had to work this afternoon, remember? I'm tired. We're

staying in tonight."

"Okay."

On Sunday afternoon, I drove back to Fayetteville, stewing on the Baylor loss as I passed through towns like De Queen and Y City. To compound my woes, guilt-ridden thoughts chased after me. Having been raised in the Methodist church, I was of the persuasion that premarital sex was a sin, and sin carried consequences. Just as I imagined my mother in miniature perched on my shoulder at a Razorback games, now God sat on my conscience.

But who needed God, anyway? Throughout my college years, I had drunk deeply of secular ideas and values. I'd found this way to be easier, freed from any religious taboos that might curb my impulses and throttle certain behaviors. Even so, I realized that my desire that weekend to do what *felt* good had overcome any desire to *be* good. It seems that I hadn't put God away entirely. Driving northward, I wondered if the Razorbacks' loss was the price I had to pay for what I'd done (repeatedly) that weekend. Was this God's way of punishing me?

That's the thing about being a fan; whenever something good or bad happened to my team, I always took it personally. It was absurd to view any collective endeavor so subjectively. Such self-absorption was practically a sin in itself. Yet the fact that the Razorback players, the coaches, and every other Hog fan felt this loss too didn't help me one bit. The season-spoiling defeat was a singular burden I couldn't share, and I had to process it in my own way, bringing to it all of my accumulated baggage.

During my final semester of college in the spring of 1983, I got one last oddball dose of football when several enterprising fraternity brothers hit upon a creative idea: To raise money for charity, our Sigma Chi chapter would stage a full-contact football game against the highest bidder, which turned out to be the Sigma Nu fraternity. The game was called the Charity Bowl and, not surprisingly, more was involved than mere undergraduate altruism.

The Charity Bowl was like a fantasy camp for about 35 washed up high school football players from each side. In the lead-up, there were weeks of practice and months of trash talk. For any participant, this vanity game had it all: The players were to wear full pads, there were to be referees and a live clock, and, remarkably, the action was to take place at Razorback Stadium.

Game day brought a brisk wind, and the springtime pollen was thick. With my hay fever, I was a sneezing, runny-nosed mess. At Razorback Stadium, I sat midway up the stands on the west side, my usual placement, like a moviegoer who always takes the same seat, no matter if the theater is empty or packed.

In a scene out of *The Bad News Bears*, the two teams of make-shift players charged out onto the sidelines, and that's when it sank in on me that as a boy I'd dreamt of quarterbacking the Hogs like my hero Bill Montgomery, but now I couldn't even make it onto the field at Razorback Stadium in a contrived game between two frat houses. The players were hyped up and it was obvious many of them considered this game to be a really big deal—perhaps the highlight of their entire college experience—even though Razorback Stadium was mostly empty and lifeless, with no colorful Razorback Band, no stirring sound of the Arkansas Swing March, no leggy pompom girls on the sidelines, no blood-curdling Hog Call from the voices of the tens of thousands. All of the pageantry that mattered was absent. Even so, I realized that if I were down on the football field, I'd have been amped up to the point that I wouldn't have slept last night, like it was Christmas Eve when I was nine years old.

A few players in the Charity Bowl flashed talent: the quarterback only two years removed from his high school glory days, the thick guys who moved forcibly in the trenches, the twitchy wide receiver who once threatened the state record in the 100-yard hurdles (this cat also occasionally leapt over cars as they idled in traffic on Maple Street). Regardless, the execution on both sides of the line of scrimmage was less than crisp, and at times near comical. It seemed a bit sacrilegious to watch these guys attempt to act out a real game on the field at Razorback Stadium, which was hallowed ground to me.

The Charity Bowl, played two months before my graduation, was the Football Gods' way of confirming for me that my college days were over. It was time to move on from Fayetteville, if not from Razorback football itself.

14

Real Life

Upon graduation, my job prospects were not altogether encouraging. Maybe I shouldn't have been so dismissive of one of my fraternity brothers, a practical-minded accounting major, who, when I'd told him I was pursuing a degree in English, leaned in with a befuddled look on his face and said, "Okay, so what exactly do you study?" I had seen no point in telling him that the chief glory of the English was their language, much less that I'd lately been into the Irish poets, especially Auden and Yeats.

The default post-undergraduate choice of my generation was law school, that giant holding tank for 22-year-olds who didn't know what else to do. Though I had applied to and been accepted by several law schools, I had no particular passion for the law. So to avoid this fate, I had to get creative.

Sure, I could tuck tail and go back home to Jonesboro. The year before, my father had gotten a call from a Londoner who urged him to fly over to check out a new product called a tanning bed. My dad, prescient spotter of money-making trends, soon began to manufacture these tanning beds. He was on a roll.

However, in pursuit of my own job-related interests, on a

sunny afternoon in May, I went to the offices of a magazine publisher in Little Rock. I'd always loved newspapers, books, and
especially magazines, going back to my devoted readership of *Dave
Campbell's Arkansas Football.* "Is Alan Leveritt here?" I said to
the receptionist. Back in February, I'd heard the publisher of the
Arkansas Times speak to a group of journalism students. The flyer
on the bulletin board in the Journalism department had noted that
Alan's speech would begin at 8:30 a.m., an inconveniently early
hour as far as I was concerned. But on the appointed morning, I
had managed to get myself out of bed.

With unruly brown hair and worn patches on the elbows of his
corduroy jacket, Alan Leveritt exuded the earthy verve of a young
man on the make. In a small, relatively poor state like Arkansas, it
took a hardy soul to even try to profitably turn out a slick monthly
magazine like the *Arkansas Times,* but he was somehow pulling it
off. A former obituary writer and moonlighting cabbie, nine years
earlier he had scraped together $200 to start his publication. On
that February morning, I'd made a mental note to someday look
Alan up.

But on this sunny May afternoon, the publisher wasn't in
his office—another dead end in my job search. Then, on my way
out the front door, I ran into Alan as he bounded up the steps. I
introduced myself, then got to the point: "I'd like to work at your
magazine. I'm fond of it."

"Do you have any experience in magazine publishing?"

"Not really."

"Well," he said, not unkindly, "I'm sorry, but I'm afraid I don't
have a job for you."

Before he got away, I threw a Hail Mary and offered to work
for free for a few months. I had relatively few expenses (which
means I was living with my Treasured Girlfriend, who'd recently
moved to Little Rock), and I assumed that my father would be
okay with my offer as long as it soon led to a permanent job. Also,

I had just sold my prized baseball card collection and had a few extra bucks.

Alan, a scrappy tightwad who'd once appeared in an advertisement in his magazine featuring a picture of himself sitting in profile on a commode a la Rodin's *The Thinker*, was intrigued by the prospect of free labor, if not exactly overwhelmed by my skill set.

The following Monday, I started work gratis on the business side at the *Arkansas Times*. Initially, my job was to coordinate International Fest, a three-day celebration of the diversity of Little Rock. (Mind you, this was 1983—long before diversity became the *sine qua non* of American society.) Meanwhile, I immersed myself in the ins and outs of how to run the magazine's circulation department, which was a backwater. I became intrigued with how to attract and retain subscribers. Two months later, I had a salaried job.

Alan often said publishing was a business of ideas, and I found it interesting to work at a company that employed men and women to write stories. The editors and writers at the *Arkansas Times* plumbed topics like the race riots of 1947 in Elaine, Arkansas, wrote articles such as "A Pollster's Definition of Just Who Is The Average Arkansan," penned essays on such Southern staples as "The Black Iron Skillet," and editorialized "On The Need For A State Dog."

While the publisher had played defensive end on his high school football team, if any of the writers at his magazine considered Razorback football at all, it was at best as a puzzling cultural phenomenon, or at worst as a head-shaking example of herd-like thinking that can cause fans to descend into madness. Regardless, at the *Arkansas Times,* I'd found a way to somewhat nourish my literary side, while working on the more practical business side of the magazine. Too, it was quite handy that I now lived in the city where War Memorial Stadium was situated.

Unfortunately, during my first autumn in Little Rock, the Razorbacks had a season to forget. Lou Holtz's team lost to Baylor on November 5, to Texas A&M on November 12, and to SMU on November 19. *They remembah Novembah.* September and October had not gone so well either, with losses to Ole Miss and, of course, Texas. Despite going 9-2-1 the year before, Coach Holtz was on the ropes. Not that he was unaware of the hazards of his chosen profession. "I have a lifetime contract," he once quipped. "That means I can't be fired during the third quarter if we're ahead and moving the football."

Despite a season-ending win against Texas Tech, Lou Holtz resigned. Or he was pushed out by Athletic Director Frank Broyles.

Meanwhile, my career in magazine publishing proceeded apace. At night, I managed a telemarketing campaign to sell subscriptions to the *Arkansas Times.* It wasn't glamorous work. But the *Arkansas Times* was a worthy magazine and, at $9.95 for 12 monthly issues, it was a relatively easy sell.

One night, as I rummaged around in a desk drawer, I came across a thick business plan for a new publication called *Southern Magazine.* This was Alan Leveritt's dream, a concept he'd developed with an editor and a consultant. When I saw this business plan, with its narrative detail and rows of financial projections, my imagination took flight.

At the time, the publishing scene across the American South was dominated by *Southern Living,* which, as Alan wryly noted, was, at its essence, about how to make a better fruit salad. His new magazine would be "not of the Old South, or of the New South, but of the South that is today." *Southern Magazine* would feature the South's best writers like Roy Blount, Jr., Willie Morris, Barry Hannah, and Geoffrey Norman. It would be launched with a circulation of 200,000 subscribers, almost 10 times more than the *Arkansas Times*, and have advertising sales offices in New York, Chicago, and Atlanta. Unfortunately, securing the many millions of dollars required to launch such an ambitious new magazine was about as realistic as the 1983 Arkansas Razorbacks, at 6-5, receiving an invitation to the Orange Bowl.

By the summer of 1985, I had worked at the *Arkansas Times* for two years, and it was time to broaden my professional horizons. In this, I was as impatient as my entrepreneurial father. I set my sights on attending the week-long Stanford Publishing Program, which I'd read about in a trade journal.

I went to inform Alan, whose office was festooned with posters of the Spanish Civil War, an enthusiasm of his. From behind his paper-strewn desk, he mulled over my plan to head out west. "Boy," he said. "It's really gets hot and humid in July in Arkansas, doesn't it? California sounds wonderful. I think I'll go with you."

The mid-1980s were a golden age of magazine publishing. Television offered only a limited number of channels and the Internet was over a decade away. Amid mass-market stalwarts like *Rolling Stone, People, TV Guide,* and *TIME,* advances in printing technologies had enabled the rise of innumerable niche magazines. All of this cultural and commercial churn excited the dreamer in me. On some evenings after work, I went to B. Dalton Bookseller in Little Rock to peruse their newsstand and to try to think of an idea for a magazine I could launch.

Attendees at the Stanford Publishing Course were tasked with presenting a concept for a new magazine to a jury of publishing executives. Our group of eight pitched *Southern Magazine,* which, per Alan, was to "combine the grace, style and humor of the *New Yorker* with the probing insights of *Texas Monthly*." A natural raconteur and a terrific salesman, he captivated everyone in the packed auditorium in Palo Alto, including a New York-based publishing executive with roots in Dried Prawn, Louisiana.

That night, Alan and I made our way to San Francisco for some fun. The sock-hop-cum-hippie bar in Haight Asbury had waitresses in bobby socks and Buddy Holly on the jukebox. Yet it also looked like the kind of joint where you could score some drugs if you had a mind to do so: Think *Happy Days* meets *Midnight Cowboy*. The hours passed in a blur. Alan, a devotee of Evan Williams bourbon, was well into his cups, and I was on my third beer, a lot for me. Both of us sensed that something momentous had happened that week at Stanford. Improbably, we had breathed life into Alan's bold idea for a new magazine.

When we landed in Little Rock, I got unwelcome news. My mother and father had separated. For the sake of dramatic interest, I would like to say that this cast a pall over my life and prompted in me what could be called a quarter-life crisis. But that wasn't the case. I was a self-absorbed twentysomething, and aside from my adventures in publishing, I had grown close to my Treasured Girlfriend. Also, as ever, Razorback football served as a steadying influence. In just three weeks, the Hogs, in Ken Hatfield's second year, were to play Ole Miss at War Memorial Stadium, just like the season I was born 25 years before.

It would turn out to be a very successful season, with the Razorbacks going 9-2, but to me the private highlight of that year was a bold prank by a fraternity brother of mine. Laddy Diebold, a younger Sigma Chi still at the University of Arkansas, decided it would be really cool if he, too, could run through the giant Arkansas "A" as the Razorback players took the field. Like me, Laddy had dreamed of doing this since he was a boy, and while he'd played in several of the annual Charity Bowl games at Razorback Stadium, that was a pale imitation of being a real Razorback player at a real Razorback game.

When Laddy mentioned his crazy idea to backup Hog defensive end Brother Alexander, he set the precondition that he would only follow through if he could wear his old high school number, which was 56. With his persnickety demand, Laddy figured this would be the end of it. But only days later, Brother scrounged up just such a jersey, threw it down in front of Laddy, and said, "We're going to do this thing!" Using the gear of injured players and a few redshirted players too, Brother gathered up a helmet, pants, high-top black cleats—everything Laddy needed to look like a real player when he charged through the "A."

On the November day of the game against SMU, as the Razorback players made their way from the team bus through the horde of adoring fans to their locker room at the Broyles Center, Laddy simply fell in line with his accomplices and acted as if he were one of them. Inside the locker room, he went to the locker that Brother had arranged for him, calmly dressed and even had his wrists taped. Then came the moment he had long anticipated: actually running through the "A" as Arkansas Fight blared. Of this, Laddy later said, "I was so high I felt my knees were going to hit my chin!"

When Laddy reached the sideline, Brother instructed him to avoid making eye contact with any of the coaches. At halftime, when the Hogs trotted back to their locker room, Laddy slipped away from the stream of players, jettisoned the more cumbersome parts of his uniform, and returned to the stands to watch the second half with his wrists still taped and still wearing his number 56 Razorback jersey (without shoulder pads).

When I heard about Laddy's triumph, my first thought was to call him to offer my hearty congratulations. I was impressed that he'd been motivated by a sense of aspiration and a yearning to be part of the team, not by any desire to mock the players or undercut them with irony. My second thought was that I was too small to ever pull off a caper like this. The best I could do was to serve as a stand-in for a placekicker of, say, Garo Yepremian's stature.

Thank goodness the 14th-ranked Hogs defeated SMU 15-9, or else Laddy's prank would've summoned a nasty backlash.

Soon after Laddy's bold gambit, several well-heeled executives from *Southern Living* magazine, including publisher Emory Cunningham and his right-hand man, Don Logan, flew to Little Rock to learn more about our plans for *Southern Magazine*. When they arrived, we learned of problems with the heater in their Learjet. Poor fellows. I wish I had seen the look on their faces when Alan picked them up at the airport in his yellow Ford Escort. Shortly before their arrival, Alan had been in a fret when he realized an alley cat had crawled in through the open window of his car and peed in his backseat. In a bind, and perhaps harkening back to a trick he'd learned as a moonlighting taxi driver, on his way to the airport he stopped at a convenience store and bought a strawberry-scented odor eater to hang on his rearview mirror.

Because the Poobahs from *Southern Living* had jetted up to see us, we couldn't just take them to lunch at Sims Barbeque, Alan's favorite for ribs and fixins'. Fortunately, a few executives at a prominent investment-banking firm in Little Rock had taken an interest in our plans for *Southern Magazine,* so they invited all of us over to their offices, where we had a proper three-course lunch, cornbread included, in a wood-paneled dining room. As it turned out, however, the *Southern Living* people were just kicking our tires; their interest in our formative project was only in passing.

The good news was that the executives at the local investment-banking firm had become more intrigued themselves. Investment bankers require empirical proof of likely success, however. They wanted more numbers showing that our idea for *Southern Magazine* made good business sense.

So, Alan and our group, along with a magazine consultant,

hatched a plan. We had hired a renowned direct mail copywriter to design a direct mail offer, which asked a representative sample of 180,000 people across the South to subscribe to a magazine that didn't yet exist. If enough of these 180,000 people chose to subscribe to our new magazine, then we'd know the numbers would work. If too few of them chose to subscribe, we would send their money back and call the whole thing off. Such test mailings were a tried-and-true way to launch magazines.

The only catch was that Alan Leveritt and our team at *Arkansas Times* didn't have the some $130,000 it would cost to conduct such a test mailing. A proposal ensued: If I could come up with the funds to do the test mailing, Alan would sell me a stake in both the new magazine and the *Arkansas Times*. I pitched the idea to my entrepreneurial-minded father. If this test worked, it would prove a good investment. If it didn't, I'd come back home to Jonesboro and work in his burgeoning tanning bed factory.

The day after Christmas, our team mailed out subscription offers to the targeted list of 180,000 potential readers. As head of the circulation department, I spearheaded this effort, with the help of a consultant. The response rate we had to hit was 3.7 percent, or 6,660 prospective subscribers. Anything less and it would be too expensive to garner the 200,000 subscribers *Southern Magazine* needed from the get-go to lure national advertisers.

Each morning, I went to the post office and stuffed responses into a canvas satchel. I could fairly accurately gauge the number of responses we'd gotten each day by the weight of this canvas satchel. In the end, we hit our 3.7-percent target, and, before long, the local investment bank invested $6.3 million in a joint venture to publish *Southern Magazine*.

In October 1986, the same weekend the eighth-ranked Hogs beat New Mexico State, the first issue of *Southern Magazine* came out with articles probing the quirky quintessence of the South, including Willie Morris' rumination on whether or not the South really existed. "Is it nothing more than personal nostalgia codified? Are Virginians and Mississippians connected by anything other than the fact that their ancestors lost a war together? What is innately Southern anymore?"

These were all good questions.

15

Torments

The arrival of the 1987 football season at last gave me something to look forward to. Eight months earlier, my Treasured Girlfriend and I had gotten married, but it had been anything but a smooth transition.

The night before our scheduled wedding, I had told her I couldn't do it, that I was too unsettled about such a commitment. I had put off this reckoning for months, and here, at the last minute, I was blowing everything up. A portrait in courage I was not. She was in tears. I was in tears.

Outside the apartment building, my best friend, Rick Angel, waited. He grabbed me by the shoulders and looked me in the eye and told me to drive my car to his house in West Little Rock—he would be there in 15 minutes, right after he went inside and consoled my fiancée. And me? I promptly got into my car and drove north towards Jonesboro.

To that moment, the ongoing separation of my mother and father had seemed to have little impact on my life. Their separation was no mystery. Mother had long ago embarked on a spiritual journey and changed from the person she was when she and my father married at age 20. Also, as my father had more successes as an entrepreneur, he'd no doubt changed. They had both evolved, but in different ways. Nevertheless, during the two-hour drive to Jonesboro, I realized I wasn't sure whether I should go to my mom's house or my dad's.

I chose to go to my mother's. She and I had always been emotionally close. Though I was exhausted, we talked for a long time. She had always been fond of my Treasured Girlfriend and after much prayer—teary-eyed, I knelt beside my old bed in my old bedroom—my mother and I decided that I should drive back to Little Rock the next day and get married. After all, my Treasured Girlfriend was a good woman, and I might never find anyone, save my parents, who loved me the way she did. Getting married was what I *should* do, especially since my Treasured Girlfriend and I had lived together for more than three years.

So that's what I did. But unfortunately, and perhaps predictably, the marriage lasted only six months. I think it's safe to say that I had never looked more forward to a Razorback football season.

For the Texas game, War Memorial Stadium was packed and to get to my seat I had to navigate past the knobby knees of 10 other red-clad Razorback fans seated down the long row. *"Excuse me. Sorry. Go Hogs, y'all. Sorry. Excuse me."* The women swung their legs to the side to let me pass, but the men stood up, our encounter ranking somewhere between a clumsy handshake and a full-on embrace. When I finally landed at my seat, I spotted a man selling drinks at the end of the aisle from which I'd just come: "Ice-cold bottled water!" he bellowed. Tempting. Yet I didn't dare pass my money down the same line of folks I'd just climbed over, so I did without.

I felt lifted when the Hogs took the field. Just steeping in the charged atmosphere surrounding the Texas game gave me much-needed emotional fuel. Yet I also knew I would be crushed in just a matter of hours if the Hogs lost this game. This would be a totally binary experience: either elation or heartbreak, compounded by my divorce.

This year, however, I was more confident than usual, with the Hogs at 4-1 and ranked in the top 20, despite losing 51-7 to Miami three weeks before. Meanwhile, this Texas team, at 2-3, was hardly a juggernaut. For the season, Longhorn quarterback Brett Stafford had thrown one touchdown against 10 interceptions, one of the worst such ratios since the dawn of the forward pass in 1906.

With 1:48 to go, Texas trailed 14-10 and had the ball on their 44-yard line. Then the heretofore-woeful Brett Stafford caught fire. He converted a crucial fourth and 10, and as the Longhorns steadily moved towards the goal line, it was all I could do not to turn away in fright. This was a rerun of the same horror show I'd watched two seasons before, when the Longhorns had beaten the fourth-ranked Razorbacks 15-13, after the Hogs' kicker had missed three potentially game-winning chip shots.

But hold on, I told myself. The Razorbacks just might escape disaster; they just might keep me off the ledge. With only four seconds left on the game clock, every Razorback fan in the stadium rose and screamed in an effort to rattle Brett Stafford. The noise was earsplitting. Then Stafford dropped back and found Tony Jones in the end zone for the winning score.

Both teams spilled out onto the field, and amid the intermingling of opposing players and coaches, my eyes found Razorback coach Ken Hatfield. Near midfield, he shook the hand of the Texas coach. Hatfield had his back to me, yet as he turned and walked towards the tunnel at the north end zone, I could see, in his ashen face, bowed neck, and hunched shoulders, the full weight of what had just happened. As a key player on the Arkansas Dynasty team of 1964, Hatfield certainly knew beating Texas was the overriding goal of every Hog fan. Do this, and practically all else is forgiven. Fail in this, and woe unto thee.

The next day, I watched Hatfield's weekly Sunday television show. To the annoyance of athletic director Frank Broyles, himself more of a results-oriented secularist, Hatfield, who was sometimes derisively called Saint Kenny, always opened his show by quoting scripture. This week, he led with, "Jesus wept."

I was annoyed that Hatfield made no mention of the earthly causes of this defeat, namely his unimaginative, one-dimensional offense with 62 running plays and only four passes. Even so, I appreciated how he had conflated this Razorback loss with the fate of Jesus Christ. Also, he had presumed that Jesus was a Razorback fan and, by implication, that Jesus' Roman crucifiers, and even the Devil incarnate, were in the Longhorns' huddle. Bully for him. In all this, Hatfield cast the Razorbacks in the role of the martyred, which I guess he thought resonated with Hog fans like me who preferred to feel we're persecuted.

And he was right, martyrdom pairs well with our nagging sense of inferiority. To Hog fans, the footballing world just wasn't fair. The referees in the Southwest Conference, most of whom lived in the state of Texas, were always screwing us. The national media never gave us enough respect. Our victories were overlooked, our defeats magnified. We never rose as high in the national polls as we should have. Poor us. Poor me, suffering this loss to Texas on top of my blundering divorce. *Jesus wept.*

16

Thank You, PBS

A mong the many satisfactions of fandom was being able to watch a game on TV that I otherwise thought I'd have to miss. It was midway through the following season, and I was in Alexandria, Virginia, where my old pal Chuck Gschwend and I were visiting Sandy Brown, a mutual friend now pursuing a master's degree at Georgetown Law School. Sandy was happily married to a woman he'd met at the University of Arkansas and they had a daughter. The stability of his life was a sobering counterpoint to my half-a-year marriage.

I wasn't thrilled to be spending this weekend on the East Coast in the first place. Chuck, who these days was front running as a fan of the ascendant Miami Hurricanes, had initiated this trip. I preferred not to stray too far from home during the middle of any football season, but especially this year with the Hogs at 6-0, including a win over Texas the week before. Nevertheless, with the Hogs playing an away game in Houston, I had grudgingly agreed to cut myself off from Razorback football and had come along in the name of friendship—nowadays especially, I really needed my friends.

But I soon discovered that the Public Broadcasting Service

(PBS) station in northern Virginia was telecasting the Arkansas-Houston game. Such a minor miracle was made possible by the U.S. Supreme Court's ruling four years earlier that the NCAA no longer had exclusive rights to televise college football games, which in turn meant ABC Sports was no longer the only network to carry college football. Houston, at 1-4, was a bad team and the crowd down at the Astrodome was only 16,354, but who cared if no one in Houston was interested in this game? Stranded in Alexandria, I was all about it. *Turn up the volume on the TV, y'all!*

The Hogs got out to a 13-0 lead, but Houston scored a late touchdown to make it closer than it should've been. When the game was over, the local PBS station segued into a fundraising drive. That's what PBS stations do. Constantly. The talking head on television was making a big deal out of each donation: "Mr. and Mrs. So-and-So from Roanoke have pledged $150...."

To show our appreciation for PBS, Chuck, Sandy and I decided to make a contribution. The logic of our enthusiasm was perverse. The avowed mission of our nation's Public Broadcasting Service is to educate the American public, but this particular telecast, a feed from a regional network called Raycomm, had the unintended consequence of causing my friends and me to forgo our planned tour of the Smithsonian Museum. In other words, PBS's airing of this particular football game between Arkansas and Houston actually served to *uneducate* us.

I dialed the number on the TV screen, whereupon a pleasant-voiced lady took our pledge. It got complicated when she asked who was making the donation. Ordinarily, I would've just given her my name, but I figured that when the talking head announced our pledge on TV, my friends would want to hear their names called out too.

So I gave the PBS lady my name, then Sandy's, then Chuck's. Through the phone, I heard her struggling with Gschwend, a weird German name with a lone vowel thrown in among seven consonants. To help her out, I spelled Gschwend slowly at least three times. "You sure you got it?" I said, before I hung up.

Chuck, Sandy and I sipped our post-game refreshments and made plans for the evening. I was eager to explore Old Town Alexandria and at least dip my toe into the history of the area, since my family had roots in nearby King William County, going back to 1701. Ten minutes later, the talking head on the public television station finally got around to us: "*And from Alexandria, we have a donation from...blah, blah, blah... and Mr. Gus Chewin.*"

This mangled announcement, and the comical mishearing that had led to it, even elicited a reluctant laugh from the man whose name was just butchered.

Southern Magazine was at a crossroads. After more than two years and the publication of 26 monthly issues, we had 285,000 subscribers and had attracted numerous national advertisers. But we were also coming to the end of our $6.3 million in funding. To carry on, we needed a new infusion of cash, or another business partner, or both.

Eventually, our original investor, the local investment bank, found another willing investor/partner in Southern Progress Corporation, which published *Southern Living*. The year before, Southern Progress Corporation had been acquired by Time, Inc. for almost half a billion dollars. So, in essence, our magazine was being acquired by one of the world's largest magazine publishers.

Not long after, Don Logan, CEO of Southern Progress Corporation, showed up at the offices of *Southern Magazine*. He'd last visited us four years before, prior to our magazine launch, when he'd flown to Little Rock in a Learjet to sniff out what we were up to. Logan was a taciturn man who'd once been a computer programmer for NASA, and now one of his many duties was to inform me that, due to corporate duplication, my job as Circulation Director had been eliminated. After six years in magazine publishing, I was out of a job.

Postscript: Half a decade later, I would read in the *Wall Street Journal* that Don Logan had been promoted to CEO of Time Warner. Somehow, I felt better to learn that I'd been terminated by a man who was now one of the most powerful media executives in America. It called to mind a friend's story about his grandfather, who'd had the satisfaction of knowing he'd been wounded in a World War II battle led by Erwin Rommel, the great German tank commander. At least he'd been taken down by a worthy opponent.

As for *Southern Magazine,* after the Poobahs at Southern Progress Corporation took it over, they changed the name to *South Point: A Metropolitan Monthly*, and brought in a high-powered editor, John Huey, Jr., formerly with *Fortune.* But somewhere along the way, the soul and spirit of the publication got lost, and eventually they killed it. I suspect the executives at Southern Progress Corporation never wanted *Southern Magazine* around to begin with.

17

Ivy League Interlude

In the wake of the sale of *Southern Magazine*, I reinvented myself as a student at Harvard Business School. After dealing with sharpies in the worlds of magazine publishing and investment banking, I knew it wasn't enough to have a degree in English, or English Literature, or whatever the heck anybody wanted to call it. I sought more education, plus a catalyst to perhaps change careers. Rose, my girlfriend of a handful of years, decided she would move to Boston too. She had no real ties to Arkansas, having lived there only because she'd gone to a small liberal arts college in the state. Soon enough, she had a new job producing television commercials and a new apartment.

Harvard Business School has been likened to a boot camp for capitalism. The program was intense, immersive, challenging, exhausting. Then there was the sharp-elbowed competition, which was to be expected when 720 overachievers were graded on a forced curve while vying for six-figure job offers. Day by day, I was grinding it out. There were an endless number of case studies to prepare for, and many useful personal connections to be made. I had to be laser focused, to bear down and get it done. Yet the football season had started and, with the eighth-ranked Hogs off to a hot start, it was hard to break old habits.

At noontime several days each week, I pulled away from the country club-like environs of the Harvard Business School campus to walk over Eliot Bridge, across the Charles River, past the Kennedy School of Government, to Out of Town News, a 500-square-foot brick and limestone kiosk in the heart of bustling Harvard Square. This blessed newsstand, a marvel of the old analog era, was stocked with a remarkable selection of newspapers and magazines from around the world. This was where a political science professor nabbed the latest issue of *Foreign Affairs*, where the Parisian expat bought a week's worth of *Le Figaro*, where a student from Japan got copies of the *Tokyo Shimbun*. Crucially, Out of Town News was also where I purchased week-old daily issues of the *Arkansas Gazette*. Giddy with anticipation, I tucked my stack of newspapers under my arm and walked to the nearest trashcan, where I discarded every section of the newspaper except the sports pages. Then I marched across the street to the restaurant in the shadow of the Harvard Coop (bookstore), where I ate a solitary meal and devoured every news story about the Arkansas Razorbacks that I could get my eyes on.

As I lunched with my sports pages, I was fully aware that around me teemed a world full of exciting intellectual and professional possibilities. My heavens, just wandering into the nearby Harvard Square Bookstore was a mind expander. Yet I was more interested in how many total yards quarterback Quinn Grovey had piled up in the 39-7 romp over the Texas-El Paso Miners.

On the weekend of my 29th birthday, I watched the Arkansas-Texas game at a sports bar on Massachusetts Avenue. By design, I was alone. Sure, I'd made new friends at Harvard, but I wasn't ready to share the deeply emotional experience of a Texas game with any of them. Moreover, Rose, my girlfriend, while whip smart and adventurous, didn't get football at all. Even though the Longhorns, at 3-2, were unranked, I had a not-sosneaky feeling that the 5-0 Hogs were going to lose. As if on cue, it happened—again.

The next week, the Hogs' regained momentum with a 45-39 win over 12th-ranked Houston, at which point I hit rock bottom when I called Rick Angel, my old friend from undergrad days. We made small talk—yada, yada, yada—and then got down to business as he positioned his phone next to the TV in his living room back in Little Rock, so that I could overhear the Sunday-night broadcast of *The Wally Hall Show*.

Oh, boy. Here I was at one of the world's great centers of learning, glued to the landline telephone in my tiny dorm room while listening to a quite popular local sportswriter who, though I read his newspaper column whenever I could get my hands on it, was hardly a riveting television personality. But, man alive, I was so starved for news—any news—about Razorback football that I was more than willing to stoop to this hillbillyish form of eavesdropping. And given the relatively great season the Hogs were having, I considered my behavior wholly justified.

Before matriculating to Harvard, I imagined it to be a place full of smart folks, and certainly it was. Yet I was also coming to appreciate the nugget of truth behind William F. Buckley's assertion that he'd rather be governed by the first 300 names in the Boston telephone directory than by the faculty members at Harvard. I, too, was growing skeptical about the wisdom inside all these ivy-covered walls. So, thanks to the weekly telecast of *The Wally Hall Show*, I was staging my own little anti-elitist rebellion, such as it was.

On a cold, cloudy November day, I rode a chartered bus down to New Haven, Connecticut, to attend the Harvard-Yale football game, played at the mostly empty 64,269-seat Yale Bowl. My mission was to get away from my studies and watch some college football, no matter how much it resembled that played in high school. Though almost three months into my first semester at Harvard, I still felt like an imposter, and sitting among all the Ivy League swells only amplified my sense that I was perpetrating a con. At any moment, I expected a gray-haired eminence wearing a knee-length raccoon coat to tap me on the shoulder and say, "Young man, what in the world do you think you're doing here?"

For the first 10 minutes or so of this game between Harvard and Yale, I entertained the possibility that I could play defensive back for either of these teams. My self-talk: "That little fella who just missed another tackle is not much bigger than me, and I'm not sure he's much faster either."

Broadly speaking, the more important college football is at a university, the more the university lags when it comes to academics. Accordingly, at Harvard and at Yale, football was wholly irrelevant—though it hadn't always been this way. Historians contend that American football was *born* at Yale, with their first game played in 1872, their 27 national championships, their legendary coaches like Walter Camp and Amos Alonzo Staggs.

But, man, that was a long time ago.

This particular game was college football as played by true student athletes. None of these players were physical freaks, and the rosters of both teams were filled with guys from prep schools like Phillips Exeter Academy, Andover, Deerfield Academy, and Choate. It was all delightfully amateurish which called to mind another contrast: At Football Schools, football was about money, but the school itself was not so much about money. But for Ivy League institutions like Harvard and Yale the reverse was true: The football wasn't at all about money, but the school itself was very much about money. I figured that someday a number of these guys down on the football field would be floor traders on the New York Stock Exchange.

Then there was the halftime entertainment: Such performances at Razorback games, as at any self-respecting Football School, are highly choreographed affairs, with the marching band dressed in crisp uniforms, the majorettes twirling their batons, the synchronized flag wavers wrangling their flags. Much pageantry and pomp is always involved. Musical performances might include a medley of patriotic songs, or a musical tribute to the movie *Star Wars*, or, to really spice things up, renditions of hoary rock 'n' roll classics like *Stairway to Heaven* or *We Will Rock You*. At any Football School, it doesn't really matter *what* songs the marching bands play at halftime, the point is that the entire performance is conducted with earnest sincerity and a respect for decorum and tradition.

But nothing so stilted was remotely possible at any Ivy League football game, where the so-called scramble bands assumed a we're-too-cool-for-this attitude towards the entire concept of a traditional halftime show. Scramble bands aren't really marching bands at all. They wouldn't be caught dead marching in formation while playing *Stars and Stripes Forever*. Such bands are merely the backdrop for stunts, antics, tomfoolery, and satire, all intended to convey sophistication, as well as intellectual and cultural superiority. It's all purposely silly, though I'll concede that I wish I had been in the crowd at the Harvard-Yale game in Boston 15 Novembers before when a helicopter landed on the field at halftime and disgorged a student conductor/impersonator who was a dead ringer for Leonard Bernstein.

All in all, I found the Harvard-Yale game charming, an adjective I have never used to describe, say, an Arkansas-Texas Tech matchup out in Lubbock. But I wasn't about to change colors and become a live-and-die fan of the Harvard Crimson. My Harvard classmates found it *tres interessant* that I hailed from Arkansas. Like our fellow classmates from South Korea or the Philippines, I represented an intriguing kind of diversity. Yet I was mindful not to go overboard in revealing my passion for Razorback football, which would only have furthered the impression that I was outside the bounds of the norm. I kept it as my private refuge, a way to disengage from my studies and gain distance from my peers. (Though, candidly, if my classmates thought much at all about my home state, among the most flattering associations they could make was with the Razorback football team.)

At Harvard, my classmates tended to be older, with an average age of 26. I was 29. Most of us had been knocked around a bit by life. Yet as the first semester progressed, it turned out that not everyone made it through the Boot Camp of Capitalism. There was the eyebrow-raising case of the young man who, during the middle of his first exam, rose up and walked out the stately front door of Baker Library, never to return. One of guys in my four-man study group was forced to withdraw when his father unexpectedly died. Another guy in my study group went back to Southern California at Christmas break, not surprising since he'd worn his lime-green flip flops into December. Conversely, as deep winter set in, I had gone and bought a serious coat of the kind not found back home. It was made of thick shearling.

The Chinese restaurant was perched atop a hotel, and from up here I could see the heart of Boston, a city I had not gotten to know as well as I'd have liked over the past two years at Harvard B-School. Before coming north, I had imagined myself spending evenings beside a roaring fire in an oak-paneled study while discussing the meaning of life with learned classmates, not sitting alone in my dorm room calculating discounted cash flows for a case study about a company called Carborundum Abrasives.

It was the night before my graduation, and at the big dining table my mom and dad sat on either side of me. Even after their divorce, my parents made a point to get along. I had never heard my father, now remarried, say one bad word about my mother. As for Mother, my father was the only love of her life, yet she had put it behind her. Our group included my girlfriend, Rose, and my grandmother too, now sipping Coca-Cola because she had long ago given up her Canadian Club. My grandfather, not present, had considered my two years at Harvard to be a waste of time, yet my father hardly viewed it this way. I saw in his eyes that he was proud of me, though when I had left for Boston he'd no doubt been concerned that I wouldn't return to Arkansas after graduation. My mother, on the other hand, was worried that after two years in Boston I would become even more secular and more relativist, by her spiritual lights.

But neither parent should've worried. The previous year, as a side venture, my dad had formed a company called Action Graphix, which made so-called tri-vision signs, which were basically billboard-sized signs that rotated to show three faces of advertising. He'd seen these signs on a business trip to Europe, and then, in typical start-up fashion, had a ragtag crew of employees cobble together a passable product. Considering the money he'd invested, the company had gotten few customers and little traction. But I was going to return home to take this flailing business to new heights. I considered my choice a virtuous one. I was different from my lemming-like classmates at Harvard Business School who endured the rigors of the recruiting process in order to land jobs in consulting or investment banking. Yet considering my background, my choice to return to Arkansas after graduation was an entirely predictable act of conformity.

Our group at the big table atop the hotel ate, drank, and made toasts with wine and Coca-Cola and, in my mother's case, water. I was happy, bullish about my future, and thankful that Rose, too, had decided she'd had enough of New England and was returning to Little Rock with me. Certainly, my decision to come back home was not overly influenced by Razorback football. The previous season, the Razorbacks had gone 3-8, a complete reversal from the 9-2 campaign of the year before, after which Ken Hatfield had bolted for Clemson, purportedly fed up with the meddling of Athletic Director Frank Broyles. In a panic move, Broyles promoted offensive coordinator Jack Crowe to head coach.

Back in early October, the Hogs had lost at home to TCU by four touchdowns, and that's when I had quit schlepping to Out of Town News in Harvard Square to buy week-old *Arkansas Gazettes*. From there, the Hogs went into a seven-game tailspin, and by mid-November I'd found myself more interested in the Boston Celtics than I otherwise would've been.

Graduation day was warm and sunny, as, according to legend, such days always are for such ceremonies at Harvard. I kissed Rose, adjusted my mortarboard, and assumed my place in the long line of classmates standing on Eliot Street, just outside Emerson Gate. Finally, we entered Harvard Yard single file. A large crowd was spread across the great lawn, and I took my seat amid the crowd. All graduates and all guests then endured a forgettable speech by Eduard Shevardnadze, the Russian Minister of Foreign Affairs. When the ceremony was over, I wandered through the Yard, looking for my clan. I was hardly surprised to find my strong-willed grandmother seated in a prime spot at the base of the steps to Widener Library, the perfect vantage point with a sweeping view over the quad.

18

The New Reality

Over the previous two seasons, Arkansas coach Jack Crowe had gone 3-8 and 6-5. Already, he was on a short leash, and in their 1992 season opener in Fayetteville, the Hogs lost to The Citadel, a Division 1-AA team heretofore only familiar to me as the alma mater of Pat Conroy, who drew on his school days there in his novel *The Lords of Discipline*. This was as maddening as the loss to Tulsa back in 1971, and apparently I wasn't the only one ticked off about it. The Citadel game ended before sundown on Saturday. By noon Sunday, Frank Broyles had fired Jack Crowe. It was Pavlovian: Stimulus, then response. Cause meets effect.

In attending Harvard Business School, I had gained more respect for the prowess of managers, starting with what my father had accomplished, and extending to what Broyles had achieved in Fayetteville—including his latest coup, which was to move Arkansas from the waning Southwest Conference to the mighty Southeastern Conference. As head coach for almost 20 years, Broyles had built Razorback football from nothing. Then, as athletic director, he'd built Razorback basketball from nothing. Then he built the entire athletic department at the University of Arkansas from what had been nothing. A manager of his competence could lead any organization he set his sights upon. Broyles just happened to channel his managerial talents into Razorback football and all the rest. By my lights, he was the prototypical producer/builder, like Howard Roark in *The Fountainhead*.

I was thrilled by the decisive swiftness with which Broyles had fired Jack Crowe. I imagined him watching the Citadel debacle from the press box at Razorback Stadium and all the while thinking, *I'm going to fire our coach.* Then, at home that night, he probably talked it over with his wife, and a few friends by phone, all of whom said, "Now, Frank, don't do anything rash. The sun will rise tomorrow." Yet each time Broyles awakened during what was surely a restless night, his first thought was, *I'm going to fire our coach.*

Reportedly, Jack Crow went to Broyles' house that morning where they had the following exchange:

"I guarantee we will win next week at South Carolina," Crowe said.

"I'm not sure I can wait that long," Broyles replied.

"I'm going home. Call me later if I'm still your head coach."

Broyles never called.

The message to future head coaches of the Arkansas Razorbacks was clear: lose to nothing teams like The Citadel and you will be gone by lunchtime the next day.

Such tight justice was another of the many things I admire about college football. It's dog-eat-dog in a way that not even corporate America can match. We live in a world where few people are held accountable for much of anything. Rappers spew lyrics full of misogyny, violence, and over-the-line behavior, yet shun any responsibility. In corporate America, executives find endless ways to avoid accountability. But college football coaches are ruthlessly held to account. How much better would the world be if more people—including politicians, for crying out loud—were similarly answerable?

124

The iron-sharp dagger of justice aimed at Jack Crowe is why I've never resented these coaches for making big salaries. Theirs is a cutthroat profession and, unlike endeavors in business and/or government, it's a zero-sum game: Any success necessarily comes at the expense of someone else. There are only so many wins to go around. College football coaches don't change the rules of the game to better suit them, or play accounting games to make their quarterly numbers look better, or overpromise their voters and then evade the consequences by raising taxes. During any given season, college football coaches get only get 11 or 12 chances to win, or not. Their no-excuses world boils down to a hard-nosed saying of my grandfather's: "Don't tell me how much cotton you've picked; show me what's in your sack."

As fans, we have to be careful what we wish for. We tire of the old and yearn for the new, but when the new gets here, we wish the old were still around.

I had been all in favor of the Razorbacks' move to the mighty Southeastern Conference. It only made sense—money sense, especially, with more resources for building palatial athletic facilities. Fayetteville, Arkansas, would soon enough be home to a sports-industrial complex unrivaled by any Football School (except, of course, each of the 11 other members of the Southeastern Conference). But so far, the first year of the Razorbacks' transition to the SEC had not gone so well. After beating South Carolina under Interim Coach Joe Kines, the Hogs had lost to Georgia, then Alabama, and now they were matched up against the fourth-ranked Tennessee Volunteers in Knoxville.

On the eve of my 32nd birthday, I watched the game at Rick Angel's house. A next-level Razorback fan for sure, Rick now worked at one of the leading law firms in the state and had a solid marriage to a former Razorback cheerleader. With three minutes left, the Hogs trailed by 24-16 and a resigned silence had settled upon the living room. Rick and I had yelled at his TV throughout most of the game, turning our ire on Joe Kines, who sometimes seemed clueless; up-and-down freshman quarterback Barry Lunney; and the Hogs' porous defense, which got no help from an offense that had scored only 20 points over the last three games.

Rick and I had always bonded over the picking of such Razorback nits. We were withering critics and, as a lawyer, Rick could be especially prosecutorial. But I was certainly no piker either.

The Hogs were about to drop the fifth game of their last six, and both of us were mightily concerned about where all this was headed. Clearly, with the Hogs' recent move to the SEC, virtually everything familiar to us about Razorback football was gone. It was as if we'd entered an alternate realm. As a kid, Rick, like me, had been wowed by The Big Shootout, and as lifelong fans he and I had followed the same trajectory, passed the same signposts. Every season, *until this season*, Razorback football had helped both of us hold on to traditions and rituals going back to our youth. Arkansas football was a constant, and we knew it all by heart.

Every year, until this year, the Razorbacks had played two or three non-conference cupcakes, then TCU was our first conference game. In mid-October came Texas. We played Rice in early November, then closed each season with Texas Tech. Sprinkled in were games against SMU, Baylor, Houston, and Texas A&M. In a typical season, the Hogs would beat most of these teams and wind up somewhere between 8-3 and 10-1, with a loss to Texas. Sure, there'd be a down season or two, such as Lou Holtz's final year and the just-ended Jack Crowe experiment. But any such clouds soon passed and the sun came out again. Like the cycles of nature, we could count on the rhythms of these football seasons.

But hereafter, with the move to the tougher SEC, each season was apt to be one long thunderstorm. Occasionally, beams of sunshine would break through, and for a stretch there'd be a bit of brightish weather. But, predominantly, the skies would be overcast, and at times menacingly so. The stable was now unstable, the predictable unpredictable, the generally winning now the too-frequently losing.

This new reality had settled in on me three weeks before, during the Alabama game. It had been my first visit to War Memorial Stadium in three seasons, but, really, little about the place had changed since my father's first visit in 1954. Sure, the scoreboard had been modernized and the press box expanded, yet everything else was old-times familiar. The trouble was that practically nothing down on the gridiron was like old times. As soon as the Alabama football team ran onto the field, I'd known there was something different about these players from Tuscaloosa. Was it their throwback uniforms, including their plain helmets? Was it their mystique, enhanced by 11 national titles? Was it their much-ballyhooed team speed (a euphemism for a team's predominant blackness)? This game had been my first up-close experience with the violence of football as played in the top-tier of the SEC: the sped-up rush of footsteps, the crisper sound of pads popping, the oohs and aahs riffling through the crowd after the most bone-crushing collisions.

And now, in the wake of that eye-opener against Alabama, Rick and I stared trance-like at the TV as the Hogs were about to go down again. But the two of us snapped out of it big-time when Orlando Watters returned a Vol punt 71 yards for a touchdown. Suddenly, it was 24-22.

As the Hogs lined up for the two-point conversion to tie the game, my best friend and I paced and shouted commands, most of them contradictory:

"Don't just run the ball up the middle!"

"For God's sake, not another slow-developing sweep!"

"Take your time at the line of scrimmage!"

"Hurry, don't let the play clock run down!"

Despite the propulsive force of our instructions, the Vols stuffed the try at the two-point conversion.

Still down two points, the Hogs lined up for an on-sides kick, which triggered another round of frantic, contradictory exhortations:

"Don't telegraph where you're going to kick it!"

"Get more bodies on the short side!"

"Kick a line drive off a Tennessee player's chest!"

"Squib kick it and make the football pop up in the air!"

After Rick and I bathed our dry throats with beer, a Razorback player somehow recovered Todd Wright's onside kick. With time running out, the Hogs' offense came back onto the field, and my best friend and I knew exactly how to attack:

"Pass the ball; we're almost out of time!"

"Run it! Tennessee is back on their heels! Hurry, Lunney, dammit!"

As the Hogs moved the chains, our shouts gained urgency:

"Watch the clock! We're on the 29-yard line—that's close enough for a field goal!"

"We've got time for two more plays! No, run one more play and line the ball up in the center of the field! Hurry, Lunney! Spike it! Spike it!"

With two seconds left, Todd Wright trotted out to attempt the game-winner. All our exhortations ceased. There was no use yowling at the field-goal kicker. We'd only jinx him. Rick and I watched in arms-folded silence as Wright's kick sailed through the uprights. Arkansas 25, Tennessee 24.

Oh, the joy! Rick and I high-fived and strutted around. Out in his garage, we popped the tops on more beers, and even managed to eke out some praise for the gutty Razorback players, who, unlike us, had remained positive and persevered. For sure, the two of us had behaved like head cases the entire afternoon, yet with this unexpected victory we were on common ground, casting us back to our days as roomies in college when the Razorbacks had played in the old Southwest Conference. Sharing this victory with my best friend was all the sweeter when I pondered the damage inflicted on Tennessee's fans. I knew the path they were on. I could walk down it practically blindfolded, and that's what made it so delightful to contemplate their agony, which I considered their just reward for the injustice the Hogs had suffered in the Liberty Bowl back when I was 11.

19

Fleeting Pride

During the rocky Razorback season of 1992, a couple of really good things happened. One, Rose and I got married and bought a house in Little Rock. And two, Bill Clinton was elected 43rd President of the United States. I didn't vote for Clinton, having finally started to trend Republican, but I recognized that he put forth a decidedly positive image for my home state. He was articulate, smart, a well-educated Rhodes Scholar and a savvy policy wonk with a genius for relating to the Bubbas across Middle America. Sure, he was slippery and a bit of a rascal. But this was well known from his many years as our governor. In any case, his election lifted my inferiority complex about the state of Arkansas.

Meanwhile, my business, Action Graphix, was struggling, but had possibilities. The three-message sign was a product enabled by the rise of digital printing and the obsolescence of old-fashioned sign painters. To a paltry degree, I was riding a technology trend. Billboard companies across America were buying our signs, and they were popping up in football stadiums, major league baseball parks, on the Strip in Las Vegas, and even in New York's Times Square.

One of the only cracks in my world, aside from three straight seasons of mediocre Razorback football, was that my new wife wasn't happy that I was spending four days a week at my company's factory in Jonesboro, which was two hours away. Moreover, when she'd lived in Boston, she had developed an interest in becoming a film editor, which was difficult to do from anywhere in Arkansas. It's often difficult for young career-minded couples to get their work life and their love life in the same place, and in this Rose and I were no exception.

Unfortunately, my new marriage and Bill Clinton's ascendance coincided with even more of a downturn in Razorback football. Despite the upset win over highly-ranked Tennessee, the Hogs finished the 1992 season at 4-7. Interim head coach Joe Kines was let go, and the job went to Danny Ford, who'd won a national championship at Clemson in 1981. The way Danny Ford became head coach of the Hogs was rather clandestine. Early in the 1992 season, in the wake of firing Jack Crowe, Athletic Director Frank Broyles had smuggled Ford in as a consultant. At the end of the season, he was promoted to Coach.

Hangdog in posture, his mottled face as pockmarked as the moon, and typically with a chaw of tobacco in one cheek, Danny Ford was a caricature of the Southern rustic football coach. He was always at a loss for pretty words, and dangerously blunt, so it was painful to hear him speak to a reporter: "Well, Anthony's got that knee. Got that knee and, you know, you never can tell about that knee. I'm not a doctor. You know it could be a couple of days, maybe more. Might be 10 days. Hell, let's just call it two weeks."

Yet Danny Ford was also a hard-nosed, rub-a-little-dirt-on-it taskmaster, and I liked that about him. He'd learned from the best: Ford had played at Alabama in the late 1960s, and it wasn't hard to imagine Bear Bryant yelling down from his practice tower at his starting left tackle, "Son, give me 100 up and downs!" "Yessir!" Ford would shout back, and then he'd drop down and do as he was told until he puked.

Some coaches fit their team and some don't. In many ways, Danny Ford fit the Arkansas Razorbacks. Yet his I'm-just-a-redneck-football-coach-from-Arkansas shtick was undermined by the fact that Bill Clinton, Arkansas' favorite son, was now President of the United States, and nobody in the world thought Clinton was a tongue-tied hayseed. So ole Danny Ford was rather out of synch with the historical moment. Regardless, he was who he was, and by 1995, his third year at the helm of the Razorbacks, his players had finally responded to him.

A season that started with a 17-14 loss to SMU somehow ended with the Razorbacks playing in the SEC Championship Game against Florida. Improbably, Ford's Hogs had won eight of their last 10 games. But the SEC Championship, a 34-3 loss to Florida, summoned my old, familiar feelings of inferiority—namely, how preposterous it was to think that the Razorbacks could compete with schools situated in more fertile recruiting grounds. In 1992, 112 Florida high school players had signed with Division I schools. By comparison, that same year only 10 players from the state of Arkansas signed with Division I schools.

If, according to *Sports Illustrated* of November 8, 1965, Arkansas was once the New Dynasty, then Florida, under Steve Spurrier, was now the New, New Dynasty. In the SEC Championship Game against Florida, the Razorbacks were as physically and schematically overmatched as Rice, TCU, and Texas Tech had been when the Hogs played them when I was a kid. My team was doomed to mediocrity, or worse, and I had new reason to feel bad about my state.

20

New York Daze

After five years of marriage, Rose and I divorced. She had decided to pursue a career in film. Years before, she'd gone to Los Angeles to take a six-week course in film at USC, and just before our parting she'd attended a film academy in Camden, Maine. One weekend while she was there, we met up in Greenwich, Connecticut, at a friend's wedding. Solemn vows were said between the Jewish bride and the Catholic groom, and a new marriage brings hope to all marriages. Rose and I held hands. But later, as we drove north to Maine, the spell waned. She told me what I already knew. She wasn't coming back to Arkansas—ever.

This parting stung more than my first divorce 10 years before. So to break out of my funk—to both lose myself and find myself—I up and moved to New York City. I'd always loved New York, but this was a lark born of heartbreak. I entrusted my company to my quite capable business partner, with the proviso that I would try it for three months and I'd return to Arkansas every other week, which was relatively easy thanks to direct flights between Memphis and New York. Meanwhile, in New York I was working on a novel. In my opinion, this was a great plan, a chance to stretch myself in a way that would make for at least one less late-life regret.

My small apartment, rented from a gay snowbird gone to Miami, had white walls, pin lights everywhere, a very cool black toilet, and a walk-in closet that my mother envied. Yet there was no cable television, only a black-and-white TV with rabbit ears. But thanks to the wonders of cable, Razorback games were often-enough on TV, so I sought out various sports bars around Manhattan, a hit-or-miss endeavor, typically ending in a desperate plea to a bartender: "Hey, I'm not trying to be high maintenance, but is there any way you could turn on the Arkansas-Louisiana Tech game?" Whereupon, the bartender might or might not pick up the remote to search out some obscure cable channel.

On one crisp Saturday night during the 1997 season I found my way uptown to Mickey Mantle's Restaurant, partly owned by the Yankee slugger until his recent death. Already, the Arkansas-Auburn game was on one of the big TVs in the bar. I was eager to get off my feet, as I'd spent the entire afternoon shopping. Fashion-wise, I was on a mission. When I had moved to New York nine months earlier, I quickly noticed that I didn't exactly dress the part. With my cuffed, double-pleated khaki pants and plaid shirts (black is New York's team color), I looked suspiciously like a fellow who'd bought his clothes at Dillard's Department Store in Little Rock.

To remedy this, I had gone to Barneys, the mecca of New York style, where a clerk suggested I try on a pair of blue jeans by a designer named Helmut Lang. These low-rise, tight-weave jeans were a miracle of fit, as if expressly made for my shape. And so began my obsession with the iconic Vienna-born designer, a fixation that had led me to a second-hand store in Chelsea, a boutique in Soho, to Century 21, the discount emporium near the World Trade Center, and to Bloomingdale's on the Upper East Side.

Admittedly, my Jekyll & Hyde behavior on this particular Saturday was wildly contradictory: On the one hand, I'd shopped all over Manhattan in an effort to reinvent myself via a new street-smart wardrobe, while now I sat down to watch a Razorback game on television in a ritual that harkened back to when I was nine years old. But I loved everything about this contradiction. I found it enormously stimulating.

Before arriving at Mickey Mantle's, I'd purposely not eaten much. One challenge of holding down a seat at any sports bar for three-and-a-half hours was to pace my consumption of food and drink. I had to drag out the process in an effort to make it last longer than a seven-course meal at La Grenouille.

I started with a glass of iced tea, followed by a club soda, had a small salad, ordered a beer, then stuffed potato skins, another club soda, nursed a refill of the iced tea, then ordered a hamburger with no fries, another club soda, then a second beer, another club soda, cheesecake, decaf coffee, another club soda and so on to perpetuity.

Auburn had won four of their last five against the Razorbacks, and from the opening kickoff this game was a tough go. Trailing 23-7 early in the fourth quarter, the Hogs closed to within one score with 7:03 left. Despite Clint Stoerner's two touchdown passes, it wasn't enough.

The game ended around 10 p.m., early by New York standards. The City can be a lonely place and I'd spent the entire day by myself, though not without good reason. Pray tell, who else wanted to spend the afternoon scouring Manhattan for Helmut Lang clothes and then pass the shank of the evening watching the Arkansas-Auburn football game?

I walked up Broadway towards the vortex where the bustling avenue intersected with 72st Street and Amsterdam. The air was crisp, and I caught a whiff of the char of chestnuts from a food cart. I was down about the Hogs' loss, yet as ever the buzz and energy of the great metropolis buoyed me. My somewhat unhinged move to the City nine months earlier had given me just what I needed: In all ways, it had jarred me out of my post-divorce lethargy. Heck, it was even helping me maintain a balanced perspective on

Razorback football (though coming off last year's 4-7 campaign, my expectations this season had been low).

Moreover, back in February I'd met a new someone at a Super Bowl party. I had noted her graceful manner, beguiling almond-shaped eyes, and obvious lack of interest in the game between the Packers and Patriots. As always in New York, our conversation started with, "So, what do you do?" and I had tried not to betray any mid-life confusion. I listened attentively, got her name, her place of employ. Two days later, I called her at the financial services company where she worked. "Wow," she said, "that's some good sleuthing."

Her name was Rebecca, and our first date was at Montrachet, in Tribeca, with the kind of daunting wine list that you would expect of a restaurant named after one of the great wine-growing appellations in Burgundy. From the front window, we watched the snowfall as she perused the menu, then ordered the guinea hen, a breed familiar to me because Alan Leveritt kept a flock on his farm back in central Arkansas to help tamp down the tick population. She was from eastern Massachusetts, a Catholic and an Ivy League grad with an artistic side: her mother was a painter. Thereafter, we'd spent springtime Saturdays in Central Park, gone to the opera at the Lincoln Center, had brunch on Sundays on Columbus Avenue. Rebecca even arranged a summer share for me in a house out in Amagansett.

I'd told her that I would be at her apartment, just off 72nd and Broadway, at 10:30. She had declined to join me at Mickey Mantle's, considering my passion for Razorback football yet another irredeemable quirk of my lineage, like my drawl. Yet in her defense, when it came to college football, there was good reason for her indifference. On any given Saturday in New York, with its endless amusements, entertainments, points of interest, and cultural diversions, there were at least 143 better things to do than to waste one precious moment on college football. As Rebecca saw things, college football was for those who lived in flyover country, places where there was nothing going on *but college football.*

She and I went out for a late dinner at Café Luxembourg, just around the corner, even though I was still stuffed from the three-hour eat-drink marathon at Mickey Mantle's. I was thankful to be with her. She was wise to the City, and tough, too, in a good way, yet her heart was as warm as her almond-brown eyes.

After dinner, Rebecca and I went back up to her cozy apartment and fell into each other's arms.

Into my second year as a part-time New Yorker, my world had broadened. I knew the subway routes of Manhattan, the hot restaurants and the buzziest neighborhood bars. My Helmut Lang wardrobe was filling out nicely. I considered myself more sophisticated, more cultured, and more worldly, even if the Razorbacks *had* gone 4-7 the previous two seasons.

In mid-September, one of my Harvard Business School cronies invited me to his apartment near Grammercy Park to watch the Arkansas-Alabama game. Mind you, he had no intention of watching this telecast with me. A Northwestern fan and a Big 10 guy, he was off to dinner with his fiancée. Yet his thoughtful offer saved me from having to traipse all over New York in a search of a Razorback-friendly sports bar.

Going in, Alabama was 2-0, as were the Hogs, who, under new coach Houston Nutt, had only beaten Southwestern Louisiana and SMU. I figured that soon enough I'd turn off the TV in disgust and head out to dinner in Soho. Early on, Alabama went up 3-0. But after that, the world as I'd known it was turned upside down.

The notion of our beating Alabama by 36 points was akin to my waking up one morning and being six-feet-four-inches tall. It just wasn't humanly possible. Yet, after this historic 42-6 thrashing of the Crimson Tide, I was as high as the nearby Empire State Building.

Clearly, with average coaching, even a program like Alabama's was vulnerable. Mike Dubose was not a bad coach. He just wasn't a special coach, and that's what Alabama had had with Bear Bryant from 1958 to 1982, and then under his doppelganger, Gene Stallings, who'd left two years before in 1996. Those who claimed that any coach can win at a top-tier program like Alabama were delusional. Mike Dubose—*any coach*—just got his fanny kicked by Houston Nutt, two years removed from head coach at Murray State. The margin of defeat in this game was the most against an Alabama team since 1957.

I was like an innumerate who'd just won the lottery. I wanted to kiss Rebecca (who was spending the evening with her girlfriends) and to walk around nearby Union Square and say "Hi, y'all!" to anyone who dared make eye contact with me. I called my father to gloat, but within the concrete canyons of Manhattan, the reception on my new Nokia cellphone was spotty. *"How about that?! Great game… Amazing, wasn't it?…When are you coming home again?…I love you."*

The night was relatively young and I made my way to Soho. I often went there to watch the people on the cobblestone streets and admire the Italianate cast-iron architecture. Sometimes, as I trod these cobblestones, I wondered what I was doing in New York. Sure, I was enjoying myself, but, really, why was I here? I was in middle age with no wife, no children, no home to speak of. I was dogged by a sense that I was wasting my life. My disorientation was such that only weeks before, I'd had my palm read by the swarthy lady who sat outside the upstairs bathroom at Raoul's bistro.

But on this night, no such melancholy stalked me. God, I loved it here in New York! And I loved my home state too! And, plainly, I loved both places even more when the Razorbacks won.

I stopped at Fanelli Café, with its cockeyed neon sign that

faced Prince Street. Open since 1847, the place was timeworn, yet convivial and always crowded. It seemed as if the burgeoning life of the City was contained within these four walls. Yet not a soul here had any idea how happy I was. For most New Yorkers, college football was beyond their experience or understanding. Many attended colleges in New England or the mid-Atlantic, where football was an afterthought. Any New Yorkers who were football fans were typically supporters of NFL teams, the Giants or the Jets. Not to say a good number of the folks who lived in New York weren't college football fans. On any given Saturday, the sports bars across Manhattan were packed. But these fans weren't true New Yorkers. Like me, they were émigrés from Texas or Ohio or Nebraska, people for whom New York was their life's destination, at least for now.

I wrangled a seat at the bar, ordered a Guinness Dark and a cheeseburger, and watched a late-night West Coast game on the small TV. Soon, a ribbon of scores from that day's football games crawled across the bottom the screen, and when the Arkansas-Alabama result appeared, I was tempted to stand on my barstool and lead a rousing Call of the Hogs. *Woo Pig Sooie!*

Instead, I just sat there with both elbows on the bar and daydreamed. Like a time machine, the victory over Alabama cast me back to an era before the six lean seasons under Danny Ford, Jack Crowe, and Joe Kines (with a combined record of 29-37-2). The Hogs were obviously on the rise, and already my focus was shifting from the not-so-mean streets of New York (for these were the orderly years of the mayoralty of Rudy Giuliani) to the soybean fields of Arkansas. I began to plot just how soon I could attend a Razorback football game, in either Fayetteville or Little Rock.

In early November, with the resurgent Hogs at 7-0, I found my way to Fayetteville with my buddies Bob Childress and Scott Willhite. Bob was now a partner in an accounting firm in Little Rock, and Scott, after long ago returning from Colorado, had his own law practice.

With Ole Miss at 6-2, this should've been a good game but the Rebels were lethargic, especially in the second half when the weather turned menacing. Despite that the Razorbacks now played in the SEC, Fayetteville, Arkansas, has never had much to do with the American South. But it's not situated in the Midwest either. It's in a hilly off-grid quadrant with its own fickle climate.

At kickoff, it was balmy, with the temperature in the high 60s, weather typical of, say, Winona, Mississippi—no doubt Ole Miss felt at home in such conditions. The second quarter brought cooler air and a driving rain, but still Ole Miss held up to it reasonably well. At halftime, they were down only two scores. Then the rain kept on, but the wind switched and temperatures plunged into the mid-30s. The first real cold of the season swept down with a vengeance from the plains of Kansas, and the Ole Miss players looked as if they just wanted to get this game over with and fly home to Oxford, never again to return to the northwest corner of Arkansas during the month of November.

Fortunately, Bob had risen at 6 o'clock that morning to buy all three of us waterproof ponchos at Walmart. Otherwise, I'd have been as ill prepared for this hoarfrost as were the Rebel players. Yet my five-dollar plastic poncho could only do so much. I was wet, which can sometimes be fun in a kid-like way, but the bone-chilling cold amplified everything. I cringed when hard-hitting safety Kenoy Kennedy separated an Ole Miss receiver from his helmet. I shuffled my feet to make the blood flow, and I couldn't even sit down because my keister would get wetter.

Bob and Scott and I rolled our eyes at each other and wondered aloud if the concession stand was still sold out of hot chocolate. I had never been this uncomfortable at any Razorback game.

Not even close. How bad can a good time be?

At age 38, I was too old for this—such punishment was for the crazed guys in the student section with their bare chests covered in red paint. Yet all this winning by the undefeated Razorbacks had induced a kind of what-the-hell euphoria in me and my friends. Our suffering was proof to the players and coaches—really, proof to ourselves—that we were willing to do whatever it took to contribute to this Dynasty-Year-in-the-making. So, in weather fit for only the hardiest of migratory waterfowl, my pals and I stuck it out until the scoreboard flashed 00:00.

The next day, I drove back to Jonesboro, where I stayed at my mother's house, as I always did when toggling between New York and Arkansas. Mother's kitchen smelled of beef stroganoff, and the Dallas Cowboys' game was on the TV in the den. I'd decided I liked the Dallas Cowboys, mostly because Jerry Jones, the owner for the last nine years, had played on the Razorbacks' 1964 national championship team. For me, when it came to football at any level, all roads led to and from Fayetteville, Arkansas. Yet I was still so euphoric over the Hogs' eighth straight win the day before that I changed the channel and, for the first time, watched *The Houston Nutt Show*.

This was another of those formulaic half-hour coach's shows, during which the head coach rambles in Coachspeak for 15 minutes and the television station airs 15 minutes of commercials. *Brought to you by State Farm. Proud sponsor of Razorback football.* Such shows are merely a way for the head coach to rake in some extra bucks, and the entire genre—no matter the coach or the team—can be painful to endure. You have to be almost brain dead to sit through an entire telecast.

But this season, to liven up the proceedings, the producers of *The Houston Nutt Show* had introduced a segment during which Coach Nutt, in the jubilant Razorback locker room after each game, wrote the team's unblemished record on a large white board, *8-0*, prompting a deafening roar from his players. The filming of Nutt's post-game ritual was a bit of reality TV injected into the Hogs' inner sanctum. As a Razorback fan starved for winning football, I immediately deemed Coach Nutt's show to be must-see TV.

21

Agony and Redemption

The following week, the undefeated and seventh-ranked Hogs faced undefeated and second-ranked Tennessee in Knoxville. With a win, the long-sought Dynasty Year was within grasp. There's nothing like a big game to look forward to. Anticipation is half the joy of it, and I was positively giddy, my excitement heightened by the prospect of a special visitor from New York.

Rebecca and I had been dating for almost two years, and owing to plans we'd made back when the notion that the Hogs would win their first eight games had never crossed my mind, she was headed down to the Mid-South on the weekend of arguably the biggest Razorback game since December 6, 1969.

Rebecca and I spent Friday in Jonesboro, where I showed her all three houses I'd lived in when growing up (each in the same neighborhood), the high school I'd attended, the small factory at my manufacturing company, Action Graphix. I pointed out the new mall as we passed by. Jonesboro had grown and progressed, yet there were oddities like the fact that Craighead County was still dry. But my dear father had even arranged a work-around for that. About eight years earlier, he'd been granted two liquor licenses from then-governor Bill Clinton (I never asked how he got them). These were the only liquor licenses in the county outside of places like the Jonesboro Country Club, the Elks Club, and the Eagles Lodge. So, during Rebecca's stay, she and I had dinner and a glass of wine at the restaurant my dad owned.

Regardless, Jonesboro was a bit pastoral for Rebecca's tastes, so on Saturday morning I drove her over to Memphis. My mission was to impress her with the charms of the River City, such as they were, as well as to make an effort at bolstering my liberal bona fides. As a conservative in New York, I was as rare as the sight of a meerkat. Rebecca and I sometimes gently argued about politics, or had conversations like this:

"Do you feel safer in New York," I asked, "now that Rudy Giuliani is the mayor?"

"Yes," she said. "The city is definitely safer. Even Central Park is safer."

"So, you like Mayor Giuliani, right?"

"No, I hate his smarmy guts. Why would you even ask me a silly question like that?"

In downtown Memphis, I took Rebecca to the National Civil Rights Museum, in part to further convince her that as a Southerner I wasn't a closeted racist. But it's dangerous to even try to convince a New Yorker that you possess any sort of liberal instincts at all. Once you start down this path, nothing you can do or say will ever convince a New Yorker that you're liberal enough. They will always one-up you.

Because Rebecca and I had first paid a visit to Sun Studios, we arrived at the National Civil Rights Museum later than I expected: The kickoff of the Arkansas-Tennessee game loomed at 2:30 p.m. on CBS, and our tour was a rushed experience that made me look worse than if I hadn't taken her to the museum at all.

We hustled out to my car, then headed east on Poplar Avenue. Desperate, I found a sports bar off Mendenhall, located a two-seater table near a suitably huge TV, and ordered iced teas; my girlfriend, like me, wasn't an afternoon drinker.

This sports bar was dumpier than I'd have preferred, with rickety wooden chairs and the odor of stale beer. I should've planned better, but it was too late now; kick-off had arrived and I was riveted. Meanwhile, to my astonishment, Rebecca reached into her oversized purse and pulled out a paperback copy of Thomas Hardy's late 19-century literary classic *Tess of the D'Urbervilles*.

"I started reading this book on the plane from New York," she said, melting me with her beguiling eyes.

"Sure," I said. *What in the hell is she doing?* I thought.

The crowd at the sports bar was a motley mix of Tennessee and Arkansas fans, and occasionally Rebecca glanced up from her reading to see what all of the fuss was about. But mostly she stuck to her *Tess*. Despite my initial shock, the English major in me couldn't help but grudgingly admire her. This woman was no mere reader of trendy chick lit. Yet I was so obsessed with this game—was in fact in a zone in which everything on planet earth was subsumed to it—that it never occurred to me that she would've preferred to be doing something else. *Anything* else.

During a TV timeout, I came up for air. "How's your book?" I said, even as she strained to read in the dim light. She finally marked her book with the wrapper of a straw, and said, "Fine. How's your game?"

"Good, so far. Long way to go, though."

Rebecca nibbled at a nacho, then went back to her *Tess*. Meanwhile, with the Hogs ahead 24-10 with 11:43 left in the third quarter, a familiar logic set up in my mind. In a high-stakes game like this, at some point I become convinced the Hogs are going to win and I play out all of the positive consequences; in this instance, the national recognition from beating the nation's second-ranked team on their home field; the Hogs' jump into the top three in the national rankings, perhaps even the top two; a berth in the

SEC Championship Game and an odds-on shot at the national championship.

As the third quarter progressed, I banked all of these wonderful aftereffects somewhere deep in my soul. I knew it was dangerous to do this, yet with under two minutes left in the game, I was even more convinced. The Hogs had the football and a 24-22 lead. It was second down. All the Porkers had to do was run a few plays to milk the clock, then punt the ball deep into Tennessee territory. I stood up, so overwrought with excitement that I playfully put my hand over *Tess,* pinning Rebecca's book to the table and when she looked up, I surprised her with a kiss squarely on her mouth.

"We will go somewhere nice for dinner," I said with a big smile. "I'll make this up to you. We'll have a great night."

Then, with 1:43 left, the damnedest thing happened. Clint Stoerner took the snap from center, tripped over the left foot of Hogs' right guard Brandon Burlsworth, lost his balance and, to steady himself, he literally sat the football on the ground. All this occurred with no contact whatsoever from any Tennessee defensive player.

Staggered, if I'd been stabbed in the heart with a sharp object, I sank back into my rickety chair. The replay, repeated multiple times in slow motion, only twisted the knife in deeper. With little resistance from the demoralized Razorback defense, Tennessee went on to score the winning touchdown.

This confounding game ended at that awkward hour of late fall when the sun has set and it feels late, even though it's not. Somehow, I had to get through the evening hours.

In downtown Memphis, Rebecca and I had dinner at Automatic Slim's Tonga Club (considerably tamer than the name implies), where I had a serious and no doubt annoying case of the blank stares. "Are you okay?" she said, more than once.

I couldn't summon the energy to explain why this game mattered so much to me, and any attempt to do so would've only made me more depressed than I already was. Thankfully, there were no orange-clad Tennessee fans sitting near us, or I'd probably have said or done something I'd have regretted.

When I crawled into bed later that night, I was still trying to process what had happened. I tossed and turned, and whenever I awakened long enough for a cogent thought to form in my head, my mind went straight to the game's bizarre ending.

Daylight brought no relief. This ache certainly wasn't going away anytime soon. The instant Clint Stoerner had laid the football on the ground, I knew that what had happened would stay with me for as long as I was able to draw a breath. Before Rebecca and I headed to the airport to fly back to New York, as if trying to breathe life into a corpse, I bought a copy of *The Commercial Appeal* to confirm my lingering hunch that the Hogs had dominated this game statistically. They had not.

It was an easy flight from Memphis into LaGuardia Airport. On our approach, we skirted the edge of Manhattan, towering and magically real yet also a bit Lego-like with its man-made high rises. This was another world, and the jarring sight made me think about my behavior with Rebecca over the past weekend. There was so much to unpack. I hadn't been a barrel of fun, I realized, and in my ongoing funk I regretted that I hadn't exactly presented the best side of myself. But should I have trimmed my behavior and pretended that the game hadn't been terribly important to me? If Rebecca and I were serious about our relationship—and we were—should I have pretended to be somebody I was not?

What if she had behaved the way I had? What if she were a nutso fan of the New York Giants, and she'd had a meltdown after they'd lost the NFC Championship game or some such? I said I loved her, but was it right to inflict this on her? And in doing so, did I narrow my range of suitable mates? Was I looking in the wrong places? Was she? For sure, Rebecca was different from me, yet in telling ways she was similar. We both viewed ourselves as strivers in the world of business, yet we also fashioned ourselves as being attuned to things literary, or at least to being reasonably well read. I really liked that about her. How adorable was a woman who subscribed to *The Economist* and read meaty books like *Tess of the D'Urbervilles*?

All that aside, though, it didn't matter if I was back in my home state or in New York, I couldn't get away from myself. And I was stuck with the reality that my team had once again lost the big game in the most Arkansas way possible.

One year later came another crack at Tennessee, undefeated and on course to play for their second straight national title. The Hogs were mired at 5-3; nevertheless, I relished the prospect of inflicting a soul-crushing loss on the Vols, who wouldn't have won squat the year before without the improbable botch by quarterback Clint Stoerner.

Yessiree, I could feel it: The Hogs were about to write another chapter in the all-too-thin book entitled *Epic Redemptive Victories in the History of Arkansas Football*. The Tennessee Volunteers were about to enter a version of Dante's Contrepasso, where they would endure their own counter-suffering. Just as the false prophet must eventually go forth with his head twisted around backwards, last year's score of 28-24 in favor of the Volunteers would swivel to 28-24 in favor of the Hogs.

I schlepped to Fayetteville and met up with my chums Bob Childress and Scott Willhite. This was an opportune weekend for me to be away from New York. The longer Rebecca and I were together—we'd dated for almost three years now—the more apparent it became that a crucial choice loomed. Either I had to become a New Yorker. Or she had to become a Southerner—an Arkansan, no less. Such a reckoning was coming.

Bob, Scott, and I arrived early at Razorback Stadium to bask in the pre-game buzz. Like every Razorback fan, we'd waited an entire year for this game. To help us burn off nervous energy, Bob fished around in the trunk of his car for a toy football, as essential to any game-weekend road trip as a spare tire. But my friends and I, full of edgy anticipation, didn't just loll around in the north end zone parking lot and casually toss the football back and forth. Rather, we aired it out as we ran short down-and-out patterns and long fade routes, using the third man in our triumvirate as a defender. We maneuvered around parked cars, tailgate tents, and hordes of red-clad fans. To channel traffic, the police had put out blue saw horses, which made nifty sideline boundaries over which we, as receivers, had to stretch to stay inside this imaginary boundary. It was as if I was back in fourth grade, playing Hut-Two with my dad out in the front yard.

The possibility that our behavior was inappropriate for three men approaching the age of 40 never entered our minds, and nobody in the crowded parking lot seemed bothered by our jejune game of pass-and-catch. One of the joys of fandom is that on game-day Saturdays we're all granted some leeway to act as if we haven't grown up. Whenever one of our errant tosses was gathered by a bystander, he typically assumed the pose of quarterback, pumping the football a few times and motioning for one of us to go this way or that, so he could fire a pass to his intended receiver.

At the heart of redemption games like this one is the act of repossession. At root, they're about righting a perceived wrong, and as such they are fraught with peril because if the victory can't be repossessed, then the original affliction is only magnified. With such high emotional stakes, it's not surprising that different people deal with the stress in different ways.

I lost it when punt returner Rossi Morreale fumbled a punt. Luckily, he recovered the football. But then he bobbled another punt, and with each of his flubs I stood and let out sharp, full-throated yells, "Come on, Rossi! Get your head in the game! Jeez!" And when Rossi Morreale trotted to the sideline, I yelled at him again in the conceited hope that the irritant of my voice would somehow spur him to clean up his act.

The Vols led 24-14 in the second half. But the Hogs cut the lead to 24-21 and, with four minutes left, were driving. This game, as so often is the case, came down to a crucial third-down play. The crowd held its collective breath. On my left was Scott Willhite, bestowed with an unflappable calm that served him well as a lawyer: As the game had tightened, he'd only grown quieter. On my right was Bob Childress, among whose clients at his accounting firm was a legendary pro football coach; they'd golfed together at Pebble Beach. Certainly, Bob was no stranger to adversity, having weathered the death of both of his parents before he was old enough to drive a car. Yet, as the players approached the line of scrimmage, and with every fan in Razorback Stadium on their feet, he plopped down in his seat and said, "I can't watch. Just tell me what happens."

Moments later, Clint Stoerner dropped back and found Anthony Lucas in the back of the end zone to put the Hogs up 28-24. The stadium erupted in a cathartic release, as Scott and I each grabbed one of Bob's lank arms and raised him from his seat.

But the game wasn't over. Tennessee took the ensuing kickoff and drove down the field. On a fourth-down play, with every fan on their feet, Bob again cowered, head down, as Tee Martin's pass into the end zone fell incomplete. Over the roar of the crowd, he looked up from his seat with plaintive eyes and said, "Did we win?" as if the outcome was only official when he heard it from me.

After the game, we lingered in the stands as the crowd cleared. Down on the near sideline, the Razorback players were locked arm in arm as they swayed and sang, "Oh, Lord, it's hard to be humble if you're an Arkansas Razorback fan." One of the best things about winning was to see how happy the Razorback players were, to share in their jubilation and vicariously experience their joy. When the Razorback Band quit playing, the stadium went quiet. Behind me, I overheard excited conversation. I turned and, about six rows back, I saw practically the entire Morreale family of Fort Smith, Arkansas. Like groupies, practically all of them wore number 24 Razorback jerseys, Rossi's number. I slowly turned back around, trying not to call attention to myself, and stood with my back to the Morreales, hoping no member of their clan walked down from the bleachers, tapped me on the shoulder, then reared back and punched me in the mouth. But in the wake of the Hogs' redemptive victory, most sins, even perhaps all, were forgiven. Everyone concerned was in good cheer, at least on the Razorback side.

22

The Pompom Girl

My stint as an ersatz New Yorker had ended. At heart, I wasn't a New Yorker, and Rebecca wasn't a Southerner either, much less an Arkansan. It was unwise to try to turn people into something they were not. I was content to be back full time in Jonesboro, which was said to be a good place to raise a family—though at age 40 I had no wife, no children, nor even any romantic prospects.

Then, two years after my return home, I met a special woman at a health club in Jonesboro. She was seated on a leg press machine, and I'd been furtively casting my eyes in her direction when she looked at me in the floor-to-ceiling mirror and said, "Do I know you?"

She was vaguely familiar, yet I couldn't quite place her. So in a hopeful tone I said, "Maybe," and introduced myself.

Some 20 years before, Susanne Williams and I had both attended the University of Arkansas, but we hadn't known each other. Then, when she mentioned that she'd been a pompom girl, it hit me: During my college days, I'd admired her from afar—from high in the stands at Razorback Stadium, to be exact. She had fantastic legs.

Call me shallow, but this connection to our Razorback-related past caused a vibration inside me. I considered this link as valid as any of our other mutual associations: Susanne had grown up in the same nearby town in eastern Arkansas where my father had lived until he was 12, and, as is typical in a small state like Arkansas, she knew people I knew, and vice versa. She'd even been a member of the same sorority as Darla Lacey, the coed with whom I'd had the non-date blind date to the TCU game more than two decades before.

Just weeks after this chance encounter, I went to the 2002 Cotton Bowl with my dad and my sister, where, on a bitterly cold afternoon, we sat through one of the Five Worst Razorback Games of All-Time, a 10-3 loss to Oklahoma during which the Hogs amassed a whopping total of 50 yards. *Fifty yards.* In a stat I'd never seen, the Hogs ran more plays (55) and had more yards in penalties (54) than they had in total offense. Watching this game was about as much fun as counting the number of white pickup trucks parked out in the surrounding acreage of the Texas Fairgrounds.

Nevertheless, I was hardly soured on Arkansas football. I was on to romancing the pom-pom girl of my not-so-distant memory.

The following season provided the first opportunity for Susanne and me to watch a Razorback game together. We were at Houston's Restaurant in Memphis, where the second half of the Tennessee game was on both televisions in the crowded bar. Houston's attracted an older, somewhat classy clientele—this wasn't some raucous sports bar—and among us were some Volunteer fans, a few Razorbackers, and several with no obvious rooting interest. Such a mixed crowd was typical in Memphis, which is barely in Tennessee, just east of Arkansas, a tad north of Mississippi, and even fairly close to the Missouri state line. For all those reasons, a respectful protocol was observed by all patrons in the bar. During this battle between teams from neighboring states, there'd be no displays of excessive partisanship. Together, we would all watch this game with the dispassion of a television commentator.

Such tacit neutrality suited me because it gave me cover. Thus far in our relationship, Susanne had not been exposed to my game-watching histrionics, and certainly she wasn't apt to get too enthused about any of the in-game particulars herself. Though ostensibly a Hog fan—the front of her SUV bore a "Go Hogs" license plate—to her, Razorback football evoked her days as a pompom girl, the packed stands at Razorback Stadium, the electricity in the air. The actual game itself didn't much matter to her. I still wasn't convinced that she even knew 10 yards were required for a first down, or why this was important.

Into the tense fourth quarter of this game, I let loose with a few under-the-breath comments and muted exhortations, particularly when the Hogs scored a touchdown with 3:45 remaining to tie the score. My restraint generally held up even through the first overtime as both teams traded field goals, though granted I was distracted by my conversation with Susanne, whose mind was still on her looming custody battle with her ex-husband over their 15-year-old son.

She and I had spent the afternoon in the office of Bert Hodkins, a lawyer in West Memphis whose law practice focused on underdogs, particularly women in divorce or custody proceedings against powerful husbands. Susanne had insisted that I be there. During our get-to-know-you conversation, Bert had rambled on about his experiments with mushrooms and LSD back in the '60s, a confession perhaps triggered by Susanne's mention that she'd once worked as a psych nurse: She sometimes had that effect on people. I could still see Bert Hodgkins, with his spindly arms and pallid face—he was old enough to be our father—and how he'd told us to forget about all this custody stuff and leave it to him. "I have all the files and I'll call you if I need anything else," he'd said. "We'll get together again as the custody hearing comes closer."

Beneath the lights at the bar at Houston's, Susanne sipped her wine as she ate the Evil Thai Jungle Salad, her favorite. "I feel really good about Bert Hodkins as my lawyer, don't you?"

"He's a good fit," I said. "He understands your cause."

"I think he listened to what I was telling him. I believe he's going to do right by me."

"Yes, he will."

As the second overtime unfolded, the Razorbacks had to settle for a field goal. But then the Hogs' defense stiffened and Tennessee lined up to attempt a field goal just to tie the game again and force a third overtime, and that's when I let out an impolitic gasp when the Vols' kick was partially blocked, yet somehow barely crawled over the cross bar. Had I been anywhere but among this bipartisan crowd at this somewhat upscale restaurant, I'd have shouted at the TV. *How on earth can that happen?!*

Into the third overtime, Susanne continued on about her custody battle, talking rapid fire: "My ex-husband once claimed he was going to have me put in an orange jumpsuit because one Wednesday night I didn't deliver the kids to him at his house, which is 50 miles away. We had a court hearing over that incident and when my son complained about being tired at school from all of the early morning rides back to Jonesboro for school, the judge said, 'Well, you get up early to go duck-hunting with your grandfather, don't you?' And my son said, 'Yeah, but I don't go to class all day after that.' Can you believe a judge would say something like that to a teenager?"

"No, I can't believe it," I said, still in shock that I hadn't let out a blood-curdling shriek when Razorback kicker Brennan O'Donohoe had missed a game-winning 38-yard field goal.

She continued: "And when this custody battle for my son is

over, we will have another custody battle in two years over my daughter. You know how this will play out, don't you?"

"We're on to the fourth overtime," I noted. "It's totally nerve-racking, isn't it?"

Plainly, Susanne and I were talking past each other. To this day, I have no idea what mysterious power stopped me from hurling my cloth napkin at the nearest TV when Tennessee's Jabari Davis fumbled into the end zone, only to have a teammate fall on the football for a Volunteer touchdown.

Even more remarkably, I maintained my composure through the fifth overtime and even the decisive sixth. Granted, my repeated shows of restraint were a plus for my love life. But later, in the wake of the Hogs' 41-38 loss, I felt like a wimp for the statesman-like way I'd behaved. All this was the counterfeit me, induced only by the fact that I was with my new girlfriend, and that we were out at a nice restaurant in Memphis, surrounded by nice people. At some point, the real me would be exposed. Like Prometheus, I'd be unbound, eventually.

Seaside is a portrait-perfect, moneyed village on the Emerald Coast of Florida's Panhandle where high-dollar shotgun houses are painted in the pale pastels of the sea, sand, and sky, where teenagers play hacky sack on the great lawn, where the smell of saltwater mingles with fresh-baked calzone from the pizzeria. This paradise of New Urbanism architecture isn't the real America. But it isn't surreal either, like Disneyland. It hits a sweet spot just in between.

Out in the blue waters, swimmers bobbed in the sunshine and a few dolphins frolicked. Susanne and I walked hand in hand on the white sand beach. Just out in the shallows, a group of men tossed a football. I caught the eye of one of them and broke into a trot, one arm raised like a wide receiver. His pass led me almost perfectly, and I made a nifty back-shoulder catch as an incoming wave undercut me.

"Razorback fan," I shouted over the roar of the ocean.

"Go Hogs," the passer said, with a chortle.

Behind me, I heard the claps of several bikini-clad women who sat under a tent adorned with a big Georgia Bulldog "G" in a red oval. This entire area along the Gulf Coast was a kind of St. Tropez for football-obsessed Southerners, who touted their fandom with their sunbrellas and hats and T-shirts and towels bearing the logos of the LSU Tigers, Alabama Crimson Tide, Auburn Tigers, or some such.

Later, Susanne and I made our way to the open-air bar at Bud & Alley's Restaurant with its sweeping view out over the surf. Down on the beach, a well-to-do couple was being wed. The bartender clanged a rusty ship's bell to mark the evening's sunset. That day's winner of a free drink was a doctor's wife from Atlanta who'd guessed the exact minute the sun slipped below the horizon.

Susanne squeezed my hand. "This is great!" she said with her luring smile. We'd been together over two years, and this vacation was intended to take her mind off her recently-concluded custody battle over her son, which she'd lost, plus the pending custody battle over her younger daughter. Susanne's grudge match with her ex-husband was likely to go on through their kids' college years, the marriages of their children, the births of any grandchildren.

"Maybe we should just both move down here," she said, as the wind ruffled her blond bangs. "It would be heaven."

I listened with psychiatric silence. As rattled as Susanne was by her serial legal battles, I couldn't rule out the possibility of her up and leaving Jonesboro, even though she took an aspirational view of my hometown much as I did of New York. It was where she'd always wanted to live.

"I couldn't do it though," she continued. "I couldn't move down here. I'd miss my kids."

"I know. You're right."

I drained the last of my frozen margarita and watched a squadron of pelicans fly low along the beach. The horizon was washed with purple and orange, yet my sunset view was broken when a half-drunk blaggard walked past wearing an authentic, down-to-his-knees LSU jersey. This sight, of course, caused me to think about football, which in turn called to mind the fate of poor Mike Price.

Hired the previous December as the head coach at Alabama, he'd been fired only five months later after he visited a strip bar in nearby Pensacola called Arety's Angels, where he conspicuously dropped hundreds of dollars on drinks and lap dances. He'd wound up in a hotel room with a stripper named Destiny Stahl, who dinged his credit card for $1,000 in room service. She'd ordered at least one of everything on the menu in to-go boxes.

Most of us are guilty of an overinflated view of ourselves, but apparently Mike Price had no idea what he represented as the head football coach at Alabama. Perhaps he could carry on like this out in Pullman, Washington. Who cared how he'd spent his evenings when he'd been the head coach of the Washington State Cougars?

But unleashed down here on the playground of what's affectionately known as the Redneck Riviera, Mike Price had naively thought he could behave as if he were just another fun-seeking good ole boy with a wad of 20-dollar bills in his hip pocket. (Too, he didn't account for pesky Auburn fans—one in particular with the avatar of EagleKlaw on autigers.com—who ratted him out.)

A lady walked by our table wearing a black-and-white houndstooth blouse with the Alabama "A" emblazoned on it. It was too much.

"Why are you laughing?" Susanne said.

"Well, you see, there was this football coach and he went to a strip club down here..."

She looked at me, puzzled.

"Ah, never mind."

Susanne could hardly be expected to share the impish delight I felt over how Alabama had screwed up its most-recent coaching search. Nor did she appreciate that lower Alabama was the epicenter of the college football universe. On our drive down to the Gulf Coast, we'd stopped at a flea market where I'd showed her a glass-enclosed display full of books about the glorious history of Alabama football. This display was well lit, the glass spotless as if the tomes inside were signed first editions of *To Kill a Mockingbird*. Unfortunately, her mind had been on scouring the flea market for bowls and vases made of cut glass.

But I was crazy about her, anyway.

23

Lifeblood

Recruiting is said to be the lifeblood of every college football team, and each year in the lead-up to National Signing Day in early February, I regularly visit the recruiting forum at Hogville, the fan-based website. This has always been a waste of my time. Nothing I learned and none of my hopes about recruiting have ever changed a single thing, because I'm up against the whims of 18-year-old high school boys.

Even so, I can't resist Hogville. When it comes to recruiting, two threads of drama propel my sustained interest: The first is how many of the highly recruited in-state prospects would sign with the Razorbacks. Then there's my perennial hope that the Hogs will lure numerous top high school players from Texas, Louisiana, Missouri, Tennessee, Georgia, or wherever. I've always considered such recruits to be like the Hessian mercenaries enlisted by the undermanned British back during the Revolutionary War.

When the inevitable recruiting betrayals occur, when the hotly recruited kid turns down the Razorbacks' scholarship offer and chooses to play for another school, I fantasize about someday dissing him, like the time I popped off to Al Franken when, by chance, I walked by him as he sat on the stoop of a brownstone on the Upper West Side of Manhattan. At the time, Franken was clearly feeling his comedic oats, having just published *Rush Limbaugh Is a Big Fat Idiot*. In my view, writing a book like that was not only a bit thick with East Coast condescension, it was also just too darned easy. Similarly, whenever a prized high school prospect spurns the Hogs, I imagine a day when this young man needs something from me—a job, a personal referral, a five-dollar bill—and I'll cut him a look and say, "Well, I'm sorry, young man, but you should've thought about this moment when you didn't sign with the Hogs." Then I'll shut the door in his face.

My obsession with recruiting has accounted for much of my interest in professional football. I've always followed Razorback players as they moved on to the pros, and, irrational though it may be, I've believed that any success they had in the NFL would help the Hogs on the recruiting trail. I imagine a blue-chip prospect sitting in his parents' living room, watching an NFL game on a Sunday afternoon, and saying, "Gee, Steve Atwater is an All-Pro safety for the Denver Broncos and he played college ball at Arkansas. So I think I'll sign that scholarship offer from the Razorbacks and turn down my offers from Oklahoma, Alabama, Ohio State, Michigan, Texas, and USC. Please, somebody hand me a pen, right now!"

Of course, each year when National Signing Day finally comes around, I fixate on the players the Hogs didn't sign, the big fish who wriggled off the hook, and I take for granted any of the decent-sized fish hauled into the boat. No matter how many promising recruits are signed in February, I stew over the four-star player who spurned the Razorbacks. Then, say, by July 4, if you were to put me on the spot, I won't be able to recall the name of single Razorback recruit we'd signed, much less any of the big fish who got away.

Yet whenever I'm tempted to get down about the Razorbacks' struggles in recruiting, there's always the hope of the home-grown freak athlete who might be lurking in the margins of the class the Hogs just signed, the football equivalent of one of those 10-carat diamonds they sometimes find beneath layers of dirt at the Crater of Diamonds in Pike County.

One of the signees in the Razorbacks' 2001 recruiting class had been Matt Jones from Fort Smith, who, per his thumbnail picture in the *Arkansas Democrat-Gazette,* was a white kid listed at six-foot-six inches, 220, with a 40-yard dash time of 4.40. I remember scoffing when I read this. Come on, who really believed a six-foot-six-inch white kid could run this fast? Give me a break.

Yet, the following autumn, on an overcast afternoon in Fayetteville, it became evident that freshman Matt Jones was indeed Arkansas' own freak of nature. Midway through the second half against Auburn, he replaced the starting quarterback. On his first pass, he darted around in the pocket to buy time, then fired a strike for a touchdown. Because this was Matt Jones' first extensive action as a collegian, the Auburn defense was caught unaware. From high in the stands at Razorback Stadium, I watched him head up field with his long loping strides as an Auburn cornerback took an angle in pursuit only to find Jones a stride or two farther up field than expected. Three years later, Matt Jones ran a laser-timed 4.37 at the NFL Combine; if anything, his blazing time of 4.40 as reported during his high school days was understated.

Not long after National Signing Day in 2006, my grandmother passed away. Her funeral was at the First Methodist Church, which hovered like the Parthenon over Jonesboro's Main Street. Words were said over her shiny black casket and I prayed she'd gotten right with God, as my mother had always wished for the woman she considered more than merely her ex-mother-in-law. I recalled what a true Razorback homer she was, and more than that, how as a lifelong Yellow Dog Democrat from the great state of Arkansas, she was so smitten with Bill Clinton that she almost came to blows with a checkout clerk at the Winn Dixie down in Destin after the young lady criticized the President. And she could be brutal—and brutally funny—in her opinions. The night before her funeral, family members and friends had gathered in her living room, where I had watched The Big Shootout, a memory as permanently etched on me as my birthmark. Among her many mail order catalogs and so-called Funny Papers, I'd spotted *The Dallas Cowboys' Wives Cookbook & Family Album*, in which she'd written in the margins, "This is the worst cookbook I've ever read! And I paid good money for this! Bad, bad, bad!!!"

When Grandmother's funeral ended, I walked down the sun-drenched stone steps of the old church. Amid the crowd of black-clothed mourners, my eyes met my father's, and with his index finger he motioned for me to come over.

"Two things," he said, his voice reedy with emotion.

I looked at him intently, unsure of where he was going with this.

"First thing: no open casket."

This did not surprise me because my father, though he was in good health, got squeamish at practically any display of physical frailty, especially his own. Then he put his hand on my shoulder and with an equally serious look, said, "Second thing: when I'm gone have a party, because I've had a good time."

When I was a boy, it was inconceivable to me that my grandmother would ever perish, as if her flamboyance could stave off mortality. In a similar sense, through all my years of Razorback devotion, it had never crossed my mind that the game I loved might someday fade away.

But by 2006, one of the most talked-about subjects in sports was Chronic Traumatic Encephalopathy, or brain degeneration likely caused by repeated blows to the head. Accordingly, I began to fear that in a matter of time football as I've known it would go the way of the high dive at the Jonesboro Country Club.

Stay with me here.

When I was a boy, to leap off this glorious 10-foot high dive was the local equivalent of diving from the cliffs in Acapulco. I got white-knuckled just climbing up the ladder. The diving board itself was also quite bouncy, and I gained even more lift when doing can openers, front-flips, and swan dives. With a well-executed cannon-ball, I could splash the moms who sunbathed on the apron of the swimming pool.

When I was 13, I had looked on in awe as an older boy did a headfirst dive during which he tucked his hands and arms over his head and rolled over the instant he hit the water, executing what was in effect a headfirst cannonball. This was way cool, so I set out to perform the dive myself. The problem was the learning curve involved—I never really figured out how to protect myself. Every time I hit the water I took an awkward blow to the head, leaving me starry-eyed.

Years later, when the Jonesboro Country Club pool opened on the customary Memorial Day weekend, I discovered that the exhilarating high dive of my youth was gone. It had been cut down with a blowtorch, its base capped with a metal plate like a dried-up oil well. Perhaps the high dive had come to represent an untenable legal liability, or, just as likely, some concerned mothers had banded together to have it removed. Regardless, it was gone. But the low dive was still there. Even so, I wondered how long it would be until there was no diving board at all at the Jonesboro Country Club.

Many years later, it's now hard to find a diving board of any sort anywhere in America. This I began to fear was the fate of college football—of football at all levels, starting with peewee league football. First goes the high dive, then even the low dive too. In the future, we will still have something called college football, just as the Jonesboro Country Club still has what's called a swimming pool. Granted, it may be safer, but it won't be the same football as before.

24

Magic at Midlife

After losing the 2006 season opener to USC by the score of 50-14, the Hogs improbably reeled off eight straight wins. Darren McFadden, another homegrown freak of nature like Matt Jones, was emerging as a once-in-a-generation superstar, never mind that he'd missed the USC game due to a toe injury suffered in a fight outside a Little Rock nightclub. Game-by-game, win-by-win, my excitement built.

But as the season headed into its ninth week, I passed on going to Fayetteville for the game against 13th-ranked Tennessee, a matchup with such buzz that the *ESPN Game Day* crew was to be on hand. It was going to be crazy, with all the sign-waving Razorback fans clustered around the Game Day podium and that wacko Lee Corso predicting his winner just before kickoff when he'd don one of those striking plastic Hog hats.

But no worries. As the new millennium had unfolded, digital technology was on the march and the game-watching experience on TV had markedly improved. Like many Americans, I had purchased a large flat-screen TV with picture quality that was impressive. All the *ESPN Game Day* buzz aside, why did I need to travel all the way to Fayetteville for this game, when I could watch it all in bold living color from my own home?

But on the Monday before the game, Susanne informed me of our plans to attend a party on Saturday night. I was reluctant to go—the game on ESPN was slated to kick off at 6:30. But surely the party hosts, a couple neither of us knew well, would have the Razorback game on a TV at their house, right? As late as Saturday afternoon, Susanne once again assured me I'd be able to watch it at our friends' party that night, and I didn't doubt it.

When I walked in the front door of the hosts' opulent home, I immediately scoured the place for a television. Fortunately, there was a giant flat screen in the living room—but it wasn't turned on. Uh-oh. It seemed the hosts, Harry and Leana, weren't at all into Razorback football. As it turned out, Harry was more interested in entertaining small groups of his guests by performing magic tricks, and I'll concede that when he bent a handful of spoons right in front of my disbelieving eyes, I was impressed. The second time he performed this trick, I examined his spoons before he bent them and examined them after he bent them: They looked like ordinary spoons to me. But, really, I didn't care to spend much more time trying to figure how Harry bent his darned spoons. I was willing to accept that he was an illusionist on the order of David Copperfield. Whatever. *Just get the freakin' Razorback game on the giant flat screen!*

After Harry bent his spoons yet one more time, I finally persuaded him to turn on his TV. No doubt he sensed the urgency in my voice. It was awkward to basically take over his living room, but it was either this, or I had to pull Susanne aside and tell her I had to run an urgent errand, which would mean I was leaving to go watch the first half of the game at my house. And ditto for the second half.

All this made me wonder just how many social outings like this one have been redirected by die-hard fans like me? Similarly, how many men have agreed to the game-night demands of their girlfriends or wives, and wound up attending parties and social gatherings against their will (and, I daresay, against their better football-obsessed judgment)? And, in advance of these outings, how many women, to placate their man, have said, "Oh, sure, they'll have the football game on TV," while having no idea whether or not the party hosts will be able to back up her claim?

Here's the thing, though: With my running commentary and real-time reactions (this game was turning into a Razorback romp!), I managed to get the other guests at Larry's party interested in what was happening on his giant flat-screen TV. They fed off my excitement, like the scene in *One Flew Over the Cuckoo's Nest* when Nurse Ratchet won't let R.P. McMurphy (as played by Jack Nicholson) watch the Dodgers' World Series game on television, he intrigues his fellow patients by summoning an imaginary version of the game on the blank TV screen. *"Koufax's curveball is snapping off like an effing firecracker!"*

Few of us gathered in Harry the Magician's living room realized that we were watching a new innovation in college football. Any changes to the game typically came gradually and owed to better coaching, new training techniques, and bigger, faster, stronger athletes. There was so much film analysis, and every team was so coached up that it was difficult to do something truly different.

But in recent weeks, the Razorback brain trust had introduced a new wrinkle that was taking college football by storm. Necessity is the mother of invention, and the Hogs needed to get the football as often as possible to their two best players, running backs Darren McFadden and Felix Jones. So, the idea was hatched to set Felix Jones in motion, running laterally at full speed, and then shotgun snap the ball directly to McFadden, thereby eliminating the quarterback. The Wildcat it was called, and the Hogs were shredding opposing defenses with it like a cheese grater. McFadden was even tossing touchdown passes.

Sure, Tennessee had film of the Hogs running the Wildcat in several previous games. They knew it was coming. The Wildcat was a throwback to the winged T, so it had been unveiled in about 1937. My fourth-grade peewee league team had even run a variation of it, when, as quarterback, I'd lateralled the ball to the tailback, our best player, who, in turn, either ran or passed. Regardless, on this night, the Vols lacked the will to stop it. McFadden ran for 183 yards and two touchdowns and passed for one TD. Felix Jones rushed for 164.

In the wake of this victory, it dawned on me just how thoroughly this ongoing Razorback win streak, now at nine straight, had infiltrated my psyche. Over the past two months, commencing with the September 9 win over Utah State, I'd come to feel a deepening sense of personal potency.

Because the scale and breadth of football is wider than in any other sport—a Division I college football team had 85 scholarship players, nine coaches, a throng of support staff, etc.—the range of virtues required for a team to be successful is commensurately broad. These Winning Virtues included, but are not limited to, discipline, smarts, strength, passion, mental toughness, resilience, desire, focus, good decision-making, and crisp execution. Translation: This 2006 Razorback team was among the most virtuous in all of college football.

Unfortunately, most fans, myself included, struggle mightily to practice these Winning Virtues in our daily lives. It's not so easy. Yet week after week, this ongoing run of wins had allowed me to affirm these Winning Virtues, and even fancy that they'd somehow been transferred onto me. Almost nothing compared to the aura of competence I felt with the Hogs piling up consecutive victories. My life was just better all around.

Notwithstanding this nine-game roll, Arkansas coach Houston Nutt, now in his eighth year, had endured bouts of withering criticism. He was accused of being a glorified used car salesman, a waster of talent, a coddler of mediocre assistant coaches (which included his youngest brother), an unimaginative offensive mind who literally chewed his fingernails whenever a pass play was called, a lazy recruiter, a man too eager to take credit for successes and too willing to throw others under the bus when things went wrong. He was derisively called The Dale, a mean-spirited invocation of his middle name meant to put him in his place. But gosh darn it, this was Houston Nutt's second win streak of serious consequence, the first being his eight-game streak when he'd joined the Razorbacks back in 1998. Obviously, in light of my Theory of Winning Virtues, he was doing something right. The incessant criticism of Houston Nutt hit me wrong.

And so we come to yet another irony of college football—the rabid fan who, though he practiced precious few of the Winning Virtues in his own life, nevertheless expected the coach of his team to be a paragon of the Winning Virtues and perhaps even the most virtuous man on the planet. And any weakness—any failure to produce win after win as far as the eye can see—was met with harsh one-sided criticism twinned with a total lack of self-reflection.

Regardless, as win after win mounted, I too came to expect Houston Nutt and his Arkansas Razorbacks to chalk up a victory every game, at least through the end of the season and inevitable big-time bowl game. Anything less and I was going to feel personally cheated.

25

The Perils of Passion

Aweek after the Tennessee game, I was lured onto the road by the Hogs' ongoing win streak. My eventual destination was Starkville, Mississippi. Yet my overriding goal was to spend as little time there as possible. All I wanted to do was drive straight to Davis Wade Stadium, watch the Hogs put it on the Mississippi State Bulldogs, and then leave. I was determined not to give Starkville, aka Starkvegas, any chance to counter its repute.

Susanne and I spent the day before the game in Oxford, our base for the weekend (the Rebels were playing at LSU). We hung out at Square Books, dined at City Grocery, and visited Rowan Oak, the Greek Revival home of novelist William Faulkner. I'm particularly susceptible to the influence of anything dusted over with literary tradition, so I swooned over Rowan Oak with its tall white front columns straining for shambolic glory, the vaguely-bookish Victorian furniture, gauze-thin white curtains that looked as if they'd been hung by wife Estelle Faulkner herself. When I asked the docent for directions to the facilities, she pointed towards the bathroom next to Faulkner's bedroom. It felt honorific.

In the study, the white plaster walls bore the master's handwriting— his day-by-day outline of *The Fable*, the novel that had won the Pulitzer Prize. I stared at the life-sized outline, witness to the obsession of a writer, and wondered if Faulkner was much of an Ole Miss fan. Surely in his last days, he had some inkling that the Rebels were in their Dynasty Years. According to some pollsters (Sagarin, the Dunkel System, and the Football Writers of America), Ole Miss had won the national championship in 1959, 1960, and 1962. With his deep connection to the history of his home state, didn't Faulkner get some sort of charge out of this? I searched the white walls of his study for any subtle declaration of his enthusiasm: a scribbling of the words Hotty Toddy? Maybe a doodle of Colonel Reb clutching a football? But, alas, no dice. So, I went out to the back porch and stared into the surrounding forest and pondered Faulkner's hunting stories called *Big Wood*, especially the one about the obsessive stalking of that poor bear named Old Ben.

The next morning, it was on to Starkville to watch the electrifying Darren McFadden, who had a serious shot at the Heisman Trophy. It was cool and sunny, and with my usual sense of gameday nervous anticipation I made my way to the visitor's section at Davis Wade Stadium. It's well established that the cowbells in Starkville are a problem. Despite restrictions imposed by the SEC, the fans wouldn't quit shaking them. Certainly, I'd known this before I came to Starkville, just as I'd known on my first visit to London that it often rained. Nonetheless, this incessant ringing quickly got on my nerves and in due course I suffered an out-of-body experience when I found myself yelling my head off at Hog cornerback Matteral Richardson.

For reasons I could not fathom, this young man had decided his mission on this fine autumn afternoon was to single-handedly keep Mississippi State in this football game. By the second of his silly penalties, I rose from my seat. "Come on, number nine!" I screamed, invoking Richardson's number because his last name wasn't specific enough to suit me, and his first name sounded like a drunken slurring of the word "material." The air was filling with my own sulfurous exhaust: "What the heck is number nine doing?" "Get him out of there! Come on! Come on!"

A few fans turned around to see who was doing all this fussing, and at least one patron expressed his displeasure by pelting me in the back of the head with a wadded paper cup. Embarrassed, Susanne got up and went to the bathroom.

Matteral Richardson aside, Mississippi State never really threatened in this game. With eight minutes left and the Hogs' victory in hand, Susanne and I headed out for our car in a distant parking lot. Though she'd been to several Razorback games with me over the last five years, this was the worst I'd behaved, by far. As we trod along in silence, I considered blaming my eruption on the damned cowbells. Surely, I wasn't the only visiting fan ever to be unnerved by the ringing. After all, wasn't the point of it to push the opposing team and their fans to the brink of a nervous breakdown? That's right, the real culprit in all this was the Mississippi State fans and their damned cowbells. I was merely a victim.

But by the time Susanne and I finally got to our car, remorse had set in. In my ongoing struggle to mature as a fan, I had clearly regressed. Obviously, winning wasn't enough. The Hogs' streak, now at 10 games, had only raised the stakes even higher and made me more demanding, more cantankerous, more intolerant of sloppy play, more obsessed and crazed.

We battled the traffic around Davis Wade Stadium. Our goal—*my goal*—was to get back to Oxford as soon as possible. Then, just before the game ended, as if to rescue me, over our car's radio, we heard the play-by-play announcer say number nine, Matteral Richardson, had committed yet another penalty. I cut my eyes at Susanne as if to say, "See there!" But she wasn't having it. And she was right: There was no justification for my behavior.

A week later, on the day after Thanksgiving, the Hogs' 10-game win streak ended against LSU, whereupon commenced a three-game losing streak. The Hogs finished 10-4 and, not surprisingly, the critics lashed out at The Dale.

After the 2007 season, an 8-5 result in Houston Nutt's final year, I went to a bookstore in Memphis to hear Nick Hornby, the popular British author, read from his newest novel, *A Long Way Down.* Frankly, I'd come to this bookstore on false premises. I wasn't really interested in Hornby's new novel, or any of his old novels either. Rather, I'd come to see Nick Hornby solely because, 15 years before, he'd penned *Fever Pitch,* his account of his love affair with the Arsenal Gunners. His memoir, which revealed him to be a wing-nut fan of the first rank, chronicles his youthful obsession with his beloved Premier League soccer club from when he was 11 years old. Yet Hornsby's book ends when he's only in his mid-thirties, and the reader is left to presume that in the years beyond he outgrows all of his fan-driven lunacy.

Some years later, in yet another of his many writings about soccer, Hornby confirmed his maturation: "*I wouldn't and couldn't write* Fever Pitch *now, but that is not to belittle it, because the inability represents a loss, as well as growth. I miss the person who had the time and energy for all that angst and passion, and if I were to write about him now, I'd probably pat him on the head and tell him that he would become older and wiser, and the whole point of the book would be lost.*"

Hornby's progression as a fan raised an interesting question: When was a fan expected to grow up? And, if he grows up, is he even truly a fan anymore? After all, the word "fan" is a shortened version of "fanatic." If a fan loses the fire, then what's the point?

In pondering such weighty questions, I suspected that Hornby was like me, or, rather, I was like him. We wanted to be serious men. We wanted to write books that were bigger than mere soccer (or football). We wanted to outgrow our youthful passions and become great-souled elders.

But contrary to Hornby, as a fan I'm not at all sure I've grown wiser as I've gotten older. I haven't matured in a straight line like he apparently did. Season by season, even game by game, I seem to jump around chronologically, acting at times like a man of my age should, but at other times behaving as if I were back in fifth grade. Too, when I reflected on my deceased grandmother's life as a fan, it seemed that as she got older she never quit caring deeply about the Razorbacks; instead, her nerves gave out. She hardly gave up her fanaticism, she just got the willies.

After Hornby finished reading from his new novel, I waited in line for him to autograph my well-worn copy of *Fever Pitch*, which I had with me, going so far as to make the store clerk aware that I'd brought it in. When I presented Hornby my book, he gave me a doleful glance, annoyed that a member of his audience was passing up his new novel.

"So, how's Arsenal's season going so far this year?" I said, hoping to lure him into a conversation, or better yet entice him to follow me to the restaurant next door where we could have a long talk over a pint of beer. I had a few questions for him: As he got older, did he worry that moderation could be overdone? Could a certain dull evenness set in? Moreover, did he agree that soccer was a feminized, philosophically-absurd strain of American football, a game in which a player like Lionel Messi, at five feet, five inches tall, was feared for his physical prowess (i.e. quick feet)? Would he concede that even the world's greatest soccer players were not as athletically gifted as any random member of LSU's secondary? Could he rebut my thesis that the popularity of soccer presages a nation's descent into complacency and softness?

Hornby took my worn copy of *Fever Pitch* and mumbled on in rapid-fire British-speak about Arsenal's disappointing season. Then he asked me where I wanted him to sign his name in my book, whereupon I swiftly turned to one of the many dog-eared pages. At this, he shot me a look as if he got me and then penned his name and underneath wrote, *"They will return..."* and sent me on my way.

26

Memento Mori

A week before the 2008 season opener, Susanne's ex-husband, a prominent doctor in eastern Arkansas, suffered a fatal heart attack. On a sweltering day in late August, he'd attended his mother's funeral in Blytheville. Ever the dutiful son, after the service the doctor had gathered the sprays of flowers from his mother's grave and delivered them to her friends. Then he ate dinner with his father, drove to his home nearby, and collapsed in his driveway. His son, John, a junior at the University of Central Arkansas, rushed him to the hospital. Only hours before, his daughter, Emily, had set off on her return to Fayetteville, where she'd just begun her first year of college.

Three days later, at the same cemetery, there was the long black hearse, the doctor's heavy coffin, the smell of burnt stubble rising in a plume from a fallow rice field in the distance.

After the doctor's burial, I went for the first time to his house, the red-bricked Georgian manse he and Susanne had built in the final years of their 16-year marriage. While the doctor's family and friends were gathered in the huge kitchen, Susanne showed me the custom window panes in the garden patio from a Memphis firm, which also made stained-glass for churches, the stately mahogany fireplace mantles, and the claw-footed dining table bought from an antiques dealer down in New Orleans. The foyer was adorned with a teardrop crystal chandelier, and years ago, just before Susanne had moved out during the course of their divorce; she'd stripped it in ire of half its finials. The chandelier hung high above, denuded and spindly, like a glass scarecrow.

What interested me more, however, were the many photographs throughout the house: prints in color and black and white, large to small, professionally shot to amateur stills, framed and unframed. Each photo was of the doctor with his kids, John and Emily. The house was practically a father museum, like those commonplace mansions on New York's Upper East Side that are unique only because of the artwork on their walls.

Through one of the many windows, I saw lightning flash across the sky like a short-circuited strobe. Out by the back door, I ran into Emily, who'd mourned and brooded considerably over the past few days.

"So much has been lost," she said as she stood there in her elegant heels. "He was a good dad. He liked nothing more than making me happy."

"It's going to be okay."

"I'm not sure it will be."

"Better days are ahead," or something similarly inadequate, was all I could manage to mutter.

Later that night, Susanne and I drove back to Jonesboro, passing by the turn-off to Dyess, the New Deal-era colony where Johnny Cash was raised, and then through several other small towns with only one stop light. A sprinkling rain had resumed, an echo of the earlier storm, and the rural dark was like a blanket, yet all I could think about were the photographs on the walls of the doctor's manse. There was a lot of love behind all those photos, I knew. I wasn't sure I was capable of such love. It seemed to come from sources I lacked, or had failed to develop, probably because

I hadn't had children of my own.

Finally, out near the giant food processing factories on the eastern edge of town, we came upon the first lights of Jonesboro.

"It's so sad what's happened," Susanne said.

"I know."

As the days passed, she and I continued dating, as we'd been doing for almost seven years. But, for her and her children, and even me, the doctor's tragic death was a turning of the page.

In times of great change, we reach for familiar rituals. The week after his funeral, September arrived and football was in the air. Like me, Susanne's children had grown up with Razorback football. Their father, who'd played guard on the Blytheville High football team, had been a faithful fan with the Hog license plate on the front of his car and many trips over the decades to games in Fayetteville and Little Rock. The doctor's father was also a devout Hog fan. Years before, upon first meeting his prospective son-in-law, a Tennessee fan, he'd said to this young man, "You know you stole that Liberty Bowl game from us back in 1971."

Tell me about it.

This season, Razorback football was in transition as well, with Bobby Petrino, formerly of the Atlanta Falcons, as the new head coach. His predecessor, Houston Nutt, had won eight straight games in his first season. But the Southeastern Conference, fueled by top-tier coaches like Nick Saban at Alabama, and ever-increasing monies from television rights, had gotten even tougher in recent years. The challenge Bobby Petrino faced was huge. Building a winning college football team is difficult managerial work, requiring long hours, perseverance, much attention to detail, emotional intelligence, the ability to teach, and a high degree of skill in dealing with young people.

Under any new coach, what I wanted to see was a steady progression. A desultory 4 and 8 season will lead to a so-so 6-6 season, which is the foundation for an encouraging 8-4 season, which translates to a sterling 11-2 season that includes a win in a big-time bowl game. Along the way, it's a test: How much suffering can fans endure? We desperately want to feel a sense of gathering momentum. It's all about the story we tell to ourselves and to others: the narrative. I can, and will, endure adversity as long as I feel better days are just ahead. Houston Nutt was gone because Razorback fans had quit believing in the future—well, his future, anyway. And this was despite his winning 18 games in his last two seasons, including a thrilling overtime victory over top-ranked LSU in his final game.

On a muggy September night, in Bobby Petrino's second outing, the Hogs were matched up against Louisiana-Monroe (ULM), a team from the not-so-mighty Sun Belt Conference. The game was at War Memorial Stadium and any such matchup against a cupcake opponent like ULM always involved a decidedly asymmetrical set-up. On the Razorbacks' side, everything was the same as for any other game—same aging stadium, same players, same coaches, same band, same fight song, same perky cheerleaders and pep squad, same voice over the public address system: *"Another Arkansas Razorback first down!"* It's just that the team on the other sideline was thought to be lacking.

I was fine with such a mismatch. With the doctor's tragic passing, my emotions were still raw. What I needed was a calm, reassuring performance from the Razorbacks, with a lead of four touchdowns or so late in the game, when I'd get to watch the younger players on the roster take a few snaps.

Adversity struck early when Alex Tejada blew two field goals. I squirmed in my seat, as Susanne's son John and I traded uh-oh text messages. (I was thrilled to hear from him!) By the third quarter, with ULM up 17-6, my innards were in full churn. The Hogs were stuffed on a fourth and two, and in no time the ULM lead stretched to 24-6. The prospect of losing to a have-not of college football like ULM totally stressed my psyche. The previous season, Nick Saban had likened the Crimson Tide's loss to this ULM team to both Pearl Harbor and 9/11. I'd snickered at this: Saban came across as a man so addled by football that he'd lost any sense of historical perspective. A Razorback touchdown and two-point conversion cut the deficit to 24-14, but with 12:56 remaining, ULM went up 27-14, and, given my already fragile state, the historical parallel that shot through my mind was more along the lines of Hitler's humiliation of France.

With three minutes remaining, the Hogs, down by six points, had one last chance. Casey Dick converted a fourth-and-one pass into double-coverage to the ULM 10-yard line. With 1:22 on the clock, the Hogs finally took the lead. But ULM wasn't finished: With 36 seconds remaining, their 45-yard field goal to win was barely wide.

It was a bad win, meaning it felt like a loss. Emotionally, I felt as if I'd been pie-faced, and I was clammy with sweat as if I had played the entire second half. The stress of this game was exactly what I *did not need right now*. Ultimately, though, I had confidence in Bobby Petrino. I sensed he was a good coach with a sound plan. Even if the Hogs had lost to ULM, while it would have been yet another unnerving blow, I wouldn't have hit the panic button.

Conversely, if the Hogs had played a clunker like this under Houston Nutt, I'd have called for supremely harsh consequences (at least in the privacy of my mind). Such is the power of the better-days-are-ahead narrative in college football—and in life in general, for that matter.

The following week, the stock market dropped precipitously, and venerable Wall Street firms like Lehman Brothers went belly up. Amid all this tumult in the nation's financial system, I decided it was time to shut down my company. Action Graphix manufactured a product made possible by the rise of digital printing technology, and, the current financial crisis aside, the product was surely fated to be overtaken by new technologies, namely digital signs. Besides, the company's sales were tanking and cash flow was an issue. So I hatched a plan to wind down the venture, which, for me, had amounted to a 17-year-long false start.

I had tried to imitate my father's success by going into manufacturing (and this, during an era when American manufacturing was waning). But the product was too faddish, too limited in appeal, too vulnerable to new digital technologies. I'd also missed windows of opportunity in the first decade to sell out at a tidy gain. Sure, I'd had some good years. But I hadn't been able to sustain them. In all this, I was like a football coach with a middling record, or even a team with a flawed game plan to begin with.

Among the best things about a football-game weekend in Fayetteville is that it draws people together. Ostensibly, I trek to the campus for the game, but I also go to see friends, family, long-lost frat brothers, even frenemies. Half of the fun is wondering who, or what, I might run into.

On this trip, Susanne was with me, eager to spend some time with her daughter, Emily, who was still reeling from her father's death only two months before. For them, the upcoming Ole Miss game was merely a backdrop for a weekend of socializing with friends and family. I, on the other hand, was in knots over the worrisomely incestuous matchup against the Rebels, now coached by Houston Nutt.

When we arrived, we dropped by Carnall Hall, the boutique hotel on the edge of campus. I wandered the gracious lobby and took in the oil paintings by former Razorback linebacker Barry Thomas (who countered the stereotype that all linebackers were philistines), the photographs of the prim coeds taken back when Carnall Hall was a women's dormitory, the enlarged black-and-white shot of President Nixon as he sat in the stands during The Big Shootout. Near the hotel, on the edge of the sprawling front lawn of Old Main, my name was etched in the sidewalk in an honor accorded graduates of the University of Arkansas, beginning with the inaugural class of 1905. It was called Senior Walk, and I considered it a marker of my accomplishment, though it was a bit eerie to see my name set in concrete, as if I were looking at a premature gravestone. The name on the sidewalk was the same as my father's, same as his father's, same as his father's father, same as the young Englishman who sailed from England back in 1701.

On the wide porch at Carnall Hall, I ran into my former Treasured Girlfriend/ex-wife. This was our first encounter since we divorced over 20 years before. Yet of all the places she and I could possibly have met, it figured to be here. When we'd started dating back in college, she had lived only a block away on Reagan Street. Just across was the Sigma Chi house and the nearby apartment I'd shared with Rick Angel.

I greeted her with a quick hug, then introduced Susanne, thankful for the grace with which my girlfriend was handling this awkward moment. My former-Treasured-Girlfriend-and-ex-wife was still spunky and, of course, still dark-haired and blue-eyed, and, though she and I never communicated, each year she continued to send my mother a Christmas card signed "Lots of Love Always." So I knew that she had remarried not long after our divorce, moved with her second husband to Springfield, Illinois, and birthed three daughters.

She and I made small talk, and if she still harbored any bad feelings toward me, she disguised it well. I suspected that she had long ago realized it was best that we had split up after only six months; nevertheless, when she mentioned that her eldest was pledged to Kappa Kappa Gamma sorority, it wasn't lost on me that if she and I had stayed married, I would probably have my own college-age children now.

She and Susanne talked on about their children—they were both prolific chatterers—while my gaze drifted off to the spires atop the distant Old Main. It was painful to be reminded of this chapter of my past life. How I'd told her the night before our wedding that I couldn't do it, yet hadn't had the fortitude to make it stick. How she and I had doubled-down by buying a house right after we married. How I'd handled the whole situation, beginning to end, so gutlessly.

Yet wouldn't it have been worse to have stayed in the marriage, perhaps to have a child and then divorce? There was power in quitting—or so I'd come to believe. I would've been considerably better off if I'd stopped trying to make a success of my manufacturing company years before I finally did.

Our genial conversation was interrupted when a woman in a wheelchair clambered out the front door of Carnall Hall. Then came a lull and it seemed that one of us—me or my former Treasured-Girlfriend/ex-wife—should have said something pithy and knowing and perhaps even a bit humorously conclusive, like the scene in the movie *Sex and the City* when Carrie, who'd been jilted at the altar, says, "Why did we decide to get married?" and Mr. Big, the love of her life, shrugs and says, "I guess because it would have meant something if we didn't."

But in that moment, neither of us knew what to say about all of that, and our unexpected encounter ended with the most predictable niceties.

By the one-year mark following their father's death, Susanne's son and daughter had warmed to me. It wasn't as if they ran into my arms, and I was mindful not to press in prematurely, but our relationship had noticeably strengthened. After years of being their "mother's boyfriend," I was now more than just their mother's boyfriend.

After Emily's freshman year in Fayetteville, she spent the summer in Jonesboro, where she worked as a hostess at my father's restaurant. She was a stunning young woman with blond hair, a lean silhouette, and a bright smile—all of which evoked her mother, down to the picture on my dresser of Susanne in her days as a pompom girl, with her inviting smile and the red stitching across her uniform that read, "Hogs."

When summer was over, Susanne and I made plans to take Emily back to Fayetteville for her sophomore year. The three of us were to drive across the state in a caravan of two cars, each full of Emily's clothes, bedding for her dorm room, a TV and assorted electronics, even an Oriental rug that had been her father's. But Susanne came down with a stomach bug. So Emily set out in her car, while I followed in mine.

It was a long trip across the state, and not long after we arrived in Fayetteville, trouble set in. We were one block off Dickson Street, retracing our steps, trying to remember where we'd parked our cars. The weather was blazing hot, even as dusk approached. "This is weird," Emily said. "I swear we parked right here."

I saw a flashing red light and it hit me what had happened: The tow truck driver had already hauled off my car, and, now, he was about to haul off Emily's car too.

I trotted ahead, with Emily behind me, her sandals slapping at the asphalt. At the bottom of the hill, I confronted the burly driver whose richly tattooed arm dangled out the window of his tow truck. He informed me that the parking lot vouchers I'd purchased just before Emily and I had gone to dinner had timed out.

"Come on," I said. *"Seriously?"*

"Don't get pissy with me, dude. I'm just trying to do my job here."

I remained calm for Emily's sake, as well as my own for the tow truck driver was a burly sort. I looked back at Emily's vehicle perched atop the bed of the tow truck. "Come on, man," I said. "You've already towed one of our cars. If you take this vehicle too, we'll have to walk."

"It's a $60 drop fee for your vehicle," the tow-truck driver said.

"What?! No!" I lowered my voice. "Look, let's be reasonable here. I'll give you 30 bucks."

As the tow truck pulled away, I sprang ahead and thrust three waded-up $20 bills into the driver's meaty hand. Soon he lowered Emily's car to the pavement, but before he drove off, he peered back from the window of his truck, his wide face nestled on the muscled knob of his shoulder. "It's going to cost you another $115 to get your other car out of the tow yard," he said. "Just giving you a heads-up. We tow cars out of this lot every weekend night, and this weekend is going to be busy with school starting next week with all the parents in town."

"Thanks," I replied. "Thanks for all your help."

Emily and I got into her car and followed the driver's directions to the tow yard. A "Closed" sign hung off-kilter in the front window, and the parking lot was ringed by a fence with a padlock on its gate as big as a boot. My car was parked next to a wrecked rally-yellow Camaro. For now, there was nothing to be done.

At our hotel, Emily wrote out a list of her items that were in my car back at the tow yard. I wondered how her deceased father would've handled this situation: Likely, he'd rise at dawn this next morning to go and buy replacements for his daughter's missing possessions, whether she needed them or not. He was that kind of father. A better father than I could hope to be, though with Susanne well past child-bearing age, if she and I married, my relationship with Emily and John was as close to fatherhood as I would get.

The next morning, at 8 o'clock sharp, Emily and I pulled up to the tow lot. My car was fine. All of her belongings were accounted for. I paid the $115 fee and followed Emily in my newly-freed car to the campus dormitory, a tall brick tower that faced the north end zone of Razorback Stadium.

The parking lot was already full, with mothers and fathers moving their children into their dorm rooms, load by load. The look of proud sadness on their faces recalled my father's countenance on the morning I'd headed off to Boulder for my first year of college.

Emily's fifth-floor dorm room was as tight as a ship's cabin, but large enough to accommodate all but a few of her items. We went out to my car one last time, where she rummaged through the trunk. She'd brought a half-dozen of her favorite framed pictures of herself and her dad. But with limited space in her room, several of them were headed back to Jonesboro with me.

She closed the trunk to my car and when she turned, she gave me a hug. I held on to her tight.

"Buh-buh," she said. "Thanks for everything. I really appreciate it."

"I'm proud of you," I said, my eyes teary.

I watched her bound up the front steps of the dormitory, but before she was out of earshot, I called after her. "Hey!" My voice carried farther than I'd intended, but I didn't care. "I love you!" I said to her for the first time.

"Oh, I love you too," she said, and then she walked back towards me and we hugged one last time. I couldn't wait to see her again, when her mother and I returned in a month or so for the game against Georgia.

27

Pilgrims in The Grove

From Jonesboro, Susanne and I drove east into the rising sun. Though Oxford, Mississippi, was only two-and-a-half hours from my hometown, at age 49 I'd never been to a football game at Ole Miss, where the tailgating in The Grove was said to be a bucket-list experience.

"My gosh," Susanne said, as she looked the clock on the car's dashboard. "It's barely past 8 o'clock in the morning and we're already halfway to Memphis."

"I know," I said. "It's silly, isn't it?"

Like me, Susanne wasn't a morning person, but she had risen at dawn to fix her long hair and get dressed in slacks, low heels, and new red blouse. "I still don't understand why the game starts at 11 o'clock in the morning," she said. "How is anyone supposed to tailgate in The Grove before the game?"

"Well, they don't," I replied.

Each fall, across the South, legions of SEC fans were tormented by these 11 a.m. games. As the season unfolded, start times were announced each week for the upcoming SEC slate of games. The prime slot was the 2:30 game on CBS, which was when football should be played on Saturdays in October. Too often, this mid-afternoon start time went to flagship SEC teams like Alabama. But CBS and the SEC had an agreement stipulating that no other game involving two SEC teams could be played during this prized 2:30 p.m. time slot. So all the other teams left out of the 2:30 game were either slated in night games or, worst case, shunted to the pre-noon time slot.

The 11 o'clock start affected the players, the weekend travel plans of fans, and practically every game-day ritual. The timing of the entire event was queered, and even Friday night was messed up because fans couldn't stay out late. It was ridiculous that CBS had this much power, and not just over the SEC football schedule—they also affected the cherished rhythms of life across the entire southern tier of the United States. The message to the teams involved and their fans, was, "Hey, y'all ain't no good, so get yourselves to bed early and deal with it."

As we neared Oxford, the highway traffic slowed, which only heightened my anxiety. Ever since rising that morning, I'd been on a dead run *to get to the game*. But just when I'd given up on being in my seat for the opening kickoff, I followed a car with a Mississippi license plate, figuring the driver knew a shortcut. He didn't. So I parked in an outer lot and we set out down a long road towards Vaught-Hemingway Stadium. When a golf cart full of Ole Miss fans passed by, I hollered at the driver, but he went on. At the sound of drumbeats in the distance, both of us picked up our pace, but Susanne soon told me to slow down, her low heels were rubbing a blister on her foot.

We walked past several low-slung brick buildings along Manning Way, a road named after Archie Manning or Eli Manning, probably both. All of this was part of the sports-industrial complex at Ole Miss, which included The Tad Pad, a basketball arena. Sure, these facilities were nice, but nothing I'd seen so far, including the Vaught-Hemingway Stadium in the distance, was as impressive as the sports-industrial complex in Fayetteville, and this modesty around me, relative though it was in the rich world of college football, once again confirmed in my mind that Arkansas was a far better state than the state of Mississippi, even though both states always ranked 49th and 50th in the nation in per capita income and educational attainment and in practically every other statistic that supposedly mattered. But as I walked on, I considered how much money every school in the Southeastern Conference, including Ole Miss, made these days from television monies and all the rest, and I realized that eventually Ole Miss would build a sports-industrial complex as impressive as that at Arkansas, and perhaps one day Ole Miss's facilities might be even better because more of them would be new.

But then I considered the Walmart factor and all the money it makes and all the Razorbacks fans enriched by Walmart, and how, on the drive to Oxford that morning, the landscape of northern Mississippi had looked threadbare and poor, like northwest Arkansas used to look before Walmart took over the world. These thoughts made me feel better about today's game because, no matter if the Hogs lost, the sports-industrial complex at Ole Miss would never catch up to the sports-industrial complex at Fayetteville, which probably meant we'd recruit better players than Ole Miss over the long haul and beat them more often than not. At least I hoped so.

Down 17-7 at the half, the Hogs never got over the hump in this one, yet they seemed to be on an upward trend under second-year Coach Bobby Petrino. The week before, in a 23-20 loss to top-ranked Florida, the Razorbacks had sacked Tim Tebow six times and forced four turnovers, but got jobbed by a pass interference call, followed by a personal foul. (The entire officiating crew had been suspended by the SEC.)

Throughout this game in Oxford, I was in touch with my father. The iPhone had been introduced two years before and by now even 70-year-olds had figured out how to text back and forth in order to communicate with their children and grandchildren.

My dad and I traded cryptic messages, which came in bursts: "Big play, right there!"..."What was that?!" ..."Great catch by Childs. He's money!" Or, in homage to the old *All in the Family* TV show, my father's favorite comment from Archie Bunker when things went bad, which was "Geez, Edith." Texting during a football game was almost as dangerous as texting and driving: Too much critical action could be missed. But these exchanges with my father were a pleasant distraction with a resonant connection to my past.

Before we left Vaught-Hemingway Stadium that day, I had to endure the jubilant Rebel fans and their damn signature cheer: "Hotty Toddy, Gosh Almighty, Who in the Hell Are We? Flim, Flam, Bim Bam, Ole Miss by Damn." You'd have thought they'd just beaten Alabama. My gosh, the Razorbacks were a four-loss team—such a boastful cheer made me realize just how delusional Ole Miss fans could be. It was as if these Rebel fans were trying to chant their way back to 1962. It also made me wonder just which fan base in America was the most delusional in their expectations of sustained football glory. Certainly, these Ole Miss fans had stiff competition from the likes of the folks at Auburn, who screamed for the head of any coach who lost more than two games in any season, plus all those Rocky Toppers in Tennessee with their pining for the good ole days of General Neyland. There are many other similarly delusional fan bases across college football, and, yes, I'll concede that Razorback fans, myself included, are as delusional as any.

But both Ole Miss fans and Razorback fans could be forgiven, I thought. After all, both our teams had periods of domination back during the decade or so from 1958 to 1969, the last days of all-white-boy college football. Now, though, it was hard to say which was a longer long shot: Arkansas reviving its Dynasty Years in a state that lacked enough elite black athletes to recruit in the first place, or Ole Miss returning to its national championship days of yore while trying to lure elite black athletes to a school that, when it comes to race relations, had some baggage, to say the least.

Given that the name Ole Miss Rebels was a veritable dog whistle in the ear of many elite black athletes and their parents, I figured Ole Miss fans were the victors in this unsavory competition, if only narrowly.

Susanne and I followed the crowd headed to The Grove, at heart of the Ole Miss campus. It was a short walk and she had a little giddy-up in her step. Though she didn't care much for the game of football, she loved all the trappings that came with it, and she was eager to see what all the fuss was about. I, however, was less ardent. For years, I'd heard about the wonders of game-day tailgating in The Grove, and whenever I did, I rolled my eyes. For crying out loud, it wasn't like this was a long-running Broadway musical or a soul-stirring U2 concert; it was just tailgating at a football game. What could possibly be so wonderful about it? I attributed all the hyperbole to rank boosterism, like the way Razorback fans brag about how great Dickson Street was, when really it isn't all that terrific.

But when we got to The Grove, I realized that my long-held skepticism was off base. Among the stately old oaks and elms were hundreds of red and blue tents with chandeliers and names like Vicksburg Rebels, the Dixie Dozen, and the whimsical Zebra Tent. Susanne and I dove in amid the roving crowds and the barbeque smoke that wafted through the air and the twang of live country music. This was tailgating on steroids, a cozy, yet sprawling after-game party with all comers invited. The setting was courtly, yet casual, and the Rebel fans that spilled out of their tents and milled about on sidewalks were quick to offer a smile, a beer, a bite to eat. Above all, The Grove was a powerful expression of Mississippi's culture and tradition, for as William Faulkner wrote in *Requiem for a Nun*: "The past is never dead. It's not even past." It wasn't hard to envision such a tableau back during the glory years of Ole Miss football, just before the Civil Rights movement: I'd heard rumors of white-gloved servants. Undergirding it all was certain Southern graciousness, as well as a palpable sentimentality about the way things should be. As a place, as an experience, tailgating in The Grove was indeed unique.

I made my way to see the Pryors, a family I'd grown up with back in the 1960s and 1970s. For their clan, game days in Oxford were as treasured as Easter and Christmas Eve, with their well-stocked tent serving as a gathering place for family and friends. Despite their roots in eastern Arkansas, over the past two decades the Pryors had all, one by one, moved to Mississippi. It began when the eldest daughter, on whom I'd had a crush back in first and second grade, came to Ole Miss, her mother's alma mater. The middle daughter followed, then inevitably the younger son. Eventually the family moved to Jackson, with a getaway place in Oxford. Over the decades, the Pryors had become as rooted in the soil of Mississippi as the oaks and elms in The Grove. What was their option? To return to eastern Arkansas, yet carry on as Ole Miss people?

After shuttering my manufacturing company, I looked for a new opportunity. Fortunately, back during the Dynasty Year of Razorback football, my grandfather and father had started a company that distributed thousands of parts used in agriculture. My grandfather, who'd been part owner of a John Deere dealership, was well suited for this and the company had flourished under his leadership.

The articles of incorporation for this company were filed on October 21, 1964, four days after the Razorbacks' pivotal 14-13 win over Texas down in Austin. It was the year Frank Broyles decided he would no longer have his players play both offense and defense: His switch to platoon football was key to the Hogs' ensuing 22 straight wins, including all 11 in 1964, the year the Razorbacks won their only national championship. (Arkansas football: On the excuse train since 1964.)

My grandfather had passed away in 1997, and since then my dad had driven an expansion of the company. Also, my younger cousin had a talent for the business. Given all this, perhaps this business could use my talents. Maybe, together, we could lead this company on its own run of dynasty years.

Too, my love life had moved in a promising direction. In the spring of 2010, Susanne and I were married. We honeymooned in France. Nothing unique about that; in fact, this was my second honeymoon in Paris. But this one was indeed unique because 10 other family members went with us: Susanne's son and daughter (my new stepchildren), her mother, my father and stepmother, my mother, my sister, our nieces, and a nephew. In the days before our wedding, whenever Susanne and I informed friends of our plan for a group honeymoon, they raised an eyebrow as if to insinuate that we were out of our minds. But everything went almost perfectly in Paris, as well as during the additional week we spent in a centuries-old stone farmhouse in Provence. Most of all, our group trip was a great bonding experience.

28

Lost Opportunity

The most crushing losses are those that come after I've felt that I had earned the right to experience a signature victory. It's all about the build-up. Over the past three years under Bobby Petrino, the Razorbacks had shown steady improvement, with his first season at 5-7, his second at 7-6, and, now, in his third, a 5-0 start. Fayetteville was electric as top-ranked Alabama rolled in.

On Friday night, I had dinner with my father at Bordino's, one of the best restaurants on Dickson Street and always a tough place to get a table on football weekends. Fortunately, my father and a friend of his, Larry Palmer, a manager at J.B. Hunt, had an arrangement best described as you-scratch-my-back-and-I'll-scratch-yours.

Each December, Larry spent a week in Northeast Arkansas duck hunting with my dad at his hunting club in the rice fields near Weiner. It was a gentleman's club with a simple hut that hunters used for changing into wader-boots, yet the surrounding woods were steeped in waterfowling glory. President Jimmy Carter had even hunted there. As the gold morning light slanted through the barren timber and a light south wind rippled across the waist-deep water, the ducks, thick as gnats, would cup their wings as they dropped into the hole. The shotguns were like thunder. My grandfather once turned to my father and said, "Boy, this ain't huntin'! This is murder!"

As payback for all this, Larry Palmer hosted my dad on football weekends in Fayetteville and secured dinner reservations at Bordino's, where he knew the owner. On this eve of the Alabama game, the packed dining room was charged with optimism that the Hogs had a real chance to beat the Crimson Tide. My silver-haired father sat beside his wife and chatted with old friends from around the state, including a stooped older ex-Hog player in a jaunty red sport coat. It felt like all of us were in our own private club, a kind of moveable gated community for Razorback fans.

After dinner, I stopped by George's Majestic Lounge for some live music, then drove north to the Embassy Suites, where, as it happened, the Crimson Tide football team was also overnighting.

On the morning of the game, I went downstairs for breakfast, and it was at the coffee station that I saw Nick Saban: He was just across the red velvet dividing rope, so close I could've shaken his hand. I lingered, stealing glances at him. My first impression was that Saban was fairly short, inspiring since I shared his condition. Then the thought occurred that I should somehow engage him in conversation, or just *do something* to get his attention since this was as close as I'd ever come to the legendary football coach. Quick, what could I say? But my chance slipped away as Saban disappeared into the bowels of the hotel.

It was just past noon when I got to Razorback Stadium, and cars already filled the surrounding parking lots. The tailgating was cranked up in earnest and soon the Hog players, unrecognizable without their numbered uniforms, spilled out of the buses and walked through the cheering fans to the locker room in the Broyles Center. I heard the drumbeat from the Razorback band as game time approached. I was jacked for the 2:30 kickoff (as arranged by CBS, naturally).

The Porkers drew first blood on a touchdown pass to tailback Ronnie Wingo. Arkansas coach Bobby Petrino had a reputation as a master play caller. On numerous occasions over the last three seasons, I'd watched a successful play and then, with delight, said to myself, "How in the world did So-and-So get so wide open?!' This pass to Ronnie Wingo, on a wheel route, was just such a play. He brushed off a late-arriving defender and, when he crossed the goal line, thereupon ensued the loudest noise I've ever experienced at any college football game. It was later measured at 117 decibels, literally like standing in front of the revving engine of a jet aircraft. The stands vibrated beneath my feet. I worried that they would cave in like some rickety risers in a Third World Country. I envisioned a headline in the London newspapers, *"Stadium Collapses in the Backwoods of the Ozark Mountains, Killings Hundreds, Injuring Thousands."*

Early in the fourth quarter, I looked up at the scoreboard—Arkansas 20, Alabama 14—and thought that if this score held up, I could later say, "I was there," just as I'd witnessed the triumph over top-ranked Texas back in 1981. To bank such a memory would salve many of my accumulated football wounds, and my longing for such a healing was so deep that if it meant the Hogs would hold the Crimson Tide scoreless over the next 13 minutes, I just might have agreed to have my left pinkie toe amputated.

But the Hogs' lead didn't hold up. At six foot seven, quarterback Ryan Mallett was as talented as he was tall—in the huddle, he looked like a ninth grader standing among sixth graders. But Nick Saban was a master at exploiting weakness in opponents. The previous summer, Mallett, a rowdy sort, had been arrested on Dickson Street for public intoxication, and down the stretch of this game he threw two interceptions.

I lingered in my seat, too drained to deal with the hordes that crowded the exits. I stared once more at the scoreboard, then glanced back at the press box, then looked up into the fading gray sky. I don't know what I was looking for. Solace, I guess. What crushed me was that I knew this Razorback team was really good. This opportunity to beat Alabama had been years in the making, yet high-stakes games like this inevitably turn on a few key plays. It all happens quickly, in only a matter of minutes. A play here, a play there, then it's done forever.

In the immediate aftermath of any loss, I typically find ways to minimize what's just happened. I tell myself that it's not such a big deal in the grand scheme of life, that I don't really care about Razorback football that much anyway, that, when you get right down to it, my team is nothing more than a random assemblage of 21-year-olds who just happen to wear Arkansas Razorback jerseys. Like water spilled on a patch of dirt, it takes time for any loss to fully soak in.

But no matter how I tried to rationalize this loss, the sting was immediate. Already I wondered how, or when, it could be avenged. We would play Bama again next year, of course. But, hellfire, we could never beat a Nick Saban-coached team down in Tuscaloosa. The next best shot was when the Crimson Tide returned to Fayetteville. But two seasons was an eternity in football years, and even then any redemptive victory was unlikely.

Razorback Stadium had mostly emptied out. But as I walked to the exit, a zany thought popped into my mind, and I chastised myself for not having been more aggressive that morning at Embassy Suites. I could've done something, *anything,* to get inside Nick Saban's head and throw him off his game. After all, he was such a mercurial, hair-trigger coach, apt to lose it over the slightest provocation. I could've spilled a cup of hot coffee and scalded him, or coughed with my mouth full of chamomile tea and accidentally-on-purpose spat in his face. *"Oh my gosh, Coach Saban, I'm soooo sorry. Can I get you some paper towel, or maybe a can of hairspray?"* I could've done any number of things to somehow impact a game the Razorbacks could just as easily have won.

—————— **29** ——————
Shuggie Bowl Fever

Two months after the loss to Alabama, the Razorbacks faced sixth-ranked LSU, a bid to the Sugar Bowl on the line. With the Hogs leading 31-20 in the fourth quarter, I made a move that could've proved disastrous had the Razorbacks choked away this game—I phoned the Royal Sonesta Hotel in New Orleans to book several rooms that required non-refundable deposits, including a room for my father and his wife. This hotel was on Bourbon Street, and I wanted to make it as easy as possible for my dad to participate in all the upcoming fun. He was 71, and I wasn't sure if the Razorbacks would ever get back to the Sugar Bowl during what remained of his life. Or mine either, for that matter.

The Hogs' 2011 trip to New Orleans to face Ohio State unleashed three decades of pent-up demand, as Razorback fans descended on the Crescent City in droves—among them most of the family members who'd honeymooned with Susanne and me in France, including my sister, who, invoking another of her endearing childhood malapropisms, called this the Shuggie Bowl. (When she was 11, as we'd flown over the Atlantic, Mallory had asked Dad if it was the Specific Ocean.)

In the lead-up to the game, our days were full: beignets and chicory coffee at Café Dumond, duck sandwiches for lunch at Bayona Restaurant, obligatory pilgrimages to Pat O'Brien's. Hour-by-hour, drink-by-drink, sumptuous-meal-by-sumptuous-meal, the momentum of the occasion built. No telling how many times I bellied up to the bar at Napoleon House, even for a mid-afternoon iced tea and a package of Zapp's Potato Chips. Meanwhile, I, along with my stepchildren, John and Emily, became well acquainted with the piano player in the back room of Laffite's Blacksmith Shop, a popular bar.

I dined with my father one night at Mr. B's Bistro and we sat at the table where, according to the plaque on the wall, Bill Clinton had sat on September 5, 2002, and September 1, 2004, respectively. This delighted my dad, who was proud to have been a big supporter of Clinton when he was governor of Arkansas. He had even served as a delegate to the Democratic Convention in 1992, the token entrepreneur among a caucus comprised mostly of members of the teachers' unions.

Just across from Mr. B's Bistro was the Carousel Bar, where I met a friend from Harvard Business School, a lifelong fan of Ohio State. Through the tall windows that looked out onto Royal Street, I saw hordes of Razorback fans, my kith and kin, marauding about. My friend and I finally nabbed two prime seats, and as we slowly spun around the grand bar he noted with a tone of weary superiority that, as an Ohio State fan, he'd been to numerous high-profile bowl venues in recent years—Miami, Phoenix, Pasadena—but New Orleans was easily the best venue for a bowl game. He loved it, and I did too. *Another Sazerac, please!*

Lord help me if the Razorback players were having half as much fun as I was. Fortunately, Coach Bobby Petrino was the consummate disciplinarian. The previous year, Arkansas had gone to the Liberty Bowl in Memphis and when three players missed a curfew, he'd sent them back to Fayetteville the next morning on a Greyhound bus. Message sent.

The night before kickoff, the French Quarter was off the leash, the crowd so thick I could barely bull my way down Bourbon Street. From the balconies, red-clad women tossed beads on us revelers below. Most of us in the mosh pit were Arkansas fans, and with go-cups in hand we were pretty much sauced. In a Saturnalian gesture, I wore a tri-cornered pirate hat I'd bought at a consignment store near Jackson Square, and amid the garish neon signs and frolicking fun I felt the long-simmering passion of Razorback fandom course through my Sazerac-clogged veins. It was a fever dream, like bobbing in an ocean of euphoria.

In typical Razorback fashion, the way the game unfolded inflicted a fair amount of everlasting agony. Early on, the Hogs were down 21-7. Then a comeback. With four minutes left and down just 24-20, the Porkers blocked an Ohio State punt. The football just lay there on the turf, waiting for Julian Horton to scoop it up and run into the end zone for the winning score. There was no one around. He had a clear and brief path to the end zone. But Julian Horton didn't scoop. He didn't score. Julian Horton just fell on the ground and covered the football.

This would qualify as a disaster only if the Hogs failed to score the go-ahead touchdown. Then Ryan Mallet threw an interception. All of this happened down on our end of the field, as my posse watched from the second row of the upper deck of the Superdome.

After the game, the hoodoo moon was out, and our walk back to the French Quarter had the air of a funeral procession.

New Orleans, which Mark Twain likened to an upholstered sewer, can unleash all manner of subterranean behavior, and in the wake of another crushing football disappointment I descended into the dark world of Hogville. I was already a frequent visitor to this fan-based website. In fact, I visited it daily, compelled by a logic that was perversely circuitous: During the season, I checked this website lest I miss a crucial twist or turn or some vital inside poop related to upcoming games. Then, when the season ended, I checked it regularly because I was starved for any news at all, even any conversation, about the Razorbacks. Hogville was a year-round itch I had to scratch, even if much of the user-generated content was on the level of *McGuffey's First Reader.*

But there was a difference between visiting Hogville merely to read the posts of other Razorback fans versus actually making posts on this website myself. To use a crude analogy, it was the difference between just looking at pornography versus actually churning it out myself.

I had not foreseen my eruption on Hogville. Immediately after the Sugar Bowl I hadn't stewed on the loss, although it certainly made me loathe Ohio State even more. But my levelheadedness was in large part due to the fact that I was still in the French Quarter, still with all of my family, still within walking distance of the bar at Napoleon House and the grand piano in the back room of Laffite's Blacksmith Shop. But as soon as I headed north on the interstate toward northeast Arkansas, a swarm of goblins began to gather up in my head.

The catalyst for my manic posts on Hogville was that I couldn't stop thinking about how one of the Hogs' receivers, Joe Adams, had spent the entire Sugar Bowl more interested in talking smack with Ohio State's defensive backs than he was in catching the passes that fell right into his hands. Somebody had to take the blame for this loss, and I had settled on Joe Adams and his purportedly discipline-minded head coach, the man who had returned the Razorbacks to football glory.

Understand, I wasn't a guy who, when it came to critiquing my team, saw himself as the only expert. I wasn't a man who was confident that I was the only objective Razorback fan with any common sense. I wasn't a fellow who, no matter how much of a mess

I had made of my own life, with my divorces and my lackluster track record in the world of business, believed that I was perfectly capable of coaching the Razorback football team better than anyone else possibly could. No, that wasn't me. Not by a long shot.

That said, there I was on Hogville, typing away furiously while hiding behind a not-so-clever avatar, which, for obvious reasons, I won't divulge. Herewith, an excerpt from my posts on Hogville three days after the Sugar Bowl:

Look, I concede I'm being a bit harsh here. But college football, at its highest level, is a harsh business. The thing that disappoints me is I thought we had the coach in Bobby Petrino who was harsh enough to rid our team of showboating, me-first players who crack in high-pressure, big-game situations. But, judging from Joe Adams' behavior and his performance, we don't. What I hate to see is the guys who aren't hot dogs playing their living guts out—Demario Ambrose and Zach Hocker and Knile Davis and DeMarcus Love—lose a game because guys like Joe Adams can't make plays when it counts because they are worn-out, frazzled, and distracted from all of their woofing, strutting, taunting and jack-jawing. And if Coach Petrino can't see this and do something about it, then he's the not the smart disciplinarian I thought he was. I'm sick of losing big games at Arkansas! We need to either get tough, or resign ourselves to perpetual disappointment. What's it going to be, Coach Petrino?

Amid all my bile and bilge, I chuckled when one of the regulars on Hogville suggested that the man making such posts sounded as if he was indeed a full-time football coach.

Soon enough, my angst subsided. Even so, in early February just before National Signing Day, I was shot through with a shiver of recognition when I encountered an unrelated thread on Hogville with this headline: "I'm a Razorback fan first, and an adult second."

Like a koan, this observation was laden with sideways insight. In other words, when it comes to supporting my team—or mercilessly criticizing it as well—don't expect me to act like a mature, rational, fair-minded person. Especially when I can sit at a computer and hide behind a digital disguise.

As unbalanced as I was in the wake of this Sugar Bowl loss, it seemed that my stepson John took it even harder. He and I had become closer over the past year. He needed a father and I was blessed to have him as stepson. And while his sense of life was as different from mine as was his mother's, easily the most passionate of our shared interests was Razorback football.

As the months passed, John kept bringing up the Sugar Bowl loss, and I wondered why he couldn't let it go (the notion of my urging perspective on any young fan is rich, I admit). Then I realized why: As a Razorback fan, John had no experience of winning The Big One. Born in 1987, he wasn't clued in to Razorback football until he was 10 years old or so. By this time, Arkansas had long ago made its fateful move to the SEC. When John was 11, Clint Stoerner had sunk a real chance at a Dynasty Year with his so-called Hand of God fumble at Tennessee. So, there was that. In 2006, the Hogs' 10-game win streak had ended with three losses, including Reggie Fish blowing the SEC Championship Game with a pull-your-hair-out play against Florida. Then, in the season just past, the Hogs were unable to hold onto their fourth-quarter lead against Alabama. Whenever it had been time for the Razorbacks to meet the moment, the moment had proved too big. For John, all of it was just one disappointment after another, the latest being this Sugar Bowl letdown.

What was remarkable about the younger generation of Razorback fans like John was how they continued to sustain their passion at all. The glory days of 1964 and 1965, the excitement of The Big Shootout, Lou Holtz's epic Orange Bowl triumph, the five consecutive seasons of at least nine wins under Ken Hatfield—these triumphs were to them what World War II battles were to me: events I knew to be expressions of American greatness, yet so far removed from my personal experience that it was all just bathed in a sepia-toned glaze.

As a young fan, nostalgia, the love of your home state, your father's raising, your grandfather's abiding passion can take you only so far. To confirm that all the effort to be a fan is worth it, we all need the occasional fuel of memorable big-time wins. Such triumphs don't have to come often, but like the rains that sustain life itself, they must come. That's where John was, and there was nothing I could say to pull him out of it.

30

The Fanatic At 50

After National Signing Day in February comes March Madness, then the Masters, and by early summer the NBA playoffs are finally over and major-league baseball is in full swing. That means it's again time to plan my fall travels.

It's always a challenge to arrange suitable hotel accommodations for games in Fayetteville. It's a simple a matter of supply and demand, and the hotels have the upper hand. They jack up their prices and require a minimum two-night stay, plus a nonrefundable pre-payment. They also send out their reservation forms early in the summer, forcing me to make some critical decisions: How much do I really want to go to the home opener against a dud team like Missouri State? Would it be better to go to the South Carolina game on November 5, or wait until the next weekend for the game against Tennessee? Should I commit to both of these back-to-back games? But what if the season goes poorly and I get stuck with these late-season hotel reservations? And what about the fall foliage? The hotels' early-reservation racket even requires me to predict when leaves in the Ozarks will be at peak color.

After stewing on all this for the 2011 season, I finally called the Holiday Inn Express in Fayetteville to make my reservations.

This was a complicated process, with a special form to fill out, and in due time, via a series of emails and faxes, I found myself dealing with a young man on the hotel's staff named Tyler Wilson. Now, I found this to be quite interesting because the Hogs' incumbent quarterback for the upcoming season was also named Tyler Wilson. Last year, he'd filled in for the injured Ryan Mallett and almost singlehandedly beat a Cam Newton-led Auburn team—at Auburn. Could it be that this young man I was dealing with was *The Tyler Wilson?* What were the odds of there being more than one Tyler Wilson in the vicinity of Fayetteville, Arkansas? Pretty slim, I judged. Furthermore, the year before, I had seen *The Tyler Wilson* in that very hotel; apparently his parents had been staying there.

So even though I like to consider myself a cut above all those jock-sniffing fans who God-up football players, I allowed myself to believe that this young hotel employee named Tyler Wilson was indeed *The Tyler Wilson*. It made perfect sense: During the summer months, the Hog quarterback was working at the hotel, arranging accommodations for fans like me who would, in turn, come see him play this fall. How cool was this? I wanted to reply to *The Tyler Wilson* with an email to ask how his summer workouts with his teammates were coming along. What were his thoughts on wide receiver Cobi Hamilton's ability to stretch the field this season? Any reflections on what he expected in the passing game from running back Knile Davis?

My belief that I was dealing with *The Tyler Wilson* lessened the sting of the confiscatory $239 per night rate at the Holiday Inn Express, the two-night minimum stay, and the fact that my room reservation, secured by a credit card, was not cancellable under any circumstances. Soon enough, *The Tyler Wilson* faxed over a form for me to sign, which I immediately returned, thus locking myself into spending almost $500 for two nights at a mediocre hotel next to a McDonald's just off the freeway. In all this, *The Tyler Wilson* was most helpful, and in return I wasn't about to let him down, just as with his game-day performances this season he wasn't going to let me down either. The two of us had a pact, a bond.

Summer came and went, though August, when I was most eager for autumn, dragged by with typical slowness. For the Razorbacks under Bobby Petrino, the early games of the season went as expected: a loss to Alabama in Tuscaloosa, but wins over everyone else, and, as predicted, *The Tyler Wilson* was killing it at quarterback.

On the appointed November weekend of the game against South Carolina, I checked into the Holiday Inn Express in Fayetteville. To satisfy my curiosity, I asked the young lady at the front desk to confirm that the young man named Tyler Wilson with whom I'd dealt a few months ago at this hotel was, in fact, *The Tyler Wilson.* She half-laughed at this as if I wasn't the first jock sniffer to ask such a question. Then, as though I was suddenly unworthy of trust, she asked to see my credit card and driver's license one more time.

Six days after this 44-28 win over South Carolina, on 11/11/11, Alice Walton, daughter of Walmart founder Sam Walton, opened Crystal Bridges in Bentonville, just north of Fayetteville. Her museum cost $200 million to build, and she had shelled out hundreds of millions more to buy artworks for her new repository. The Walton Family Foundation also endowed the museum with another $800 million. Certainly, such an expenditure on culture was well and good. Crystal Bridges was among the most enriching developments to hit Middle America in my lifetime. But as a long-suffering Hog fan, it was hard for me not to fantasize about what such an immense sum of private capital could've done to boost the fortunes of Razorback football.

The Walton fortune has been called the greatest ever amassed outside of a monarchy. Sam Walton had died in 1992 as the world's richest man, and it had not escaped my attention that Sam's brother, Bud Walton, soon thereafter donated half the funds required to build a state-of-the-art basketball arena. Bud Walton Arena opened in 1993, and the following spring the Razorback basketball team won the NCAA Championship.

Sometimes when I grow pessimistic about Razorback football, I fantasize about somebody named Walton finally saying, "Enough with this!" and pulling out a checkbook to money-whip the Razorback football program into Dynasty-level shape. It gives me hope to know there are people in Arkansas with the wherewithal, if not the inclination, to do just this. Perhaps a relatively inconsequential chunk of the Walmart fortune could go to the building of a new football stadium—the greatest ever in college football, a palatial showplace with annual upgrades funded by a trust that rivals even the academic endowment of an Ivy League university. A football mecca to lure a critical mass of highly-rated recruits and instantly return Arkansas to its rightful place as the next New Dynasty.

On the other hand, with their appearance in the Sugar Bowl and an 8-1 start to the 2011 season, the Hogs had returned to national prominence without any huge injection of Walmart money, hadn't they? All it had required was a top-tier coach, a man of the highest on-field standards, a man who was an innovative offensive mind and genius play caller. Despite my post-Sugar Bowl rant on Hogville only 10 months before, I was so thrilled with the Porkers' ongoing run of success, so enamored of our head coach, that I put a bumper sticker on my car that read "BMFP," which, to those in the know, indelicately translated to "Bobby Mother F***ing Petrino."

Let's be clear, bumper stickers are not my thing. I had never stuck one on any car of mine. Nevertheless, I was quite proud of it. This bumper sticker was my way of virtue signaling, like the Roman soldier who holds aloft a Roman standard emblazoned with SPQR, the ancient way to show support for the citizens of the Empire, as well as the policies of the Roman army, and even the Emperor himself.

31

Everything Going Right

In mid-November, Bobby Petrino's Razorbacks thrashed Mississippi State at War Memorial Stadium to go to 10-1. The Hogs were headed to another big-time bowl game. Winners of 20 of 24 over the past two seasons, Arkansas football was on fire.

My stepdaughter Emily now lived in Little Rock, where she attended nursing school. After the Mississippi State game, she threw a party at her rented house, the living room packed with friends from her undergrad days in Fayetteville. Encamped around the large coffee table, they talked and laughed and sipped wine and beer. The ESPN game between Oklahoma State and Iowa State flickered on the TV, and periodically the score "Arkansas 44 Mississippi State 17" scrolled across the bottom of the screen. I was in a great mood, as was the typically dour Bobby Petrino, who, in his post-game radio interview, had said, "I really like the way we're playing."

Yet all of this was so worrisomely fragile. Emily would soon be off to her first nursing job in Dallas, where an aunt lived. She was being pulled to Texas by her boyfriend from Houston, Blake Matocha, a tall, sandy-haired graduate of the University of Arkansas. Two years before, I had met Blake's parents at Bordino's in

Fayetteville. His father, an engineer, was an alumnus of the University of Texas, and his mother had gone to Texas Tech. I dreaded Emily's leaving for Texas almost as much as her mother did. As for the football part of the equation, I had long realized that, with Bobby Petrino, the Hogs had caught lightning in a bottle. But college football was cyclical. With his roaming eye, Petrino would inevitably leave for a bigger, better job. It was just a matter of time.

For now, though, the Razorbacks had a coach who knew how to win football games, and Emily still lived in Little Rock. Earlier that afternoon, she and several of her sorority friends had sat with me at War Memorial Stadium. Like her mother, Emily enjoyed the social aspect of the game-going experience, yet she was also more knowledgeable about the finer points of football, or at least more interested. But best of all, she totally got me as a fan. For some reason, I had never been able to say, "Let's go, Hogs!" This exhortation just didn't roll naturally off my tongue; instead, and since I was a kid, it had always come out, "Let's go, Hoggies!" So imagine my pride when, at various points during this game, I'd overheard Emily shout, "Let's go, Hoggies!" As the lucky beneficiary of a new family by marriage, this subtlety of language, not unlike the Archie Bunkerisms ("Geez, Edith") my father and I sometimes traded during games, made me realize how much I loved her and her brother and their mother, and how blessed I was to have my new family. I was in good health, and my parents were healthy too. I had my new work at the company my grandfather and dad had started back in the Dynasty Year of 1964. My gosh, everything was going right for me, even Arkansas football.

That night as Emily's post-game party progressed, a frisson of excitement built in the living room. Attention had turned to the game on TV between Iowa State and second-ranked Oklahoma State, now in overtime. For Arkansas fans, this game presented the opportunity for a team above the sixth-ranked Hogs to go down. The prospect of any Oklahoma State loss always tickled me more than it should, because the Cowboys had beaten the Hogs consecutively back when I was 13, 14, and 15—and two of those losses had been season spoilers.

Sure enough, in overtime the Cowboys went down to Iowa State. When the BCS Poll came out the following Monday, the national rankings were LSU, number one; Alabama, number two; and Arkansas, number three—all teams from the SEC's Western Division. In just a few days, the Hogs would play LSU, with a chance to vault to the top. *My cup,* I remember thinking, *runneth over.*

32

The Crash

It was the afternoon of April Fool's Day 2012, the day before my mother's 73rd birthday, when I received a text from John: "Did you hear the news about Bobby Petrino?"

Dear God.

Despite losing to LSU in the season finale, the Arkansas head coach who had led the Razorbacks to 21 wins in their last 26 games had been involved in a motorcycle accident. Okay, calm down. This certainly wasn't good news, but it wasn't a disaster, either. It wasn't as though Petrino were dead.

But over the next few days, other highly problematic shoes began to drop. Petrino had been riding on his motorcycle with Jessica Dorrell, an all-SEC volleyball player. Then it was revealed that he'd given her $20,000 in cash for Christmas, as well as preferential treatment in hiring her for a job within the football program. It further came to light that he had lied about all this to his boss, Athletic Director Jeff Long. Within two weeks, Bobby Petrino was gone.

Are you kidding me?

In his classic history *The Decline and Fall of the Roman Empire*, Edward Gibbon speculates about the role of chance in

Rome's eclipse. What if the Huns and the various barbarian tribes to the north had been, well, less barbaric? How would things have been different if Nero's mother had murdered him, instead of vice versa? What if Marcus Aurelius' son, Commodus, had been more like his wise father?

With a nod to Edward Gibbon, when it comes to agonizing what-ifs, the Roman Empire has nothing on Arkansas football. What if the Hogs had beaten LSU in the 1965 Cotton Bowl, thus completing their second-straight undefeated season and second-straight Dynasty Year? What if James Street had overthrown Randy Peschel on that lucky-ass fourth-and-three completion late in the fourth quarter of The Big Shootout? What if safety Steve Atwater had held on to that interception in the end zone at Miami in 1988 and the Hogs had finished 11-0? Among the most agonizing possibilities involves Bear Bryant, an Arkansas native who was traveling from Nashville, where he was an assistant coach at Vanderbilt, to Fayetteville to interview to be the Razorbacks' next head coach on the day Pearl Harbor was attacked.

I could go on with the what-ifs.

It had been a stroke of conniving luck that Arkansas had hired Bobby Petrino in the first place. Highly successful at Louisville, where he was 41-9 in four years, he had erred in 2007 by taking the job as head coach of the Atlanta Falcons. Petrino was so desperate to get back into the college ranks that he quit the Falcons with three games left in his first NFL season. He informed his Falcon players he was gone by posting a 78-word letter in his team's locker room.

And so I was left with the problem of what to do about that BMFP bumper sticker on my car, which made me look as out-of-it as those folks still driving around with a McCain-Palin 2008 decal on the back window of their pickup trucks.

Yet I wasn't the only Razorback fan in such a predicament. Only weeks after Petrino self-destructed, I had an exchange with a lady in a parking lot in Jonesboro.

"I see you took that bumper sticker off your car," she said airily, as she passed by. I nodded and stared at her. I had never seen this woman before in my life. "I took mine off my car too," she went on, talking back over her shoulder. "Painful, is it?"

"Yes, ma'am. Sure is."

I got in my car and pulled the door shut with a heavy thud. As I drove away, a speculative thought came to me: *What if Bobby Petrino weren't such a flawed human being?* Then, in a flash, the answer came: *Very likely, he would never have taken the job as head coach of the Arkansas Razorbacks in the first place.*

Like everyone else, I have a hard time coping with change. Before Bobby Petrino blew himself up, I had looked forward to the Alabama game, slated for early September of the 2012 season, more than to practically anything else in both my near or distant future. The Hogs had a loaded team returning and, with BMFP at the helm, this game would be the Hogs' chance to atone for the crushing home loss to the Crimson Tide two years before. The mere prospect of this was like a long-sought prize just waiting for me to possess.

But when the 2012 season actually rolled around, Petrino had been gone for five months, replaced by interim coach John L. Smith. Initially, I accepted the cultish logic that this Razorback team was so talented that it didn't matter *who* the coach was—I drank down a good-sized glug of this red-colored Kool-Aid. But deep in my gut, I feared that the coming season was going to be miserable, despite the Hogs' preseason Top 10 ranking. In August, just after the players reported for fall camp, the *Arkansas Democrat-Gazette* published a team picture in which one of the Razorback players had the nerve to reach behind coach John L.

Smith and make two-fingered bunny ears right above his head. (The player was not long after arrested for stealing gas from a Fayetteville convenience store.) This was fourth-grader nonsense. Smith looked like a grandfather who'd been pranked.

Yet even though I sensed that Petrino's departure had changed everything, I kept on reaching for the long-sought prize. In a willful denial of reality, even in the wake of the Hogs' shocking loss the previous week to Louisiana-Monroe in John L. Smith's second game, I went on pretending as though BMFP had never soiled himself.

On the Friday afternoon before the Alabama game, I drove to Fayetteville. First, I dropped in for a visit at the Sigma Chi house on Maple Street, and then I went to Bordino's for dinner. My dad wasn't there because his duck-hunting buddy Larry Palmer, who'd always secured a choice table for us on football game weekends, had recently died from lymphoma. Afterwards, I prowled up Dickson Street like a fiftysomething Peter Pan, sticking my head in at Maxine's Tap Room before calling it a night and going to my hotel.

On Saturday morning, per usual, I went for a jog around campus, making it a point to go and spot my name in the sidewalk near Old Main. Then, just for old times' sake, I sauntered through the lobby of Carnall Hall to take in the oil paintings by former Hog linebacker Barry Thomas. Around noon, I dressed in my usual hot-weather Razorback game outfit of khakis and a red polo shirt with a Hog logo on it and went to my sister's tailgate party, where I hung out with family and friends. In all this, it was as if I believed that by strictly adhering to my usual game-weekend rituals, I could somehow put this shattered Humpty Dumpty of a Razorback football team back together again.

At Razorback Stadium, the Alabama fans filled up the lower northeastern corner, so many of them that it seemed as if their presence was rude. Tide fans always travelled well. And why wouldn't they? The day before, I'd spotted a gaggle of them wondering around the Square in Fayetteville. Clad in crimson, but typically with a distinguishing bit of houndstooth on at least one garment, they were polite to a fault to anyone and everyone, because they knew that their well-coached team, winners of 15 of their last 16, would thrash their opponent. What must it be like to have such a feeling of serenity, magnanimity, and goodwill towards the fans of other teams? With their polite good cheer, these Alabama boosters were more like Rotarians than the typical hard-bitten fans who trekked across three states to watch their team play.

This game against Alabama got ugly early. Typically, at half-time of any Razorback game, I made a trip to the concession stand, but after what I'd just witnessed, I lacked the spirit to even get up and go to the bathroom. I just sat slump-shouldered in my seat as the Razorback Band played songs from *James Bond* movies, including *Skyfall*, *Live and Let Die*, and *Goldfinger*.

Then the Band duly performed the "Go Hogs Spellout," as the Band members raced around to form the letters in "G-o H-o-g-s," and the public-address announcer said, "What does it spell?" and the crowd returned, "Go Hogs!" and the announcer said, "Louder!" and the crowd returned, "Go Hogs!" and then the announcer said, "*Louder!*" and the crowd again yelled, "*Go Hogs!*" All of this was excruciating, particularly when the Hogs were down 24-0 and the head coach inside our team's locker room, Mr. Bunny Ears himself, hadn't a clue.

As dreadful as this game was, I didn't leave early, even when it began to sprinkle. And in a display of his sportsmanship, Nick Saban let off the gas. On the last few possessions, his tailback was a little throwback white dude named Ben Howell, who got only 18 yards on six carries, still considerably better per carry than the Hogs' measly 58 yards on 37 attempts. Yet Ben Howell was just unathletic enough to keep Alabama out of the end zone one last time.

As I watched the Razorback football program disintegrate before my eyes, I wanted to do *something*. But what exactly? I was fully invested mentally and emotionally in the Razorbacks, yet I had no influence over what happened to my team. It's not hard to figure out that the path to clout in any college football program involves money, plus a fair amount of schmoozing and politicking. Those who play that game are what're called Super Boosters—important fans who get consulted when coaches are hired or fired.

I was hardly a Super Booster. Moreover, I wasn't sure that I would want the job even if I were in a position to become one. But such whataboutism was not helpful in the wake of this 52-0 loss. As a fan, I had no option other than to stop caring, which, genetically speaking, was out of the question.

At the conclusion of this awful 4-8 2012 season, I was at Christmas party when I heard a friend—let's call him Phillip—claim that he'd been to every Arkansas football game over the past year. I encouraged him to elaborate. "Some people play golf, hunt, fish, collect cars, and things like that," he said. "I'm a Razorback fan."

When Phillip suggested that he had no peer in the realm of Hog Fandom, I mentioned the name of a mutual friend who was similarly possessed. Phillip rattled the ice in his cocktail, then looked up as if I'd called his bluff in a poker game. "Yes, well," he said, "he's certainly in my league." Then he bolstered his case by noting that he'd only missed three Razorback football games in 10 years. Overhearing this, his brunette wife, after conceding that she'd dozed off when they'd attended a Hogs' basketball game in Little Rock earlier that week, said, "I'm not a Razorback fan. But when I married Phillip, I *became* a Razorback fan."

The couple's son had recently become engaged, and not surprisingly the father had warned about the timing of the wedding.

"I told him that 12 weekends this fall were off-limits. He's got 40 other weeks to choose from." Then Phillip trotted out a story about the Alabama couple who flat-out told their kids not to get married on the weekend of a football game. "They didn't go the wedding," he said, as if this was only to be expected. "If that happened to me, I'd eventually acquiesce. But it would be hard."

On one level, I tipped my hat to the devotion of fans like Phillip. On the other hand, was I to consider myself a lesser fan for not attending *every single game* the Hogs play? One plausible explanation for Phillip's behavior was that he was indeed a Super Booster and, as such, he had some influence over decisions made within the athletic department. As for other similarly obsessed fans, all I can do is suggest that they need to get a grip.

33

Some Healing

After the disastrous 2012 campaign under interim coach John L. Smith, Arkansas undertook a coaching search, which put every fan through a cycle of fantastical dreaming, then optimistic hoping, then the inevitable squaring off with who, realistically, can be hired for the job. This particular coaching search, like any coaching search, was as much of an emotional roller coaster as a campaign to elect the president of the United States. Every fan, myself included, was surprised when Bret Bielema of Wisconsin was named the new coach.

Bielema's inaugural season in 2013 started well, with three wins against cupcake opponents. But the Hogs dropped their last nine, including another 52-0 loss to top-ranked Alabama.

In his second campaign, Bielema fared better and, at season's end, the six-loss Razorbacks were invited to play the six-loss Texas Longhorns in the 2014 Texas Bowl. Of course, in any game against Texas my history haunted me: Through my youth, and even through my 20s, the Hogs had lost 17 of 23 games to the Longhorns. Mercifully, this one-sided rivalry had ended 22 years before, when Arkansas had pulled out of the Southwest Conference, a nine-team league of which eight were in the Lone Star State. The

Razorbacks were done with Texans and their swaggering pride, their easy oil money, their biased referees. In joining the SEC in 1992, the University of Arkansas, like a wayward outpost of the former British Empire, had asserted its independence.

Now, however, countertrends were eroding our newfound sovereignty. When visiting Fayetteville in recent years, I'd heard carping about the influx of students from the state of Texas. The campus was said to be crawling with them, prompting lamentations that the University of Arkansas was becoming the University of Texas at Fayetteville. A frat brother had informed me that his daughter, a freshman, was rooming with three girls from the Lone Star State, making it sound as if she were a hostage. "My stepdaughter now lives in Dallas," I'd chimed in. "And she's dating a boy from Houston. They met when they were both students here, and they're getting pretty serious."

From the opening kickoff, the Razorbacks controlled the Texas Bowl. Nevertheless, like an abused child who's never quite right in the head, I expected the momentum to swing to the Longhorns at any moment. S*omething* would go wrong—a holding penalty on a just-converted third down, a missed tackle by one of the Hogs' safeties, a fumble by a running back—and the game would turn.

My paranoia aside, this wasn't the olden days when Arkansas was physically overmatched and men-among-boys like Earl Campbell free-ranged in the Hogs' secondary. Since then, Americans had grown so beefy that the size of college football teams had been democratized. Hence, a once perennially scrappy, undersized team like Arkansas could now push Texas around as if they were the 1976 Rice Owls. Late in the fourth quarter, Arkansas had more points than Texas had total yards.

Up 30-7 and with the ball on Texas' 13-yard line, Arkansas' quarterback Brandon Allen took a knee to run out the clock. Warped by my history, I rose from my favorite chair and screamed at the TV set, "What are we doing! Run it down their throats one last time!"

Bret Bielema, who never lacked for bravado even when he should've kept his yap shut, described this moment of mercy as "borderline erotic." This was a bit raw for sure, but the man had a point. The Longhorns only managed 57 yards of total offense, their worst showing in 71 years. Yet, in the aftermath, I was surprised at how unsatisfying this victory was. Sure, a win over Texas was better than another defeat. But going in, these two teams had lost a combined 12 games this season, so this was hardly a signature win. Mostly, though, I had moved on from hating the Texas Long-horns, especially when they fielded a team this middling (they'd lost 41-7 to Brigham Young earlier in 2014). Life was often like this: We become fixated on a certain outcome, and by the time it comes to pass the world has moved on and the outcome we'd longed for doesn't mean as much as we'd thought it would.

After the Texas Bowl, to torture myself I watched a replay of The Big Shootout on YouTube. Over the intervening half century, I'd overlooked a play in the second quarter when Bill Montgomery threw a 21-yard touchdown pass to Chuck Dicus to put the Hogs up 14-0. But the play was called back for offensive interference. It seems Bill Montgomery had called an audible at the line of scrimmage, but amid the crowd noise the Hogs' other wide receiver, John Rees, missed the call. Though John Rees was 20 yards from where Chuck Dicus caught the football, he was flagged for chicken fighting with the Texas cornerback. The Razorbacks were forced to punt. If that play hadn't been called back—if John Rees had heard the audible, or, heck, if he'd just stood there when the ball was snapped and done nothing—Arkansas would likely have won the national championship back in 1969. And, as it turns out, John Rees was from my hometown of Jonesboro.

When pondering such tortuous twists of the football fates, it's hard not to fall prey to fatalism. It's so darned tempting to cross over to the dark side, to occupy a world of no light, no optimism, no perspective. But just when I'm about to go there, when I'm about to lose all hope, the Football Gods will deign to cast a broken-toothed smile on my team.

One of the biggest smiles came in early November of the 2015 season. The Razorbacks, mired at 4-4, were at Ole Miss, which at 7-2 had beaten Alabama and, with a win, was headed to the SEC Championship Game for the first time ever. After seven lead changes during regulation play, the score was 45-all.

In overtime, Ole Miss got the ball first and immediately scored. The Hogs had to match it, or the game was over. Three disastrous plays led to a fourth-and-25. Yet Hog quarterback Brandon Allen inexplicably threw the ball only 12 yards downfield. As tight end Hunter Henry was being tackled—just before his butt hit the turf to send Ole Miss to the SEC Championship Game—he hurled the football backwards as far as he could. The ball bounced high, then found the hands of running back Alex Collins: Off went Collins for a 31-yard scamper. After this remarkable fourth-down conversion, Arkansas scored a touchdown and then made the two-point attempt to win.

The Heavenly Heave, as Hunter Henry's hurl came to be known, was a miracle play for the ages. Even Jimbo, who could not abide the Razorbacks, called it the smartest play he'd ever seen *in any sport at any level.* Not surprisingly, my take was that this was merely payback for the Ole Miss field goal that referee Tommy Bell had ruled good in Little Rock back in the year of my birth, the game-winner that my dad still swore was wide.

34

The Uses of Romanticism

Generally speaking, I don't care for movies about football. There have been a lot of them—films such as *The Longest Yard, North Dallas Forty, Remember the Titans, Friday Night Lights, Rudy, We Are Marshal.* Such movies seem contrived, and I find myself resisting them even though they're the kinds of movies I should like. The only exception is *Brian's Song*, which retains the power to make me weepy-eyed.

But no football movie had ever been made about a player for the Arkansas Razorbacks. So when *Greater* was released in the summer of 2016, I made plans to catch the movie at the local theater. On our drive to the Malco, Susanne was on her phone, talking to our son John about a party to celebrate the second birthday of his daughter. My wife had only agreed to come along to the Malco because I'd coyly pitched this as our date night out together. I had glossed over the movie itself, other than to mention that it was something I really wanted to see. But when Susanne finally hung up, she said, "Okay, now what exactly is this movie about?"

I attempted to make the plotline of *Greater* sound interesting, while downplaying any mention of Razorback football. *Greater* is the story of the too-brief career of Brandon Burlsworth, a walk-on lineman for the Hogs who became an All-American. (Yes, I'm obligated to remind you, this is the same Brandon Burlsworth whose foot Clint Stoerner had tripped over against Tennessee back in 1998, resulting in Stoerner's improbable fumble.) Tragically, Burlsworth had died in a car wreck just 11 days after being drafted in the third round by the Indianapolis Colts. The movie was produced by Marty Burlsworth, Brandon's brother, and was a low-budget independent production.

"What else is on?" Susanne said.

To help me out, I dialed my mother, who, over the speaker in my car, noted that the movie espoused Christian values, something rare in any film released in theaters these days. Basically, she confirmed that *Greater* was more than just a rah-rah movie about Razorback football. Meanwhile, as we idled at a stoplight, I Googled the movie and then eagerly noted that on Rotten Tomatoes, *Greater* had gotten an audience score of 86%, tantamount to a thumbs up from viewers.

Still, my wife was skeptical about any movie having to do with Razorback football being at all watchable, and I must admit that at this juncture my zeal for the Hogs wasn't exactly off-the-charts, either. Notwithstanding the Heavenly Heave against Ole Miss, too many games over the course of the 2015 season had been diabolical misfires, foremost the back-to-back home losses to Toledo and Texas Tech. But good grief, it was the dead of summer, just when I was starved for anything football-related, and now, lo and behold, the local Malco was showing a movie about Razorback football in 15 minutes. Nothing on the face of the earth could stop me from going to see it. As we pulled into the theater's parking lot, I said, "Look, if the movie is no good, we'll get up and leave. I promise."

Two hours later, when the lights came up in the theater at the end of *Greater*, I was ready to lay the wood to somebody. Films have a way of validating and romanticizing anything they touch, even Razorback football circa 1997, a 4-7 result. Events, or people, depicted in movies typically gain a strong foothold in our psyche. Much of what we know about certain historical figures has been so powerfully communicated by films such as *Patton* or *Lawrence of Arabia* or *Gandhi* that it practically blots out everything else.

Brandon Burlsworth was certainly no historical figure. He was a once-pudgy overachiever who grew up in a broken home in Harrison, Arkansas. But he did live a resonant life worth dramatizing and remembering. *Greater* is about a kid who's told he's too fat and too slow to ever play college football, yet he perseveres to become an All-American lineman. As such, the movie reinforces the human-interest stories behind every college football team.

Driving home, I could only imagine the galvanizing effect *Greater* had on the Razorbacks' current roster of players. Perhaps it would inspire them to do something special in the upcoming season (only 34 days away!). Then again, maybe these guys rolled their eyes when they saw the film, especially the depiction of Burlsworth as a principled teetotaler.

Regardless, *Greater* instantly became my favorite football movie, largely because I deemed it to have serious brand-building potential. Quick, how could the Hogs' coaching staff get this movie into the hands of every four- and five-star high school recruit in America?

In early September of 2106, the Hogs played TCU in Fort Worth, and since Susanne and I were in Dallas to see our daughter Emily, and since Emily's boyfriend, Blake, was also in Dallas to see her, he and I drove out to Fort Worth for the game. What else were we supposed to do? As a graduate of the University of Arkansas, Blake was as nutty about Razorback football as I was: a genuine next-level Hog fan.

Our outing got off to a promising start with an afternoon

tailgate party thrown by a friend-of-a-friend-of-a-friend. The venue was an ideal barn-like setting with a full bar, a spread of savory beef brisket, cushy couches, and a huge TV. I watched with glee as Central Michigan got a fluke score on the last play of the game to ruin Oklahoma State's season.

To my surprise, out here in north-central Texas who should I run into but Rick Angel, my former college roommate. Even though he and I had drifted apart over the past couple of decades, seeing him warmed my heart. Like my spouse, Rick's wife was a former member of the Razorback spirit squad, a cheerleader, and as we all visited, I noted the relief on her face when I confirmed that my seat for that night's game wasn't close to where she and Rick were sitting, thus nullifying any chance for Rick and me to feed off each other and relapse into our old game-watching histrionics.

Suitably fed and watered like a herd of wandering cattle, a group of us rode in a van to the not-so-nearby Amon Carter Stadium. In the parking lots surrounding the stadium, Blake and I milled around among the tailgating TCU fans. Obviously, the disposable income of TCU Nation was high enough for chi-chi designers to produce entire lines of clothing and accessories in the team color of the Horned Frogs; I had never seen such tasteful renditions of purple dresses, shirts, pants, loafers, cowboy boots, belts, purses. TCU had enjoyed much success in recent years—the previous season, they'd played in the Rose Bowl—and their fans exuded a we're-all-about-it attitude, which was quite a reversal from my youth, when Arkansas beat TCU 22 straight and fans like me assumed similar airs.

Inside the stadium, Blake and I sat high in the end zone. From the opening kickoff, he was more vocal than I was, which, for once, cast me as the calmer and wiser older man, a role that hardly came naturally. Arkansas jumped out to a 20-7 lead, and early in the fourth quarter the Hogs lined up for a chip shot to extend the lead to three scores. The kicker stood well away from the other players and, like a solo performer on a grand stage, he held out his right arm, using it as a plumb bob to find the vertical reference line. Then with the studied precision of a surveyor, he methodically stepped off his approach from the spot where the holder was to place the football. Just before the snap, the kicker gave the holder his nod of approval to proceed. Despite all of these theatrics, or perhaps because of them, the kick clanked off the upright, so close to me that I could see the goalpost swaying from the force of the errant blow. The momentum of the game had shifted.

With 7:15 remaining, TCU went ahead 21-20, and I bolted from my seat to go walk around the empty upper concourse. Owing to legacy effects harkening back to the 1981 season, when I'd tried to smoke marijuana in the wake of the Hogs' 28-24 defeat on this same field here in Fort Worth, I was traumatized by the prospect of a loss to TCU. In a tizzy I paced the concourse, catching an occasional glimpse of the action on the field through the ramps that led to the stands. The reaction of the TCU fans dictated my emotions: When they cheered, I cringed. When they were silent, or better yet when they booed, my hopes rose.

With 2:05 left, TCU scored again to take a 28-20 lead. Yielding to the inevitable defeat, I returned to my seat beside Blake high in the end zone. What a horrible turn of events this was. He and I were just getting to know each other, and now our outing had taken on the flavor of a guys' night out gone bad. But as I slumped in my seat, I realized I hadn't given up entirely, even if the cause seemed lost. "We're going to win this game," I told Blake. I could feel his skepticism, so I looked up to catch his eye (he was taller than me by eight inches, maybe even nine or 10 in his cowboy boots) and said, "We're going to celebrate with our football team right over there in the corner of this end zone. Book it."

Fortunately, TCU's quarterback had been flagged for foolishly making a throat-slashing gesture after his most-recent touchdown, and this gave the Razorbacks decent field position. From there, it took the Hogs only five plays to tie the game and convert the two-pointer. Not long after, in the first overtime, quarterback Austin Allen was literally carried across the goal line for the winning score, whereupon Blake Matocha, the tall Texan, reached down and raised me high in the air with one arm as if I were a 12-year-old kid.

Like a conquering army, the Razorback players gathered in the end zone to salute their fans. I watched Dan Skipper, the 6-10 lummox who played right tackle, walk towards his girlfriend in the front row of the stands. Big Dan was a sweaty mess, his face covered in eye-black, yet the toothy grin under his thick beard announced him to be the happiest man in the Lone Star State. After he and his girlfriend embraced, she turned away with a gasp and wiped her face as if she'd just smooched a stinky bear. Then, as the celebration went on, she gathered herself and hugged it out with Big Dan one more time.

Amid the crestfallen TCU fans, Blake and I headed for yet another tailgate party somewhere in the shadows outside Amon Carter Stadium, and again I ran into Rick Angel. We high-fived and whooped it up, and in the wake of this unlikely comeback I felt a euphoria not unlike my elation following the improbable 1992 win over Tennessee when, after the game, Rick and I hung out at his house in Little Rock and drank beer. The sense of uplift I felt surprised me. I was almost 56, and at that age it was weird to think about what brought me real joy. I was blessed to have my family and friends, and no doubt I'd taken on more sophisticated pleasures and cultivated an appreciation for the finer things. Still and all, in the aftermath of the game out there in Fort Worth, I realized that the Hogs' stirring comeback victory had made me as happy as anything in my life in recent years.

35

False Dawn

The date of the upcoming Razorback spring football game was typically announced each February, and each year I was tempted to attend. One April, I actually drove to Fayetteville for this intra-squad game, but after I got there I realized I had exerted far more effort than was warranted. It was as if I'd gone considerably out of my way to hear a politician give a boilerplate speech.

Even so, with each new spring I found myself seduced all over again by the storylines trotted out by the coaches and newspaper reporters. Yet I've learned to view any reportage coming out of spring football practice with a raised eyebrow. I cringe whenever I read that one position group (wide receivers) is performing well, because this means that the opposite position group (defensive backs) *isn't* performing well.

Back in the spring of 2016, it was reported that Arkansas' defensive line was so fierce that to give the offense a fair chance during practices, the Razorback coaches had to stick to the most basic schemes on defense: no twists, stunts, or blitzes allowed. As the season progressed, however, opponents such as Auburn had little trouble manhandling the Hogs' thought-to-be-unblockable defensive line—Auburn rolled up a jaw-dropping 524 yards rushing and six rushing touchdowns in a 56-3 blowout. It seems that the springtime prowess of the Hogs' defensive line was merely an indicator of how porous the team's offensive line was.

Surprises like this fed my nagging suspicion that no matter what the coaches said or the reporters wrote, I really didn't know what was going on with the Razorback football team. I was like a kid with his nose pressed against the frosted-over front window of the toy store, straining to see what the toy makers were up to. It was all fragments and shadows, shards of the real and the imagined. And what killed me was that I knew *somebody* up in Fayetteville really *did* know what was going on inside the toy store. Somebody was clued in to all the scuttlebutt, the intrigue, the inner workings, the back-fence talk. But I would be among the last to know about any of it.

After the Auburn debacle, two top-tier SEC teams were scheduled to come to Fayetteville on back-to-back Saturdays in early November. I faced a choice: It was too exhausting to travel across the state two weekends in a row. But the more I thought about it, the more I realized that this was a no-brainer because the Hogs never ever beat the Florida Gators. Forces at work deep in the universe always conspire to prevent this. So I didn't go to the game against the Gators. Instead, I watched it on TV, blissfully helpless, as the Razorbacks trounced Florida 31-9 in a game in which everything went right.

Regardless, the argument could be made, and indeed I made it, that the Hogs were peaking. LSU was up next, and my enthusiasm for the game was fed by my anticipation of my sister's tailgate party, featuring what she touted as "The best frickin' gumbo ever!" Hyperbole, perhaps. Yet after the Razorback's easy victory over the Gators, I could believe anything was possible.

Of course, any game-weekend trip to Fayetteville meant dealing with the hotels' early reservation racket: the jacked-up prices, the two-night minimum stay, the non-fundable prepayment. For once, however, I had outwitted Carnall Hall, the swish boutique hotel on the edge of campus. A friend of my sister's had offered her non-cancellable prepaid hotel reservation—I would be doing her a favor to take the room for Friday night only. Glory be, this was perfect!

I arrived in Fayetteville before dark, checked into Carnall Hall, and wandered the adjacent front lawn of Old Main, where my name was etched in the sidewalk. Then I made my way to various watering holes on Dickson Street and hit Bordino's for dinner. On Saturday morning, I got up and jogged around campus in the crisp fall air. I was enjoying myself capitally, and the weekend was only getting started.

In Fayetteville, the setting for game-day tailgating is hardly as gracious as The Grove at Ole Miss. Much of the action takes place on the hillsides around Razorback Stadium, and the tableau calls to mind crops growing on the mountainside terraces in places like Cambodia. Regardless, over the years, my sister's tailgate parties atop one of these hillsides had evolved into game-day happenings. The effort that Mallory and her second husband, Steve, expended was herculean. They had it all down to a science: What to pack into their SUV. How to deal with fussy hot and cold foods. How to unpack it all and set everything up, including the obligatory Razorback-themed decorations, a makeshift bar, and tricky electronics like the satellite television. How to take it all down and fit it all back into their SUV. The whole thing was a task not unlike the rigging up and deconstructing of a wartime MASH unit.

And what do we fans derive from tailgating that makes it such a treasured game-day ritual? Underneath a pop-up tent, we drink plenty and we eat plenty and we sit around a TV in fold-up chairs watching other football games while passing the hours until our team finally takes the field. What a blast! But is there any larger purpose served here? As citizens, we have an obligation to look out for the larger community, and through the years I've tried to convince myself that my deep caring about Arkansas football is the same thing as caring about my community. But this is a real stretch. In truth, my love of Razorback football is the opposite of caring about my community. It's little more than the self-absorbed expression of the narrowest parochialism imaginable. In a pinch, though, tailgating can be seen as a communal activity. Certainly, it adds to the sense of enlargement that comes with being a college football fan who gathers three or four times each fall with friends and family, plus the occasional stranger who just happens to show up. Before the LSU game, we invited a wandering LSU fan into our tent to try some of my sister's gumbo. His verdict? Meh. But our beer was cold, thanks. We wished him luck, sort of. He wished us luck, sort of. Then he moseyed on, beer in hand.

Much is made of the way political power is peacefully transferred in the United States, and, yes, this is indeed inspiring to behold. Equally remarkable, at least to me, is the peaceful way college football games are conducted, especially in the American South. I say this of Southerners because no one else takes college football quite so seriously. Given how much Mississippi State and Ole Miss fans detest each other, not to mention Auburn and Alabama fans, this lack of violence is noteworthy.

In wide swaths of America, college football is a quasi-religion, which can be healthy for the body politic, provided it doesn't become dark and violent. In Europe, the fans of rival soccer teams have been known to fight one another. They stir things up with their lewd chants and songs. *What do you think of Tottenham? Shit! What do you think of shit? Tottenham! Thank you! That's all right. We hate Tottenham, we hate Tottenham. We are the Tottenham haters.*

No sports rivalry in America remotely approaches the mutual loathing unleashed during the World Cup when the Dutch hate the Germans, the Spanish loathe the Portuguese, the English abhor every team in continental Europe, and the Russians just want to go into the nearest forest and fight all comers, reprising the days of Ivan the Terrible. But at college football games across America there is no riotous behavior. Granted, there's regional chauvinism and redneckery aplenty. There's too much drunkenness, and some people do brainless things: Exhibit A would be the Alabama fan Harvey Updyke, who poisoned rival Auburn's iconic oak trees at Toomer's Corner with a deadly herbicide called Spike 80DF. But for the most part, college football is good, clean fun.

What accounts for this? Is it because Americans are more civilized than Europeans? Hardly. Is it because we take the whole matter of sport less seriously? Nope. Is it because we're generally less prone to violence? Hah.

How is it that in a nation in which practically every sentient male owns at least one gun, violence between football fans is rare and tends to be interfamilial, or off-stage, such as when a female Alabama fan killed a fellow female Alabama fan because the victim wasn't upset enough that the Crimson Tide had just lost the Iron Bowl on Auburn's famous Kick Six. (The dead woman had had the temerity to suggest it was more of a downer for her whenever the Miami Heat lost an NBA game.)

Comparatively speaking, college football fans across America are well behaved. One explanation could be that American-style football is so violent that any additional expressions of violence by fans would be gratuitous. The brutality of the sport itself seems to sate us. My explanation (and if you're a hardcore blue-stater in your politics, you better skip this section): The violence among footballers in Europe has owed to the chronic unemployment, especially among young people. College football fans in America at least have jobs. From Monday through Friday, we are occupied with earning a living. Attending a football game is not an act borne of idleness and frustration; instead, it's seen as a reward for a fruitful week of labor.

If violence among fans of rival college football teams becomes commonplace here, then we'll know the push to make America more like Europe has finally succeeded. Stifling, European-style socialism will have taken root here. The stagnation of our economy, the rigidity of our labor markets, the unsettling lack of mobility that marks a statist economy like those of European nations will have finally set in, and virtually every constructive outlet for the animal spirits of hardworking Americans will have been choked off. Then the most rewarding thing self-loathing Americans will have to do on Saturday afternoons each fall is to show up at college football games looking for someone else upon whom to take out their frustrations. (And now, you hardcore blue-staters can resume reading.)

At Razorback Stadium, this game against LSU, the matchup I had anticipated all week, was a calamity from beginning to end. Typically, a match between two SEC teams delivers numerous dramatic reversals and swings of momentum—such back-and-forth is what makes these games so compelling. But this game, which included the longest play from scrimmage in LSU's 123-year history—a 96-yard run by Derrius Guice—summoned no drama whatsoever. Only pity.

What to do? Ahead of the 2017 season, my stepson John invited me to join his Fantasy Football League. He enjoyed it, spurred on by the competition with friends. They eagerly spent hours drafting players, optimizing rosters, following stats. Nevertheless, I resisted. I already had enough football on my brain, thank you very much. To me, Fantasy Football was to the football fan what the game of football was to the men and boys who played it: Like Chronic Traumatic Encephalopathy, it was a hazard of just too much above-the-neck football-related contact.

Besides, Fantasy Football was all about the NFL and I wasn't inclined to worry about Tom Brady's passing stats, or how many yards some plug-and-play running back for the Phoenix Cardinals had piled up on a given Sunday. I had to stay focused on what really mattered, like how the Hogs' quarterback play was progressing, how deep the Razorbacks were at running back given the inevitable injuries to come, what the weather forecast looked like for this weekend's game. Know thyself, right?

The Hogs started their 2017 season with a win over cupcake Florida A&M at War Memorial Stadium, followed the second week with a loss at home to TCU. Then they had a week off. This drove me crazy: Never mind the agony of losing by three touchdowns to the Horned Frogs, why-oh-why have an open date on the third weekend *of any season?* The only remotely useful purpose of such an early interruption was to kill time in hope that the searing September heat would relent.

In general, I don't at all like the open date no matter when it falls on the schedule (though any half-awake athletic director makes sure to schedule it later in the season, when the team is beat up and out of gas). No other sport but football puts its fans through this sort of nonsense. Major League baseball teams play almost every night. College basketball teams typically play several times each week, but once a week at least. Not surprisingly, given how baby's-butt soft soccer is, Premier League teams usually play twice a week. Such regularity of play is normal and expected. But football is thought to be so physically taxing that every college team must schedule at least one week off each season, also known as the open date, which, for the fans, translates to a 14-day break between games.

Of course, months ago, I'd committed the Razorbacks' 2017 schedule to memory, so I knew this early open date was coming. As for other teams, I never know when theirs will fall. Say, for example, Auburn gets on a win streak (or preferably a losing streak) and

I'm following the scores of their games each Saturday. But then at some indeterminate point (at least to me), Auburn will disappear from that Saturday's lineup of games and—after repeatedly asking myself, "Now, who does Auburn play this weekend?"—I'll finally deduce that they have an open date, for crying out loud. Too, whenever the Hogs play I have to concern myself as to whether or not that week's opponent is coming off their open date. If they are, will they be fresher than the Hogs? Or perhaps they will be rusty? And how will the Hogs respond after their 14-day break? All this sort of speculation is just too much darned work. Perhaps college football should mimic the NBA and have what amounts to an All-Star Break, during which all teams take the same weekend off. This way, every college football team can get their open date over with and then we can all carry on with the season. Together.

Meanwhile, with no Razorback game on this third Saturday of September of 2017, I was presented with the opportunity to enjoy a relaxing, stress-free weekend. The problem is, in the middle of September the last thing I ever want is a relaxing, stress-free weekend. All summer, I had endured a string of such weekends filled with sporting trivia like who was atop the leaderboard at the British Open, how the St. Louis Cardinals were faring in the National League Central, whether any racehorse had a long-shot chance at the Triple Crown. With the arrival of fall, I was ready for some sports action that mattered, and I wanted it to come at me on consecutive weekends until I was as thoroughly worn out with football as were the Razorback players themselves. *Turn on the faucet and leave it on!*

Bummed out, on Saturday afternoon I stretched out on my couch and tried to find a game between two teams I could care about. Texas was at USC, I discovered. That'll do. But my mind wandered, the eyes got heavy. I texted a friend in California who professed to be an ardent USC fan, yet knew little about his team, to ask if he was even bothering to watch this game. No reply from him. Finally, I fell asleep.

Yet after I woke up, I kept watching. Eventually, I got into this game and here's why: As a Razorback fan, I could find a tangential yet somewhat resonant thread of interest in practically any matchup between two Division I college football teams. It was all about the storyline, and the potential connections to Arkansas football were endless. It was like that parlor game of Six Degrees of Kevin Bacon. With the fewest of steps—one measly degree, in this instance—I was able to make this USC-Texas game all about me. For example, the TV image of the Los Angeles Coliseum reminded me of how I'd traveled out for the Hogs-USC game in 2005, but left in a huff at half with the Trojans up 42-10, and how the only positive note of the entire evening was when, on my walk into the Coliseum, a lady had complimented me on the ridiculously expensive shirt I was wearing that I'd bought earlier on Rodeo Drive.

Meanwhile, it occurred to me that the Longhorns loomed on the Hogs' non-conference schedule in 2021, just five seasons away. Would any of their current players still be on the team by then? Doubtful. But in five seasons, new coach Tom Herman had a reasonable chance of still being at Texas, so I watched to see why he was reputedly an offensive guru (not obvious). I even rooted for the Longhorns. My heavens, the previous year they'd lost to Kansas for the first time since 1938. I hoped Texas improved at least somewhat in the run-up to 2021, so that when they beat the Razorbacks in Fayetteville, I could convince myself the Hogs had lost to a reasonably good team.

36
It's More Than A Game, Isn't It?

Susanne wasn't keen on going to the Auburn game in Fayetteville, so I asked my mother to go. It was the weekend of my 57th birthday and as an additional lure, I reminded her that my sister would be at the game too.

The last leg of our Friday afternoon drive up the ribbon of highway from Alma was a pageant of autumnal color. In the slanted golden light, the trees across the hills and the dales seemed to vibrate in the dry breeze. This was the best time to be in the Ozarks.

Mother and I had dinner at Bordino's, no reservation necessary in the front bar. Then, after I got her comfortably situated at our hotel, I headed for the Sigma Chi house. Behind its somewhat impressive façade, the rambling white house had long suffered the predations of college-age boys; the place was like an old weather-beaten ship holding on against the waves. I lingered in the central courtyard where one night, while posing for a group photograph with my pledge brothers, I'd stood unawares as the upperclassmen on the rooftop dumped vats of muck down on our drunken heads.

Down a hallway, I spotted the composite picture of the Sigma

Chis taken 35 years before. There I was in the dollar-bill-sized headshot, goofy expression and all. Had I been any thinner in the face and through the eyes, I'd have resembled a refugee from a concentration camp.

I had dropped by the Sigma Chi house in part because this was Father's Weekend and I figured I might run into a few old frat brothers who had sons in college. No, I wasn't a father with a son in college, but I was working at being a good stepfather. My dad was a Sigma Chi too, but he'd come about it in a most untraditional way. He had pledged back in the late 1950s, but didn't stay at the University of Arkansas long enough to be initiated. For more than 40 years, this was a giant hole in his life. Then, when Dad was in his early 60s, the Sigma Chis arranged for a number of older men in similar circumstances to be initiated into the fraternity. It was, in effect, a do-over, his second chance. My father was as happy as any newly-initiated 19-year-old had ever been.

Near the large dining room, I ran into Darla Lacey, now Darla James. Her blond hair was set against her smart black dress. Hadn't she lived in San Francisco after college? I shook her husband's hand and she told me her son had just pledged the fraternity. When I mentioned our blind-date-gone-awry on the weekend of the TCU game over three decades ago, she nodded even as her eyes assumed a faraway look that suggested she didn't recall this misfire of youthful courtship quite as vividly as I did.

The following morning brought a perfect day for football. On my usual jog around campus, I passed the bronze statue of Ben Drew Kimpel in front the Kimpel Hall. I stopped, genuflected in reverence, and even rubbed the head of the statue. Ben Kimpel, educated at Harvard, was the most learned teacher I ever had. He spoke five languages and was rumored to read 100 lines of Greek every day before breakfast. As a master of many disciplines, he taught a senior-level class that plumbed the connection between the music of Bela Bartok, the writings of Flaubert, and the early art of Picasso; or the links between Dante Alighieri, Rembrandt, and Gustave Mahler. In essence, Ben Kimpel had been on a mission to civilize young folks like me, to show us how our lives could be enriched by the humanities. I reckon he was somewhat successful, though I would've had more room in my head for such things if the Hogs hadn't won their first seven games during my senior year, climbing into the top five in the AP poll.

By mid-afternoon, Mother and I made our way to my sister's tailgate party, highlighted by beef brisket, the preparation of which included injections of beef broth. Mallory and her husband, Steve, always had great fun with these parties—weeks before, when the Hogs had hosted the TCU Horned Frogs, Mallory had fried up 15 pounds of frog legs.

As darkness approached, my sister and I took turns holding Mother's arm as we four made our way down the steep hill to Razorback Stadium. Crowds of fans clogged the gates and, in the dusk, the stadium was lit up like a giant spaceship. We finally got to our seats, where Mother sat between Mallory and me, with Steve on the far end. My sister was a visceral Hog fan like her brother and our deceased grandmother, and when the two of us started talking over the top of Mother's head, she offered to switch seats with us. But sensing a too-combustible pairing, we shook her off and went on talking over her.

Snuggled in amid the brisk fall air, we enjoyed the singing of the alma mater, the obligatory flyover by a troika of Air Force jets as the national anthem concluded, the rousing cadence of Arkansas Fight when the players ran through the "A" as they took the field. Like acolytes, we stood and Called the Hogs through the opening kickoff.

"This is fun," Mother said, leaning her head on my shoulder.

And yes, this was indeed fun. Up to a point.

When left tackle Paul Ramirez drew another penalty for his second false start, I rose from my seat, the only fan standing among the many around me. "Drive killer! Get him out! Come on, Coach Bielema, earn your money!" When I sat back down, I felt my mother's hand on my back, patting me in a soothing manner as she'd no doubt done when I'd squalled as an infant. Then my phone vibrated in my pocket. It was a text from my father back in Jonesboro: He just wanted to make sure my mom, my sister, and I were all right. The four of us, oddly reconstructed at that moment, were the nuclear family of my youth, and throughout the first half of the game my dad and I traded text messages, his way of being there with us, in spirit if not in body.

The game got out of hand in the third quarter, but by then I had come to terms with the sad fate of my beloved team, set to lose their eighth of the last nine. Game aside, it was heartwarming to be with my mother and sister again, just like in the old days. And I was enjoying getting to know Steve better—he was a welcome addition to our family. Admittedly, this grateful frame of mind settled in on me only after Auburn went up 38-6 and I'd given up any hope of a win, much less salvaging what was turning out to be a very bad season indeed.

That night, in the lobby of the hotel, I spotted the tall, silver-haired Ben Hyneman from Jonesboro. I knew that Ben had once been on the university's Board of Trustees, so I Googled him and learned that not only was he still a Trustee, he was currently serving as Chairman—which explained why he looked as if he'd just walked away from the wreckage of a death-defying car accident.

I resisted the urge to go over and talk to Ben, to counsel him perhaps. Later, up in my hotel room, I played out in my mind what I could've said: "Ben, you realize Razorback fans can't endure another year of this, right?" Or, "Ben, good grief, what are you going to do now that the Hogs should be relegated to the Sun Belt

Conference?" I even fantasized about speaking to an emergency meeting of the Board of Trustees. After a solemn pause, I would launch a rapid-fire indictment: "Our coach, Bret Bielema, is driven by his appetites. He met his wife at a blackjack table in Las Vegas. He wears sandals around his office and listens to reggae music. He's far too well known among the drinking and dining establishments up and down Dickson Street. Whose brilliant idea was it to give such a man an $11-million buyout if he's fired? At some point, he's just going to mail it in. So here we are."

The following morning, I ran into Ben Hyneman again, in the hotel's driveway. He gave a forced smile, then went on loading his luggage into his Range Rover. Clearly, he was in no mood to chitchat. As he drove off, I said to myself: "And, Ben, remember, it was Bill Parcells who said, "You are who your record says you are.""

Before long, Mother and I packed up our car too, and headed back to northeast Arkansas. Four-and-a-half hours later, we were 35 miles from Jonesboro and the Auburn game had receded, somewhat, from my mind. Confronted with such mounting losses, I knew that my best psychological defense was to forgo any future Razorback games entirely, both in person and on television. But I couldn't do that. So the next best coping method was to find ways to forget about the games as quickly as possible.

Since my mother was driving, I had tried to lose myself in a book I'd bought at the Dickson Street Bookshop, a worn copy of *By Inheritance* by Octavia Thanet. That was the nom de plume of Alice French, a now-forgotten novelist who, along with her lesbian lover, had spent winters from 1893 through 1910 on her plantation in Clover Bend, Arkansas. After indulging in football all weekend, this was my feeble attempt to touch base with my more cerebral side. My mother was quite familiar with my bookish ways, going back to the days when she would drop me off at the Craighead County Public Library for hours on end. Even in my adult years she sometimes told me I had too many books, a criticism I always shrugged off since this was hardly in the top rank of my flaws.

Now I looked up Octavia Thanet online. It was wondrous what Google could summon. I instantly learned that Octavia Thanet had lived in Thanford, her three-story house overlooking the Black River. What a coincidence: Mother and I had *just* crossed over the Black River at Black Rock, an area best described as the toenails of the Ozarks. "I have an idea," I said. "Let's try to find this author's house, Thanford. According to Wikipedia, it's on the National Register of Historic Places."

After a 15-minute detour down a forlorn road, we were clearly lost. Stopping at a house for directions, I soon found myself in the dimly-lit garage of Mr. Harold Land. "Like the land you walk on," Mr. Land helpfully noted. He rummaged through shelves and bins and cupboards trying to find an old brochure about Thanford. His wife had been a schoolteacher, he said, by way of explaining why he might be in possession of such an esoteric pamphlet.

"Do you have some time?" he asked, as he searched on.

"Sure," I said, even as I knew Mother was out in the car wondering if I was ever going to emerge alive from Mr. Land's garage.

"You know Thanford burned down a few years ago?" he said.

"Really?" That important detail was not included in the Wikipedia entry I'd earlier read on my phone.

"I can't find the old brochure. But the home site is just down the road. I'll show you where it is."

Mother and I drove slowly behind Mr. Land, who pedaled his old bicycle—he was quite jaunty for a gentleman in his 70s. He led us down a field road, and finally the three of us gathered on a patch of gravel and stared at the empty place where Thanford had once stood. I walked over to the bank of the Black River, mindful that Ms. Alice French's manse had had a third-floor study that overlooked this particular bend. It was a decent view, I imagined, though maybe not worth the arduous trip required of her many guests, which had included Theodore Roosevelt, to get to her plantation.

This spontaneous excursion to the vanished Thanford was just the odd cap to Mother's and my great football-game weekend. No matter the dismal performance by the Razorbacks, we would carry this memory with us until either, or both, of us became like Dory, the memory challenged fish in *Finding Nemo,* the movie that my sister's grown children had so loved back when they were kids.

37

Habits of the Heart

We are all creatures of habit, and it seems that I am more so than others. On every workday, for years, I would eat lunch at Ruby Tuesday in Jonesboro. In college, my go-to spot was the D-Lux on Dickson Street. During my magazine days in Little Rock, I was such a regular at the Buffalo Grill that my mother left phone messages for me there. During my sojourn to New York, my place was the Union Square Café. Such fixations hold me together, it seems.

In describing what holds the United States together, Alexis de Tocqueville, author of *Democracy in America*, used the phrase "habits of the heart." Our attachments to family life, religions, and local politics were more important, he felt, than the institutions of government, the bonds of commerce, or the common culture shared among the citizens of the nation. DeTocqueville wrote this in 1839, so he had zero exposure to college football. It would be interesting to know where he placed it among things dear to the hearts of latter-day Americans.

After New Year's Day of 2018, which is to say after the dismal 2017 football season was finally over, I had lunch at Ruby Tuesday with my old friends Jimbo Osment and Chuck Gschwend (aka Gus Chewin). Though we all lived in Jonesboro, we didn't get together often. With three teenage children, Chuck was particularly busy. I anticipated a genial conversation, perhaps touching on the record-breaking cold weather, any travels we'd taken over the Christmas holiday, the latest goings-on in the NFL playoffs. But as soon as we sat down, Jimbo said, "I have a two-question Razorback Quiz for you."

This query from Jimbo surprised me, because the past season had been so forgettable that Coach Bielema had been fired literally as soon as he walked off the field after the final-game loss to Missouri.

After the waiter took our order, Jimbo leaned in and said, "Okay, first question: Do you think Bret Bielema left the Razorback program in better shape than when he got there?"

I knew better than to be blindly loyal to my team in front of Jimbo. "Well," I said, "in his first year, Bielema lost his first nine games against Power Five teams, and in his last two years he lost 10 of his last 11 against Power Five teams. So I'd say he pretty much came full circle."

The objective taint of my answer seemed to mollify Jimbo. Then he said, "Next question: Do you ever think he owned it?"

Between sips of iced tea, I hemmed and hawed and said that Bielema never owned it in public—what coach ever does? But I was pretty sure he had done so in private because, despite his stubborn illusions of playing smashmouth football with the likes of Alabama and LSU, he never seemed to break totally with reality.

From there, my two friends and I reminisced about the Razorbacks' 10-game win streak in 2006, Bobby Petrino's brilliant just-before-the-half play call against LSU in 2010, the dominance of the Hogs' offensive line in 2014, and how the defensive front seven that year, with Trey Flowers, Darious Philon, and Martrell Speight, wasn't too shabby either. Hunter Henry's Heavenly Heave against Ole Miss was brought up, and, for about the fourth time,

Jimbo told me it was the smartest play he'd ever seen *in any sport at any level.*

There was some polite mention of our children—in my case, stepchildren and new granddaughter, though it was uncomfortable to speak of my granddaughter in front of my friends because they had both known the deceased grandfather. Yet any talk of offspring was also awkward for my friends, both grads of Arkansas State: Jimbo's eldest daughter had married a rabid Hog fan, and Chuck's Razorback-loving son was now attending the University of Arkansas. At one point during our conversation, Chuck snuck in the obtuse factoid that the Arkansas State Red Wolves were the last team to beat the University of Central Florida, which had just completed an undefeated season.

Mostly, though, the three of us just kept turning over old Razorback football ground. It was as if we hadn't moved far at all from the days of our youth. When we finished our lunch, Jimbo stood up, tossed his white napkin on the table, and said, "Please don't include me in any Razorback-related text threads." With that final pronunciamento, we three walked to the parking lot and said our goodbyes, and went our separate ways.

As winter gave way to spring, Jimbo and I traveled to Hot Springs for a guys' getaway. Hot Springs always ranks among my favorite springtime excursions. I especially enjoy Oaklawn race track, with its sleek thoroughbreds, the banty jockeys in their colorful silks, the rag-tag characters in the grandstand who bet their last dollar, and, of course, those delicious corned beef sandwiches.

In Hot Springs, Jimbo and I met up with Bob Childress and Neal Harrington, our grade school chums and fellow HOCH Clubbers. Neal had long wanted to have us all down to his adopted hometown, where he and his wife had moved around the time their eldest son was killed by a lightning strike.

Friendships between males can be difficult to nourish and sustain—at least mine have been. Only in recent years had the four us gotten together with any regularity, but whenever we did, our connection was immediate. We caught one another up on the events in our lives—I was still gassed from the recent wedding of my stepdaughter, Emily, to Blake Matocha, the tall Texan, and I told them all about that wondrous night in Fort Worth when Blake had hoisted me into the air like a little kid to celebrate the Hogs' comeback win over TCU.

On Saturday morning, all of us reunited HOCH Clubbers piled into Bob's car, our destination an event celebrating the 100-year anniversary of the legendary 573-foot home run Babe Ruth had hit in 1918, back when practically all major league baseball teams held spring practice in Hot Springs. Legend had it that the Babe's colossal blast had landed in the pond at the Arkansas Alligator Farm & Petting Zoo, which, amazingly, was still there. On the way to the event, we laughed at old stories no one else would've thought were funny, while Jimbo held forth with his off-angle observations. On the radio a song from the 1970s spurred an argument over how good or bad Paul McCartney was as a songwriter.

At the site of the former Majestic Field, a small yet enthusiastic crowd had gathered near what once had been home plate, and among the celebrants I spotted the craggy face of Rick Schaeffer, a radio personality and former Razorback sports information director. During each football season, I listened to *Drive Time Sports*, the call-in radio show Schaeffer co-hosted. It was the typical sports radio show: If you loved Razorback football, you loved the show. If not, then it was patently silly.

Yet what distinguished *Drive Time Sports* was Schaeffer's role as Chief Hogsplainer, the analyst-in-residence, who, no matter the performance of the Razorbacks, never quit pumping out optimism. "Things will get better as... Pump. Pump. Pump." "The Hogs have a great opportunity to... Pump. Pump. Pump." "Just imagine what will happen when... Pump. Pump. Pump." "Yes, but you need to consider this... Pump. Pump. Pump."

Schaeffer never overreacted and never went to the dark side. He could find a silver lining in any cloud crossing the red-tinged Razorback sky, delivered to the radio audience in an I'm-the-only-adult-in-the-room tone of voice. Some among the Razorback cognoscenti considered him hopelessly Pollyanna-ish, and the wags on Hogville mockingly called him Sunshine Rick. Once, I'd even heard Schaeffer himself say, on-air, "It makes some people sick that I'm so optimistic." But over the years I had come to admire his habitually-rosy outlook, the essence of which was that what fans think is so easy, so obvious, so achievable if only *they* were in charge, is quite difficult no matter *who's* in charge. To all the armchair quarterbacks and keyboard critics, Schaeffer's consistent message was just slow your roll, come up for air, be mature, think positive.

When I spotted Rick Schaeffer in the crowd, I felt the urge to go over and pump some Razorback sunshine with him. "Say, Rick, did you see that Fayetteville was just named the 'Best Place to Live' in the SEC for the third straight year? Don't you think this is just the edge the Hogs need to recruit with the big dogs in the SEC?" But I held off while Babe Ruth's great-grandson rambled on about how the Babe grew up in an orphanage in Baltimore, and how he was a rough youngster "only slightly varnished by civilization." When I finally turned back around, Sunshine Rick was gone.

With Bret Bielema's dismissal back in November, Arkansas had undertaken yet another coaching search. Lord, what an ordeal this always was. In terms of hard-to-swallow compromises, the process of any coaching search was not unlike what I'd gone through when I hit puberty and initially set my sights on Raquel Welch, only to work my way down from there.

Chad Morris of SMU was hardly my first pick as the Hogs'

new coach. Though as a graduate of Texas A&M, he was likely disappointed to have been passed over when they'd hired Jimbo Fisher from Florida State. Predictably, though, the more I learned about Chad Morris, especially his reputed ability to recruit in the state of Texas, the more reasons I found to believe Arkansas had made the perfect choice. Pump. Pump. Pump. Golly, was it even possible that in his first season, Morris could somehow repeat Houston Nutt's feat of winning the first eight games? Pump. Pump. Pump.

Chad Morris went 2-10 in his first year, the worst Razorback season since 1952, back when my mom and dad were in seventh grade. But headed into Morris' second season, there was some optimism. It didn't last long, however, as the Hogs lost at home to San Jose State, a team which had only won three games in its previous two seasons. Despite a 2-4 start, on the weekend of my 59th birthday, I headed for Fayetteville.

Among the many fruits of winning is the buzz that surrounds each game. There's a palpable charge of energy in the air and every fan can feel it. Conversely, when chronic losing sets in, any game-related energy must be summoned from tangential sources. The timing of this game against Auburn was a major plus, as this was the only home game in October and there was a lot to like about the October weather in the Ozarks. Moreover, back in the summer when my optimism had been Pumped, I'd made non-cancellable reservations at Carnall Hall for this game weekend, and Susanne and I had made plans to meet up with our children and their spouses and our granddaughter. It was to be a great family time together. So there we all sat in the bright sunshine at Razorback Stadium, ready for yet another 11 o'clock kickoff.

Auburn quickly jumped out to a 17-0 lead. Then, with 5:29

left in the second quarter, a timeout was called and a procession ensued in the north end zone, as about 35 white men in their early 70s trundled out single file. This was what remained of the 1969 Arkansas Razorbacks, the team that had played in The Big Shootout half a century before. These old white men stood shoulder-to-shoulder at the goal line, facing the direction in which President Nixon's helicopter had landed on that cold, damp day of December 6, 1969. The end zone where they stood also happened to be where Bill Montgomery's fateful pass had been intercepted with 10:34 left in that game. Towering behind them was the north end zone complex, newly-expanded at a cost of $160 million, with its luxury suites, loge boxes, club seating, the cushy SEC Club, and, even more exclusive, '64 Club. The top story of this complex was among the choice spots from which to watch any game. This was where the parents of prized recruits were often hosted, and I couldn't help but notice that virtually every person on the top level of the complex was black. Of course, no black players had been on either team in The Big Shootout, long hailed as the last college football game of consequence in which every player was white.

During the timeout, the public address announcer recounted the exploits of this 1969 Razorback team, after which there was scattered applause from the relatively sparse crowd and then these 35 or so older men walked off the field single file.

I glanced at my phone: Already, it had gone viral. Earlier in the second quarter—at the 12:53 mark to be exact—the Hogs had attempted a fake punt, a play so lame in its design, so half-hearted in its execution, so comedic in its result (an interception by Auburn) that I had literally laughed out loud when it was replayed on the huge video screen that dominated the stadium. Now this travesty of a play was being touted on YouTube as "The Worst Fake Punt in Human History."

I wondered what the members of the 1969 Razorback football team thought about this farcical play. The team they loved, the football program they'd helped build, was clowning itself. The downward spiral of the Razorbacks was reaching historic proportions: In the seven-plus seasons since Bobby Petrino had wrecked his motorcycle on April Fool's Day of 2012, the Hogs had gone 13-46 in SEC play, including dropping their last 14 straight. Despite my determination to remain optimistic, if this losing trend persisted, and there was no end to it in sight, I would inevitably lapse into the self-pitying lament that this was *unfair to me* because I didn't have that many Razorback football seasons left. For several years, I had been fighting off just such a moan, the football fan's version of the poet's wail that life is short and getting shorter.

Amid such epic losing, I had become more nostalgic. After all, what else was there to hold onto but past glory? That very morning I had set out early to find where Bill Montgomery's name was etched into the sidewalk on the UA campus, and finally, on the north side of Mullins Library, I'd found it. Remarkably, his name was only about 300 yards ahead on the same stretch of sidewalk where my name was etched. Per the tradition of Senior Walk, every past graduate of the University of Arkansas, myself included, had their full name spelled out in the sidewalk—typically their legal name as recorded by the university's registrar. But the name etched here in the sidewalk simply read "Bill Montgomery," his football name so to speak, the name fans knew him by. Feeling triumphant for having hunted up Bill Montgomery's name, I had snapped a photograph of it and texted it to my father and to my old friend Bob Childress. As I finished texting, an older couple had approached and I'd blurted out, "Does the name Bill Montgomery mean anything to you?"

The couple slowed as I pointed down at the sidewalk. "He was my childhood hero," I had gushed, sounding every bit like some geezer fan obsessed with Elvis Pressley. "I was nine years old in 1969."

"I was nine years old in 1969, too," the lady said, before they moved on.

On Sunday morning, the day after Auburn had clobbered the Hogs 51-10, I walked from Carnall Hall to the Dickson Street Bookshop, where I went to the aisle with used books pertaining to the state of Arkansas and its history, and it was there that I found a well-worn copy of a book by J. Neal Blanton titled, *Game of the Century: Texas vs. Arkansas, December, 1969: An Absorbing Analysis of the most exciting week in college football history.* While Susanne patiently waited, I took the book to the front counter, where the hipster at the cash register regarded me as though I were insane to be spending $85 on any book about football. But I had to have it.

Emerging from the Bookshop into the crisp weather, Susanne and I walked across the street to Bordino's. The restaurant was busy, though hardly as crowded as it had been on Friday or Saturday night. We sat in the front bar and I placed the book on the table where anyone who walked by could see it. The waiter took our brunch order for Eggs Benedict and House-Made Corned Beef Hash, then disappeared. A few minutes later, he returned with two glasses of orange juice.

"Is that a book about The Game of the Century?" he said, bending slightly to study the cover.

"It is," I said. "I just bought it."

"What a cool memento."

"I know," I said. "They had the team from 1969 here in Fayetteville this weekend, and you'd have thought one of *those* players would've found this old book at the bookstore and bought it."

"Maybe one of those players dropped it off," the waiter said with a shrug. "The sad state of Arkansas football."

"Good point," I replied. "I hadn't thought of that."

While Susanne and I sipped our orange juice, I thumbed through the pages of the book. It was well done, even if larded with arcane details such as a photograph of Razorback players performing calisthenics before Monday practice of that long-ago week. But then at the end of the book there was a chapter titled, "Post Game," and as I read it I came across a paragraph about a girl in the Texas band—the same girl I had seen repeatedly, maddeningly, on TV 50 years before. I could *still* see her face as the Texas comeback had unfolded, and I recalled how her emotions during the final moments of The Big Shootout had been the mirror opposite of mine. For half a century I had wondered just who in the hell this girl was, and in my darker moments of fandom I had harbored a subversive desire to get back at her, to somehow make her atone for the happiness she'd felt that day.

And, now, here in this book's final pages were these lines: *"One member of the Longhorn band, Marilyn Edwards, a freshman clarinetist from Austin, had been seen by millions of Americans. An ABC-TV cameraman zoomed in on the beautiful brunette countless times during the latter half of the game; her expressions told the game story to television viewers with more impact than words. And after the game a final camera shot showed her in a state of complete delight."*

Epilogue

The era marred by the coronavirus is finally a memory. Who could ever have imagined such? In the lap of the grandmother, the child fidgets. She wears tiny red pants and a white shirt with "Hogs" emblazoned across her frail chest. On the floor is the Cheerleader Barbie doll the grandmother bought for her, and, outside, a cold wind blows. We are set against it, cozy and warm near the fire. The grandmother guides the child's arms and legs, moving them puppeteer-like in a familiar choreography. The child's loose limbs splay as if she's a frisky colt. "Go Hogs Go!" the puppeteer says. "Woo Pig Sooie... Yay, Razorbacks!"

I rise and throw another log on the fire, and as the blaze builds, a plausible future forms in my mind.

I am high in the stands at Razorback Stadium—each year more magnificent than ever—and I watch her every move. She is down on the field, just left of the home bench, her red and white pompoms in hand. I watch her high kicks, the bounce of her black ponytail, the gleam in her blue eyes set on the tens of thousands of fans. I wave and hope she somehow sees me. Impossible. I'm well into my 70s, grayer and slower, though still fit enough to prowl Dickson Street, or so I imagine. The huge crowd rises and the national anthem is sung, then the roar as the Razorback Band marches and Arkansas Fight blares. At the mouth of the tunnel, a fog of white smoke rises and she is among the cheerleaders that run ahead as the red-helmeted players trot through the "A." The grandmother, teary-eyed, claps wildly. Seated between us are our other grandkids, the youngest a boy near the age I was when I'd watched The Big Shootout. The sun is harsh—its low angle reminds me of those long-ago Saturday morning peewee league games—and soon the grandmother slathers sunscreen on the children's pinkish faces. I hear one of them call my name. The granddaughter in her mid-teens wants a Coke, and then all the grandkids say they want a Coke and some popcorn, too. I wait for a break in the action. Down on the gridiron, the Razorbacks incur their second penalty for five men in the backfield, and, as I rise from my seat, I feel my wife's eyes on me and then wordlessly, in chosen silence, I head down the aisle towards the concession stand.

By the third quarter, the shadow of the press box finally overtakes us. I stand next to the eldest grandson, the boy of fourteen already taller than me. We strain to find his parents, seated with friends somewhere rather far away.

"There they are!" he says. "I see them!"

"Yes," I say, though I don't trust these old eyes to confirm.

Before the start of the fourth quarter, the make-or-break fifteen minutes that Frank Broyles always said was a metaphor for manhood, every Razorback player down on the field holds up his right hand to make a four, as if to say, "We will own it." A text message comes across my phone and for an instant I imagine it's from my father. Later, on a tense third down with the crowd on its feet, I hear one of the grandchildren yell, "Let's go, Hoggies!" and I repeat this exhortation even louder, hoping it catches on with the others.

When the game ends, my mother calls, her voice weak. She'd watched on TV, and while she doesn't actually say, "Did you embarrass yourself in front of your grandkids?" she hints in that direction.

All of us leave Razorback Stadium and head up the hill for my sister's tailgate party, less elaborate in recent years as she and her husband have dialed it back a bit. But it's good to see all of our children and grandchildren there, a generational mishmash. The cheerleader finally joins us, a veritable celebrity in our midst. Our talk and laughter swell out into the cool of the late afternoon. Under our tent, the Texas Longhorns game is on the TV. I notice that the eldest grandson, the one who lives in Texas, is glued to it.

I slip away to fetch the toy football from the car trunk, and a group of us toss it around until the adults decide it's time to have another drink and eat more ribs and potato salad and spinach dip and whatever else. Tonight, I will not make it to Bordino's to dine on pasta and drink wine among friends. In fact, I haven't been to Bordino's in years.

Season by season, time moves on. Before I know it, even the youngest grandkid will be old enough to go to college. Returning the toy football to its permanent place in the trunk of my car, I wonder about all these grandkids gathered under the tent. Will they have any desire to carry on this tradition as they grow older? Will these memories stay with them? What will they remember of me?

Everything changes. Everything *has changed*. Yet through it all, these football games will go on. I walk back toward the tent, pinching my jacket tighter to my neck in the chillier air.